Vichy France and [illegible]ay Life

Also available from Bloomsbury

Britain and France in Two World Wars,
edited by Robert Tombs and Emile Chabal
Place and Locality in Modern France,
edited by Philip Whalen and Patrick Young
The Pyrenees in the Modern Era, Martyn Lyons

Vichy France and Everyday Life

Confronting the Challenges of Wartime, 1939–1945

Edited by
Lindsey Dodd and David Lees

BLOOMSBURY ACADEMIC
LONDON • NEW YORK • OXFORD • NEW DELHI • SYDNEY

BLOOMSBURY ACADEMIC
Bloomsbury Publishing Plc
50 Bedford Square, London, WC1B 3DP, UK

BLOOMSBURY, BLOOMSBURY ACADEMIC and the Diana logo are trademarks of Bloomsbury Publishing Plc

First published in Great Britain 2018
Paperback edition published 2020

Cover image: Children evacuated from Boulogne-Billancourt are given breakfast on their arrival in Guéret, April 1943. (© Archives Municipales de Boulogne-Billancourt)

A catalogue record for this book is available from the British Library.

A catalog record for this book is available from the Library of Congress.

ISBN: HB: 978-1-3500-1159-5
PB: 978-1-3501-4379-1
ePDF: 978-1-3500-1160-1
eBook: 978-1-3500-1161-8

Typeset by RefineCatch Limited, Bungay, Suffolk

Contents

List of Figures

Acknowledgements

This book is the outcome of a one-day conference organized by both editors around the theme of 'Vichy and the everyday' and held at the University of Warwick in March 2016. The conference brought together Anglophone and Francophone scholars at various stages in their academic careers in order to explore the question of everyday lived experiences in France during the Second World War. Our thanks go first of all to all of those who participated in this successful event. Amongst those colleagues who do not feature in the pages of this book, we would like to thank Kay Chadwick, Ayshka Sené, Robert Gildea and Hanna Diamond. We are grateful to Robert and Hanna for providing the concluding words to the conference and to the delegates who attended the conference and contributed to the stimulating discussions. We also thank the contributors to this book wholeheartedly for their enthusiasm, their attentiveness and responsiveness, and for their fascinating research.

The organization of the conference would not have been possible without the support of a number of individuals and bodies. First, we gratefully acknowledge the very generous support of the School of Music, Humanities and Media at the University of Huddersfield, whose financial support was invaluable. The allocation of an Early Career Researcher grant by the School to Lindsey Dodd provided not only a contribution towards the running costs of the conference, but also paid for certain speakers' overseas travel, the final translation of three chapters and teaching relief for Lindsey. Second, the University of Warwick's School of Modern Languages and Cultures provided further financial and practical support. Our thanks go in particular to Seán Hand, Pierre-Philippe Fraiture, Sylvia Howell, Harpal Singh, Elaine Robinson and the staff at both the Institute for Advanced Study at Warwick and the Warwick Conferences team. Third, we are very grateful for grants received from the Society for the Study of French History, the Royal Historical Society, the Association for the Study of Modern and Contemporary France, and the Humanities Research Centre and Connecting Cultures Global Research Priorities programme at Warwick.

We extend our thanks to the two anonymous readers who peer-reviewed the initial proposal for this book, as well as to the other readers who kindly reviewed the submitted chapters and provided such helpful feedback but who must also remain anonymous. We thank the History Division at the University of Huddersfield for funding the indexing of this book. We are indebted to Benjamin Bâcle for his translation from the French of the chapters by Camille Mahé, Matthieu Devigne and Jean-Pierre Le Crom. We would also like to offer our sincere gratitude to the team at Bloomsbury Academic and in particular Rhodri Mogford and Beatriz Lopez.

We would also like to thank friends and family for all their support. David would like to thank friends and colleagues at Warwick and in the wider 'French Studies' community; his parents (Sue and John) and brothers (James and Chris), but especially Jess and Eleanor. Lindsey thanks her colleagues and students at the University of Huddersfield, and especially Charlotte Mallinson for covering some of her teaching; she also thanks Wendy for moral support, Benjamin for language and content, and her parents for their unwavering enthusiasm.

Introduction

Lindsey Dodd and David Lees

Opening up a wartime volume of Hachette's *Almanach* is like tasting a slice of life from the past. We learn something of the preoccupations of French people during the Second World War – from advice on cat diseases, gardening, recipes and home remedies, to articles on popular science, astrology and travel, and advertisements for everyday products:

> Floraline soup. The most natural and the best for children.
> If you can write, then you can draw.
> One in five wins. Minimise risk, maximise chances with a national lottery ticket.
> The herb that kills unwanted body hair. Free recipe.
> Parcolav. A household cleaner to replace both detergent and soap.[1]

For while the Vichy regime is not absent – there are features on Marshal Pétain, information about new laws, summaries of political events – its focus lies not in the realms of ideology or high politics, but in the ordinary and extraordinary tasks of everyday life in wartime France. From illness to food, from family to savings, from work to beauty, from dressmaking to animal husbandry, such were the myriad concerns of day-to-day life during the so-called 'dark years'.

How often is L. P. Hartley's well-worn phrase 'the past is another country [...] they do things differently there'[2] invoked to encourage us to historicize past events, people and things! Yet much of the everyday is familiar to us: emotion and interaction, enthusiasm and ambivalence, certain objects and certain actions. What changes, of course, is the historical context and its attendant cultural mores; and what changes too is the historiographical context through which we see that past. For example, the material substance of cooking, washing, playing and working is profoundly altered by the historical context. In the case of France during the period 1940–44, the context is that of new and unequally-distributed pressures on a population not *at* war but *in* war. And for the period 1939–45 (the

Second World War, rather than the four years of German occupation), war must be seen as the primary factor affecting most lives at a popular level. Furthermore, the meanings attached to people's daily lives have been shaped by the frameworks through which they have subsequently been viewed. Thus simply living and being may well become tainted with the charge of *attentisme*: an absence of engagement on either side, whether 'good' or 'bad', morally judged and found wanting. Indeed, the historiography of the Vichy period in French history is morally charged, with historians standing judge, supported by their archival evidence, analysing, categorizing and theorizing the lives of the people of the past.[3]

The divisiveness of Vichy, resistance, collaboration and the shame of mass persecutions, deportations and treachery between neighbours have created a sour environment for scholars to work in, forever questioning the morality of our research topics or the court-worthiness of our sources. Our consideration of the everyday in this book raises such questions; but we side here with Richard Cobb: we must write and think with human beings in mind;[4] we must keep uppermost in our thoughts that millions of people who passed through those years did so not just as collaborators, resistants, victims and heroes. Indeed, for many, such categories are redundant. The evidence tells more than just one story, and this book creates space for others to be told.

What is 'everyday life', and why is it worth thinking about in relation to wartime France? First of all, it must be seen as a redirection of the gaze, and not a subject apart. There are so many ways of understanding what 'everyday' might mean, that it is worth pausing to evoke some of them. For Henri Lefebvre, whose interest in the everyday was political and transformative, part of the interest of the everyday was its omnipresence.[5] 'Everyday life is profoundly related to *all* activities', he wrote, 'and encompasses them with all their differences and their conflicts; it is their meeting place, their bond, their common ground'.[6] If we follow Lefebvre on this point, then the analysis of aspects of everyday life can shed light both up from the small-scale to the large-scale, and down from large to small. For another perspective, we might turn to the poet W. H. Auden. In his musings on the *Musée des Beaux-Arts*, he suggests we understand the everyday as entrenched in the simultaneity of human action:

> About suffering they were never wrong,
> The old Masters: how well they understood
> Its human position: how it takes place
> While someone else is eating or opening a window or just walking dully along.[7]

Here, we see the ordinary life of an everyday 'someone' whose mundane activities continue alongside and in ignorance of the great events and the great sorrows of the day. An analysis of the fringes, then, forces us to understand those great events and great sorrows in a context which did not put them at the heart of life; they gained their centrality and status (not without reason) in hindsight. The cultural theorist and historian Michel de Certeau encourages us to examine the epistemology of the everyday. The work of historians 'resembles that of a tramp who, as he pokes around the bins for the remains of meals or clothes, holds on the end of his stick the dream of a house he'll never enter, of meals and relationships he'll never know'.[8] Not only does Certeau suggest that we will find our everyday in the bits left over from the main story, but that we – like the tramp – can never fully know their meaning. We remain outside other people's everyday, even while it is familiar to us. In that, we must reserve some of our judgements: our knowledge is always partial. A fourth suggestion is found in Hegel's description of the everyday as:

> the prose of the world, as it appears to the consciousness both of the individual himself and of others: a world of finitude and mutability, of entanglements in the relative, of the pressure of necessity from which no individual is in a position to withdraw.[9]

Hegel asks us to consider the individual in relation to the society around him or her; we find in that world a set of inflexible limitations as well as constant movement, action and change; we find highly particular social interactions; and we find human beings organizing themselves in response their material needs, as well as acting upon desire, hope and fear.[10]

Examining everyday life in the past is, of course, nothing new to historians today. But it would not have seemed a worthwhile topic for many of our professional antecedents. Gardiner writes that the post-Enlightenment vision was of everyday life as trivial and inconsequential, the ordinary individual as illogical, irrational, and her life too mundane, too unimportant.[11] Modern academic disciplines remain, in many ways, governed by the Enlightenment thinking about reason and universalism which prevailed as they grew up. Harootunian describes how the growth of the nation state was propped up by the discipline of history; everyday life was far too contingent and fragmented to ever give a sense of the purposefulness and completeness of national destiny. The historian was tasked with giving a sense of 'the completed past' which moved the nation forwards; this completed past was pitted against 'the incomplete present', continually in motion, without logic in itself, without end –

and thus irrelevant to the great story of national pasts unfolding into national futures.[12]

Narrative interpretations of nations and destinies fell out of fashion by the mid-twentieth century, and certainly in France where structuralist dominance brought about a mode of historical analysis imbued with quantification, upon hierarchization, categorization and generalization. There was 'scant attention' to the everyday among historians, despite its prevalence in cultural studies.[13] In post-war Britain the so-called 'New History' began to emerge, opening up a history 'from below' which sought to rescue the working class from the 'enormous condescension of posterity'[14] by valuing the contribution made by working-class people to broader historical trends and events. But national historiographies follow different paths; in France, the Annales school maintained its powerful grip: sequences and series, problems and comparisons – 'serious' historians were not interested in what was unique, incomparable or subjective: that could be left to the novelist or the filmmaker.[15] Yet the small-scale was not absent. Alongside the *longue durée* macro lens of the Annales school, *microhistoire* (*microstoria* in Italy, whence the term originated) carved a place and, to some degree, challenged the Annales' totalising project. Powerful works illuminated the everyday worlds of medieval and early modern cultures: Carlo Ginzburg's *The Cheese and the Worms* or Emmanuel Le Roy Ladurie's *Montaillou* open our eyes to an everyday so alien in its beliefs and customs and yet so familiar in its passions and relationships.[16] In Germany, the *Alltagsgeschichte* movement of the 1970s and 1980s also emerged as a backlash against a depersonalized structuralist approach. Historians such as Alf Lüdke, Lutz Niethammer, David Crew or Ian Kershaw used archives as well as oral histories to investigate the everyday life of Germans during the Third Reich.[17] They were criticized for seeking to 'understand' the worlds of ordinary people who acquiesced to, enjoyed or resisted National Socialist life. Their focus on subjectivities not structures made groundbreaking research, but they stood outside the conservative mainstream, and in 2000 *Alltagsgeschichte* was declared dead.[18] It is not, of course: their research stands strong, their ideas continue to provoke new questions and ideas. Microhistory *proprement dit* is not 'history from below'; nor is it *Alltagsgeschichte*.[19] But all three require shifting the lens; all three value the everyday as a site of human exchange, from which the significant may emerge from the small; all three choose to people the past with flesh and blood individuals.

This collection contains something of each of these methodological cousins, but is not marked by the methodological structure of microhistory, the focus on the 'bottom' of 'history from below', nor the political aspiration of *Alltagsgeschichte*.

Yet the chapters are united by the contribution they make to the historiography of France during the Second World War by their attention to less well-known people (and indeed unknown people), to interpersonal interactions and to emotions at a broadly personal rather than national scale. Finding space to shift the lens inside this dense historiographical landscape is not easy. In his book *Marianne in Chains* Robert Gildea described his own attempt in 1997 to offer – through research in local archives and the use of oral history interviews – alternative stories about the period 1940–44 to those widely accepted among the French population. His were stories of people enjoying themselves, or having plenty to eat, among other things: he was confronted with hostility and left feeling that he had 'defaced the tablets of stone on which the official history of the Occupation and Resistance had been written'.[20] By trying to discuss aspects of everyday life which went against deeply-held views of resistance, occupation, collaboration and suffering, he had crossed a line. Nearly twenty years later, perhaps that line is not so sharply drawn, yet there is still a risk in seeking new ways to consider the period. Constructed by historians themselves, historical paradigms 'provide the structure for studying the field of enquiry': historians create the terms of the debate and shape its content; the readership knows what it expects.[21] Most published work on France during the Vichy years orientates its analysis around resistance or collaboration; this may not be explicit, but it is expected. Such an expectation derives in part from the orthodox narrative of how the wartime years should be understood – crystallized in Rousso's extremely influential work *The Vichy Syndrome*, which sees a triumphant resistance narrative interrupted in the early 1970s by the seeming 'revelation' of the shameful depths of French collaboration – particularly participation in the Holocaust, followed by an ongoing 'obsession' with this traumatic past 'which will not pass'.[22] The tendency of historians, even those more critical of Rousso's 'syndrome', to make use of the grand narratives of resistance, collaboration, heroism and guilt has endured: there seems no way to approach the French past without them. Colin Nettelbeck has remarked, apropos the exclusion of school-age children from historical studies of this period, that because (non-Jewish) French children lived outside the 'conflictual model out of which so much of the historical narrative has developed', they have not found a place in its history.[23] We can question, then, which other parts of the population, and how many more areas of historical experience have also been excluded because they cannot fit into the story – at once consensual and divisive – of victims, perpetrators and heroes.

There has been a shift towards understanding the period 1940–44 as part of a wider and longer wartime phenomenon. The years 1940–44 are those of the

Occupation and of Vichy; it is a specifically French periodization which distances the French experience from a European or indeed global one, and a periodization which permits an inward focus on the specificity of French experience. This militates against international comparison (which the present volume does not do), but it also confines analysis to what is specifically French about this period too: the combination of Vichy's National Revolution, French collaboration in Nazi anti-Semitic persecution and Germany's economic policy, the slow build-up of grassroots resistance and the impact of de Gaulle's Free French from London. While the dates 1939–45 rarely make it onto book covers – 1940–44 is the standard periodization – they say something important about a reconceptualization of France's 'dark years'. If we can understand the French everyday experience of 1939–45 as a *wartime* experience, not only does comparison become possible (which we hope this work will stimulate, a hope which accounts for our insistence on the full translation of all chapters) with civilian experiences in Italy, Belgium, Germany, the Netherlands, Norway, Poland, the United Kingdom and so on, but reveals a set of experiences of civilians on a home front: food, clothing, security, family life, government intervention – these were all affected *because* France was a battleground for the Allied–Axis conflict *as well as* a nation struggling against Occupation, pushing forwards new ideologies, redefining the terms of national inclusion and exclusion, and developing various relations with the occupier. In short, while the present volume does not seek to ignore the grand narratives of resistance and collaboration, it does not take them as organizing principles although they are present in many ways.

Vichy France and Everyday Life sits alongside recent work which emphasizes civilian experience of this period. From the Anglophone world, Julia S. Torrie's and Nicole Dombrowski Risser's works on civilian evacuation and the 1940 exodus respectively give much insight into the everyday living conditions of ordinary people whose worlds were upended by the events of war: in both of these books, but particularly Risser's, the agency of individuals is highlighted.[24] Lindsey Dodd's book on French children's lives under the Allied bombs situates French experience as wartime civilian experience, using oral history to probe emotion, interpretation and experience in accounts of ordinary lives. Shannon L. Fogg, Ludovine Broch and Daniel Lee have also published in recent times on everyday encounters between specific sections of the French population.[25] Lee's work on Jewish youth, in particular, forced the re-evaluation of a homogenous 'Jewish' experience of Vichy, through his use of private archives and oral testimony which bring everyday experiences – and thus nuance – to the fore.

Going back a few years, various works in the 1990s and early 2000s – such as Sarah Fishman's *We Will Wait* or Hanna Diamond's *Fleeing Hitler* – also used the small-scale to illuminate the bigger picture.[26] On the Francophone side, many analyses are structural and top-down, even when they treat what may seem ordinary: for example, Christophe Capuano's work on the Vichy and the family gives us no insight into what family life was like; similarly, Jean-Pierre Le Crom's book on the charity of the Secours National under Vichy focuses more on the 'instrumentalization' of aid by the regime than on how ordinary people experienced charitable support.[27] However, a striking trio of works have recently come out of the Presses universitaires de Rennes, pushing beyond the borders of structural interpretations and suggesting important new avenues to explore.[28] What we gain from both Francophone and Anglophone historiographies is the sense of peeling back the skin to reveal different segments of the population – bosses, civil servants, women, police, universities, POWs, Jews, prison, asylums, gypsies in camps, colonies, deportees – to understand the range of perspectives on interactions with Vichy, with the Germans and with issues of collaboration and resistance. While these help us to visualize many parts of a society struggling with the pressures of the occupation, the analytical, moral and interpretive structures remain those of collaboration and resistance.

Taking everyday life in wartime France more specifically, there are several works which precede this one, and should be read alongside it. From Amouroux's grand-scale works of the 1970s, to Dominique Veillon's masterful *Vivre et survivre en France*, the restrictions on life, as well as leisure pursuits and communications have been well documented.[29] The present volume builds on this work while also situating the activities of the everyday during this period within the wider context of war. Wieviorka has written that for the French, the period was 'everything but a warrior experience': of course, the years after defeat and before the Liberation saw no French military action (1939 and 1945 are largely ignored); but we nonetheless see the years 1939–45 as an experience of war for the French at home.[30] Even for those with no family members stuck in German prisoner-of-war camps, who saw no violent combat on the streets, or who were not bombed, war was present in one way or another. One does not have to be a soldier or a victim to experience war.

As editors of this book, and the instigators of a one-day conference which inspired it, we see a number of benefits to studying everyday life in wartime which make useful contributions to knowledge. First, a focus on the everyday valorizes the qualitative experiences of ordinary people; by 'ordinary', we mean those who were not the leading lights of cultural or political life. A history of their everyday lives looks at their lived experiences, emotions, interactions and the ways they spent their time, either by choice or necessity. On the one hand, this illuminates experiences which appeal to our nosiness about 'how other people lived'; such nosiness is inherent: why else would we watch so many films, TV programmes and read so many books set in the past? On the other hand, it exposes our historical actors' ambivalence to the events around them: as historians (and others) we focus our attention on big events and assume they affected everyone, or that everyone had a response to them. The everyday shows us that this is not the case: daily preoccupations trump bigger national issues, until those issues come knocking at one's door. Does this trivialize the past? Or does it make us wonder at how life can go on in extraordinary circumstances? Or at the seeming lack of penetration of issues we had assumed to be paramount? In the chapters that follow, we notice – as Steve Wharton suggests in Chapter 12 – that there are two sides which emerge to this everydayness: the first is those daily preoccupations themselves, the routines, activities and practices of everyday life; that is, human praxis. Jean-Pierre Le Crom and Sylvère Aït Amour both illustrate in their chapters how far those everyday preoccupations were affected by the penuries of war. The second is the idea of everydayness as mundane, ordinary and quotidian; and yet in the circumstances of war, making the extraordinary ordinary requires a process of absorption and normalization of often very abnormal events. Such a process is clear, for example, in Camille Mahé's chapter on children's play around air raids or food shortages, or in the unusual relations formed between colonial prisoners of war and French people, as Sarah Frank tells us.

Second, a focus on the everyday emphasizes the contributions made by these unimportant, ordinary and historically anonymous people to historical and social processes. Deterministic historical models posit a top-down flow of influence which reduces the individual to little more than a leaf, blowing in the winds of long-term structural change. Rather than seeing lives as purely controlled by abstract or impersonal forces, the history of the everyday recognizes the interaction between individuals and the material world around them, its processes and its institutions, and the cumulative power of small actions. This interaction is particularly evident in Matthieu Devigne's chapter on the work of school inspection teams, teachers, cooks and others to feed hungry children in their care; his specific cases show that the fine grain needs examining and that energetic individuals could effect change. There are undoubtedly benefits to generalizing about the past; but to universalize is to depersonalize; and to depersonalize is to make the reality of lived experience alien to those who lived it. Isabelle von Bueltzingsloewen shows very sensitively how an intensive personalization of the past – viewing it through someone else's eyes – reveals so much about its continued meaning into the present.

Third, studying the history of everyday life neither attributes pure agency to the individual, nor removes agency entirely: but it does admit agency nonetheless. *Alltagsgeschichte* historians faced criticism over the ability of ordinary people to ever understand, or ever to alter, the forces, structures and processes that shaped their lives: to focus on them, thus, would prove analytically futile.[31] But we would question the underlying assumption here: what does it matter if people do not understand the forces which shape their lives? What does it matter if they cannot alter them? The fact is that they live within them, and indeed, they do not live in day-to-day passivity; they act, think, change what they are able to act upon, think about and change, sometimes but not always. This comes to the fore quite clearly when we consider Wendy Michallat's analysis of student Madeleine Blaess's diary: here is a young women exerting her ability to act and participate in the Liberation of Paris, but fearing what gendered forces may then clamp down on the freedoms she had enjoyed during the Occupation. People are active in response to events around them, perhaps at a local rather than national scale. And their activity is not always resistance to such forces: if we only look through the lens of resistance to the world around, we lose the complex inner politics – the inner drives – which shape responses to stimuli. Some of those responses may be those of acceptance or conformity.[32] There are a set of pragmatic options through which ordinary people act to shape their present, in response to infinite nuances of decision and response to ever-changing circumstances at both the macro and micro levels. Such decisions may be and may remain inexplicable: irrational or imperfect, they confound our ability to draw clear conclusions about motivation; we might see that complexity in the decisions Byron Schirbock illustrates that were made by French sex-workers to consign themselves to the Wehrmacht brothels, or alternatively to risk freelance work. At other times such choices must be seen as simply making do or going with the flow: *attentisme*, perhaps, but the very substance of our daily lives. Steege et al. have written that at these 'microhistorical moments', when ideas become deeds, 'history is actually made'.[33]

Moreover, perhaps because of the value it places on the individual, or its recognition of human agency, or its attention to human emotion as a driver of historical change, or its concrete exploration of recognizable realms of experience, the history of the everyday awakens emotional empathy.[34] Richard Cobb told us that we need to write with sympathy about the people of the past: not *in* sympathy, but *with* sympathy. He urged historians to flex their historical imagination, to eschew the 'surgically cold' approach, and to understand that, above all, we are dealing with real flesh and blood individuals.[35] The history of everyday life has been criticized for the way it seeks to 'understand' the actions of the past without making moral judgements about their behaviour – a stance which can come close to excusing past actions. Yet surely trying to understand why people acted as they did, why other preoccupations prevented them acting as later commentators would have hoped, and why our retrospective categorization cannot account for the variety and complexity of past actions is worth an attempt? Shannon Fogg's chapter discusses middle-class families' sense of shame at aid offered to them by the American Quakers; if we cannot understand the powerful emotional drive to reject charity, then we cannot understand why some remained under-nourished even when resources were put before them.

If we return, finally, to the perspectives of our thinkers Lefebvre, Auden, Certeau and Hegel, we notice that each allocates a kind of spatiality to the everyday. Auden tells us of concrete places and spaces – the interior of a building from which a window is opened, a street which is walked upon dully – and likewise Certeau, who creates a dining table, family intimacy over a meal. For Lefebvre, its omnipresence situates the everyday all around us, and Hegel pulls it into the conscience of the individual. We too find it interesting to locate the everyday. All everyday activities take place in a space; they are both external to the actor and internal. Across the analyses in this book, the loci of every activity demonstrate the embeddedness of particular lived realities in real places – in Lindsey Dodd's chapter, it is place which forms the heart of the experience: the alien environment of the countryside, the uprooted child, the new 'home'. Everyday activity is located activity, and the locations are social spaces. Thus the everyday experience is not just a mirror image of an event played out on the small-scale local level; it is the interplay between the individual and his or her immediate society, the individual and his or her imagined community, the individual and his or her neighbour. Such variation and such multiplicity create a history that is diverse at every level. Certeau has warned against imposing logic, unity and structure on a past which did not have one.[36] Understanding the multiple situated contexts of the everyday creates a history which is less satisfying in its wholeness, but more real, perhaps, in its messiness.

This volume is divided loosely into two sections, with much overlap. Chapters in the first section 'Coping and helping' tend to focus more on how the great restrictions affecting all aspects of daily life in wartime France were manifested and approached. In Chapter 1, Camille Mahé draws on a range of sources to show

how Vichy slipped its propaganda into children's everyday lives, but also that children transformed the everyday of their playgrounds, inventing new games that reflected the world around them. Matthieu Devigne continues the focus on children in Chapter 2, using reports from teachers and school inspectors to suggest how the new hardships of war were creatively overcome by dedicated teaching professionals who wanted only to restore some semblance of normality to children's lives. In Chapter 3, Isabelle von Bueltzingsloewen reduces the scale to the micro-level, drawing us inside the world of Raymond, a child in 1944, an adult later interviewed, not only to illuminate the structures and strategies which permitted the family's survival, but also the lasting impact of the traumas of war down into the present. Chapter 4 by Sylvère Aït Amour again suggests the hardships faced by part of the population – this time railway workers – but also their ingenuity, adaptation and resilience; once more, the memory of the 'dark years' is evoked, this time in controversies over the SNCF's role in deportations. The next three chapters explore concerted efforts to help. Jean-Pierre Le Crom in Chapter 5 provides an overview of the work of the Secours National, Vichy's national charity, noting that politics is inseparable from everyday life, given the instrumentalization of the charity by the regime. In Chapter 6, Shannon Fogg focuses on the work of the American Friends Service Committee who established a Home Colony programme to assist middle-class families fallen on hard times; these Quakers had to tread carefully to ensure their aid was accepted by those unused to charity. And in Chapter 7, Lindsey Dodd examines the evacuation of children from the Parisian suburbs into the rural Creuse, away from the increasing threat of bombing; she suggests that these encounters were confrontations between very different ways of life, and for children, were not always easy transitions.

The second section develops the idea of 'Confrontation and challenge'. Wartime led to surprising encounters between populations unknown to each other, between ideas and practices, and as well as confrontations with the events of war themselves. In Chapter 8, Sarah Frank explores the experiences of interaction between colonial prisoners of war, imprisoned in France rather than Germany, and local white French populations; that interaction resulted not just in aid and escape, but in a sense of deception after the war when race relations returned to 'normal'. Byron Schirbock exploits German as well as French archives in Chapter 9 to expose the sexual encounters between German soldiers and French women in Wehrmacht brothels, as well as the systems established to police them, which he sees not just as the practical management of sexually transmitted diseases, but an aspect of German foreign rule as a social practice.

Chapter 10 is a close-up study of the experience of British student Madeleine Blaess through her detailed diary during the 'long' liberation of France, from 1943 onwards; in it, Wendy Michallat teases out the fine grain of Madeleine's intensely personal, emotional responses to the dramatic events going on around her. The challenge encountered in Chapter 11 is that of French people's resistance against the Vichy regime; Mason Norton, like Le Crom, emphasizes, using well-chosen localized examples, the unbreakable connection between everyday life and politics, showing that opportunities to resist, defy and protest emerged from the very fabric of ordinary activity. In Chapter 12, Steve Wharton examines cinema as an everyday practice in Vichy France, and the way in which the regime sought to normalize its policy innovations via 'everyday messages' put across in documentary film. And in Chapter 13, David Lees explores Vichy documentary film to show that the portrayal of everyday life in propaganda simply ignored the wartime context, particularly the food shortages so prominent across the preceding chapters, in favour of a vision of normality which turned documentary into fiction.

Notes

1 *Almanach Hachette 1941. Petite encyclopédie populaire de la vie pratique* (Paris: Hachette, 1941).

2 L. P. Hartley, *The Go-Between* (London: Hamish Hamilton, 1953).

3 Pertinent examples of this trend are the trials of Paul Touvier, Klaus Barbie and Maurice Papon in the 1980s and 1990s. See for example A. Nossiter, *France and the Nazis: Memories, Lies and the Second World War* (London: Methuen, 2003). The historian Serge Klarsfeld has also sought to commemorate the French victims of the Holocaust and to bring the perpetrators to justice. See for example S. Klarsfeld, *Vichy-Auschwitz: le rôle de Vichy dans la solution finale de la question juive en France, 1942* (Paris: Fayard, 1983).

4 For a stimulating discussion of Cobb's attitude to people in the past, see C. Cuttica, 'Anti-methodology par excellence: Richard Cobb (1917–96) and history-writing', *European Review of History: Revue européenne d'histoire*, 21.1, 91–110. For an example of Cobb's writing on the period in question, see R. Cobb, *French and Germans, Germans and French: A Personal Interpretation of France under Two Occupations: 1914–1918/1940–1945* (Watertown, MA: Brandeis University Press, 1981).

5 D. Schilling, 'Everyday life and the challenge to history in postwar France: Braudel, Lefebvre and Certeau', *Diacritics*, 33.1 (2003), 23–40, p. 31.

6 H. Lefebvre, *Critique of Everyday Life*, vol. 1, *Introduction* (London: Verso, 1991; transl. J. Moore), p. 97.
7 W. H. Auden, 'Musée des Beaux Arts', in *Another Time* (New York: Random House, 1940). Our thanks to Brian Sudlow for sharing this idea of the everyday with us.
8 M. de Certeau, *Histoire et psychanalyse entre science et fiction* (Paris: Gallimard, 1987), p.189.
9 G. W. F. Hegel, *Aesthetics* (Clarendon Press, Oxford: 1975), p. 150.
10 D. F. Crew, 'Alltagsgeschichte: a new social history "from below"?' *Central European History*, 22.3/4 (1989), 394–407, p. 399.
11 M. Gardiner, *Critiques of Everyday Life: An Introduction* (London: Routledge, 2002), p. 75.
12 H. Harootunian, 'Shadowing history: national narratives and the persistence of the everyday', *Cultural Studies*, 18.2/3 (2004), 181–200, p. 185.
13 Schilling, 'Everyday life and the challenge to history', pp. 23–4.
14 E. P. Thompson, *The Making of the English Working Class* (London: Victor Gollancz, 1963; 1980), p. 12.
15 P. Carrard, 'History as a kind of writing. Michel de Certeau and the poetics of historiography', *The South Atlantic Quarterly*, 100.2 (2001), 465–82, p. 468.
16 C. Ginzburg, *The Cheese and the Worms: the Cosmos of a Sixteenth-Century Miller* (Baltimore: Johns Hopkins University Press, 1992); E. Le Roy Ladurie, *Montaillou: Village occitan 1294–1324* (Paris: Gallimard, 1982).
17 A. Lüdke (ed.), *The History of Everyday Life: Reconstructing Historical Experiences and Ways of Life* (Princeton: Princeton University Press, 1995; transl. W. Templer); L. Niethammer, *Posthistoire: Has History Come to an End?* (London: Verso, 1994; transl. P. Camiller); D. Crew (ed.), *Nazism and German Society, 1933–1945* (London: Routledge, 1994); I. Kershaw, *Popular Opinion and Political Dissent in the Third Reich: Bavaria 1933–1945* (Oxford: Oxford University Press, 1983).
18 P. Steege, A. Stuart Bergerson, M. Healy, and P. E. Swett, 'The history of everyday life: a second chapter', *The Journal of Modern History*, 80.2 (2008), 358–78, p. 358.
19 B. Gregory, 'Is small beautiful? Microhistory and the history of everyday life', *History and Theory*, 38.1 (1999), 100–10, p. 103.
20 R. Gildea, *Marianne in Chains: Daily Life in the Heart of France during the German Occupation* (New York: Picador, 2002), p. 2.
21 K. Sheppard, 'Telling contested stories: J. G. A. Pocock and Paul Ricoeur', *History of European Ideas*, 39.6 (2013), 879–98, pp. 881, 889.
22 H. Rousso, *The Vichy Syndrome: History and Memory in France since 1944* (Cambridge, MA and London: Harvard University Press, 1991; transl. A. Goldhammer).
23 C. Nettelbeck, 'A forgotten zone of memory? French primary school children and the history of the Occupation', *French History and Civilization*, 14 (2011), 157–66.

24 J. S. Torrie, *'For Their Own Good': Civilian Evacuations in Germany and France, 1939–1945* (New York and Oxford: Berghahn, 2010); N. D. Risser, *France under Fire: German Invasion, Civilian Flight and Family Survival during the Second World War* (Cambridge: Cambridge University Press, 2012).

25 D. Lee, *Pétain's Jewish Children: French Jewish Youth and the Vichy Régime* (Oxford: Oxford University Press, 2014); S. L. Fogg, *The Politics of Daily Life in Vichy France: Foreigners, Undesirables and Strangers* (Cambridge and New York: Cambridge University Press, 2008); L. Broch, *Ordinary Workers, Vichy and the Holocaust: French Railwaymen and the Second World War* (Cambridge: Cambridge University Press, 2016).

26 S. Fishman, *We Will Wait: Wives of French Prisoners of War, 1940–1945* (New Haven and London: Yale University Press, 1991); H. Diamond, *Fleeing Hitler: France 1940* (Oxford and New York: Oxford University Press, 2007).

27 C. Capuano, *Vichy et la famille: réalités et faux-semblants d'une politique publique* (Rennes: Presses universitaires de Rennes, 2009); J.-P. Le Crom, *Au secours, Maréchal! L'instrumentalisation de l'humanitaire (1940–1944)* (Paris: Presses universitaires de France, 2013).

28 P. Laborie and F. Marcot (eds), *Les comportements collectifs en France et dans l'Europe allemande, 1940–1945* (Rennes: Presses universitaires de Rennes, 2015); J.-M. Guillon, P. Laborie and J. Sainclivier (eds), *Images des comportements sous l'Occupation: mémoires, transmission, idées reçues 1940–1945* (Rennes: Presses universitaires de Rennes, 2015); I. von Bueltzingsloewen, L. Douzou, J.-D. Durand, H. Joly and J. Solchany (eds), *Lyon dans la Seconde Guerre mondiale. Villes et métropoles à l'épreuve du conflit* (Rennes: Presses universitaires de Rennes, 2016).

29 H. Amouroux, *La Grande Histoire des Français sous l'occupation*, 10 vols (Paris: Robert Laffont, 1976–1993); D. Veillon, *Vivre et survivre en France, 1939–1947* (Paris: Payot, 1995).

30 O. Wieviorka, *La Mémoire désunie. Le souvenir politique des années sombres, de la Libération à nos jours* (Paris: Seuil, 2013), p. 16.

31 D. F. Crew, 'Alltagsgeschichte', p. 396.

32 J. P. Mitchell, 'A fourth critic of the Enlightenment: Michel de Certeau and the ethnography of subjectivity', *Social Anthropology/Anthropologie Sociale* 15.1 (2007), 89–106, pp. 89–90.

33 Steege et al., 'The history of everyday life', p. 372.

34 Gregory, 'Is small beautiful?', p. 101.

35 C. Cuttica, 'Anti-methodology par excellence', pp. 95, 101.

36 W. Weymans, 'Michel de Certeau and the limits of historical representation', *History and Theory,* 43.2 (2004), 161–78, p. 168.

Part One

Coping and Helping in Wartime France

1

Children and Play in Occupied France

Camille Mahé

> Without doubt, the games that our boys play – especially the five to six year olds – are largely shaped by war. One minute they are soldiers, the next they have become 'bombers', without, however, forgetting their hand-to-hand combat. You can often hear them say 'come here and fight!' And as peace breaks out in one corner, another group is hiding behind a handily positioned bundle of sticks, posing as infantrymen. At the same time, yet another group takes the injured away. Then the handkerchiefs come out, quickly folded into triangles to simulate revolvers, as planes roar and machine guns crackle.[1]

Describing a scene in a school playground in 1943, this inspection report from the Academy of Marseille tells us something of the role played by war in the imaginations of young children during the Vichy years. Although the Armistice had been signed in 1940 and French territory was no longer a battleground, the Second World War was still present in many youngsters' everyday lives, and thus in their games.

Play has a special role in children's lives.[2] It is a central activity, common to all, which takes place on a daily basis. Nicholas Stargardt reminds us that 'playing is as natural to children as speaking is to adults'.[3] First and foremost play provides an opportunity for release and for fun: games exist for their own sake, having a recreational function and providing us with a window onto children's imaginations. But in their play, children also reproduce what surrounds them: the behaviours and the words of the 'grown-up world' which is never far away. And so in Occupied France, everything found an echo in their games, from the news from the Eastern Front heard in the background on the radio, to a plane flying overhead, to the happy or unhappy times which punctuated their days. Play therefore provided an outlet, as well as a means to appreciate and understand reality. Thus its function is not just recreational, but also educational because it enables children to learn and assimilate information. And in some cases, when reality becomes too difficult, it can also be cathartic.

This multiple nature of children's play makes its study worthwhile when trying to understand childhood experiences of the Second World War in France. By thinking about the toys children played with and the games they invented, and thus by evoking their sensorial universe, we can shed light on the following questions: was war really omnipresent in people's lives? Did the conflict and the advent of the new regime constitute a rupture for young children, who could not always remember the pre-war period? To what extent did the political world of adults permeate children's lives? When it did, how did the youngest react? To answer these questions, I will make use of diverse sources including toys, children's press, oral histories and drawings, all of which reflect a material culture, or '*culture enfantine*', as Julie Delalande has called it, rooted in a specific spatio-temporal context.[4]

This chapter suggests that propaganda or news-related toys brought the Vichy regime and the world war – which nonetheless remained fairly distant for many – into children's worlds. Indeed, children were placed at the heart of Marshal Pétain's National Revolution.[5] In its effort to inculcate its values, the Vichy government used toys as learning, improving and even propaganda tools. However, even though such toys familiarized children with current affairs, it is not possible to speak here of a militarization of their play: the presence of war in children's games appears among other things as a legacy of the Great War. It is therefore more appropriate to speak about an updating of war-related games, rather than their sudden appearance. More generally, this chapter shows that while play was not initially significantly altered by the conflict – which was short-lived on French soil, although the air threat remained constant and combat returned in 1944 – it evolved, both qualitatively and quantitatively, as everyday difficulties came to the fore. The fear of bombs, as well as cold and hunger due to fuel and food shortages, progressively appeared in school playgrounds as children integrated them into their games. Finally, the changes in family dynamics due to war – absent fathers, working mothers – meant that play itself became secondary, and in many cases little to no time could be devoted to it. Children's domestic responsibilities increased, although age and gender were of course significant variables here.

Yet in France during the Second World War, children played a great variety of games, which tell us as much of their joyful and carefree lives as of their fears and troubles. It should be noted that not everything was dark during the *années noires*; on the contrary, in the countryside particularly, numerous children remained untouched by war, trauma and propaganda – which illustrates just how rich and diverse the pool of everday experience was and is.

The weight of the regime and the war: a playful and mobilizing universe

Toys designed for young children during the period of the Vichy regime show a clear and conspicuous intention on the part of the French State to use the sphere of play as a space for propaganda. Indeed, children were unlike any other group in the context of the regime's aim to 'regenerate' France: thought to be more malleable and more inclined to integrate Vichyist propaganda than adults, they represented an idealized future in which the values of the National Revolution would be perpetuated. They were seen, then, as important actors who needed to be moulded and mobilized.[6] A multitude of toys were thus manufactured, which sought to reshape children's play worlds. Such 'political' toys – which should be distinguished from merely belligerent games, although they share some of their characteristics, such as guns or military costumes – were vehicles for national or partisan propaganda.[7] Below, I consider three kinds of political Vichyist toys, and what they suggest about children's everyday lives during this period.

The first kind were toys which idealized Marshal Pétain as France's saviour. Jigsaw puzzles such as 'The Marshal's Christmas', published by the Secours National, cut-out and colouring books, and many board games all featured the 'victor of Verdun' as their central figure, styled as a benevolent, protective and very approachable grandfather.[8] His 'sacrifice' for France made him an obvious role model. Thus in one of the colouring pages of *L'Imagerie du Maréchal*, entitled 'The Gift (of his person by the Maréchal) to France', he stands tall between the ruins of a town in flames and a stormy sea, and resists.[9] The picture makes clear reference to the rapid defeat of the French army in 1940, the flames recalling the battles, the derelict town the loss of homes. Underneath, a caption quoted his words: 'Since our Victory [in 1918], THE SPIRIT OF ENJOYMENT HAS TRIUMPHED OVER THE SPIRIT OF SACRIFICE [...] I GIVE THE GIFT OF MYSELF TO FRANCE, TO RELIEVE HER SUFFERING.' There is here an evident allusion to the failures of the Third Republic. The image of a strong, inflexible and providential man fearlessly facing the storm which threatens France found its echo across children's books of the period. Gilles Ragache detailed some twenty such books glorifying Pétain, published between 1941 and 1943. He notes that in some of these, such as Yvonne Estienne's *La Belle histoire d'un chêne* (The Beautiful Story of an Oak), the Maréchal is turned into part of the natural world, linking him to the land and to 'eternal' values, in direct contrast to the modernity and decadence of urban life.[10] Some toys even encouraged children to identify with the great man. César, a toy manufacturer, sold masks of Pétain's face – but also of Laval, of various well-known French officers, of certain German politicians and even of Hitler.[11] Parisian department stores also sold Pétain costumes: thus, children could play at being among the 'greats' of the political world, and could become state or war leaders – and this was new, given that such costumes had not been available until then.[12]

The second category of toys and games was historical, and aimed to insert the Vichy regime into an overarching and grand narrative of 'French History'. The 'Great Game of French History', made by Witho, was a lottery game meant both to educate and to inculcate Vichy's messages. On the lid of the box was written:

> History is the destiny of a people as brought about not only by its outstanding heroes, but also by the continuous effort of the whole race. This game will help you learn about our history, 'the cradle of all Frenchmen's ideals'. It will teach you the names and the actions of those who have contributed to the grandeur of our legacy, and to the glory attached to the word 'French'. By playing this game, you will come to better understand your duty and prepare yourself to follow our country's traditions.[13]

Somewhat unsurprisingly, the last date featuring in the game – and thus in its retelling of French history – was 1940, when the Maréchal came to power to save France. These historical games placed France at the heart of the world, as did the map of the 'French Empire United Behind the Maréchal', which was for sale, and which shows French territorial influence.[14] Such objects presented the regime, and particularly Pétain, as the culmination of the 'Eternal France', the France of Clovis, of Joan of Arc and of Louis XIV.

A third type of playful propaganda was the moralizing game. Such objects aimed to convey the values of the French State – the only 'true' values – and, through a constant criticism of the Third Republic, to encourage sacrifice and effort. The idea was thus not just to entertain the young, quite the contrary: the French State saw toys as an excellent means to educate. This was the purpose of the 'Francisque' game (made by Labrys), a game of snakes and ladders, whose squares represented particular qualities: while 'trust', 'team spirit' and 'solidarity' allowed players to climb the ladders, 'idleness' and 'selfishness' sent them sliding back to square one. This game was also sent to prisoners of war, begging the question as to whom it was really intended for. It is, however, similar in style to other games explicitly designed for children, such as the 'Game of Life', a Happy Families-type game, sold from 1941, whose goal was clearly to instil traditional values and denounce those that had led to defeat.[15] The first card reads: 'This game was made so that you may learn, while playing, the innate and attainable qualities necessary to live a dignified life.' 'Honour', 'Honesty' and 'Ideal' are thus opposed to families such as 'Lies' and 'Idleness'. The objective was to develop a national spirit, a spirit of sacrifice in these troubled times. Play became a fictional world moulded on the National Revolution.

As Christophe Capuano has analysed, family policy was at the very heart of the National Revolution from its inception.[16] Traditional family values were seen as the basis of national regeneration, and thus there also appeared numerous toys which promoted normative gender roles in family life: the ideal family comprised a father – the *chef de famille* and bearer of all authority –, his wife and their four children. At the start of the Occupation, the Comité national de l'enfance (National Committee for Children)[17] released 'Dr Schreiber's Snakes and Ladders', a game devised to give an overview of the government's family policies, and to familiarize female players with the tasks they would accomplish later in life as mothers.[18] Three of the main themes were hygiene (square 37: 'wash your hands several times a day'), morals (square 53: 'be respectful') and, most importantly, the education of babies. Young girls were thus informed, for example, that 'all mothers should breastfeed their children' (square 1), that babies should be weighed on a weekly basis (square 11), and that their nappies should be changed often (square 35). Under the image of a girl playing with her doll, on square 47, was the text: 'Today I'm putting clothes on my dolly; when I grow up I'll dress my children myself.' Gendered stereotypes are present throughout the game. Boys were portrayed as cheeky, while girls were quieter, busily playing at 'being mummies'. From a very early age, then, games were used to teach children about the roles they were destined to fulfil as adults to further the achievements of the National Revolution.

Of course, gendered games were by no means new; yet the future roles of young girls had rarely been promoted to such an extent in written form and in games released during a period of 'peace'. There was thus a sense of novelty to those games, derived from the characteristics of Vichyist propaganda. This novelty was nonetheless relative, however: the rise of the social hygiene movement and the tribulations of the Great War had already led to the promotion of such educational toys and games during the earlier part of the century.[19] Conflicts tend to augment and exacerbate gender distinctions, especially when it comes to children.

It is therefore clear that a government can succeed in permeating children's worlds, via everyday objects and – more particularly – games, to instil a new ideology. It is worth noting here that the games focusing on family or family policies tended to target girls more consistently than boys: Vichy's propaganda centred on the two core figures of the regime's family policies, the mother and the child. The government's efforts to pervade children's daily life were thus palpable both at school and in the private sphere.

A militarization of play?

While the regime's propaganda only rarely made mention of events beyond French borders, there were numerous objects of play populating children's everyday lives which were coloured by current or European affairs. Thus there was a significant gap between Vichy's agenda – marked by the will to leave the war behind and focus on collaboration and the immediate future – and many manufacturers' intentions to adjust their production to demand. In December 1939, the Bon Marché department store listed in its Christmas catalogue a 'Maginot Line' kit, toy army trucks and officer costumes. The following year, now during the Vichy period, the Samaritaine store advertised various kinds of weapons, uniform costumes, toys tanks and the ubiquitous toy soldiers. Similarly, children's magazines such as *Fanfan la Tulipe* reported on the manoeuvres of the German Army, and offered make-it-yourself activities such as the construction of paper war planes. In doing so, they stirred up children's imaginations, in particular those of boys, and left them excited and curious to know more.

Was there really a 'militarization' of the sphere of play, though? Comparing pre-war and Vichy-era toy catalogues would suggest a negative response. Although military toys were certainly updated under Vichy – for example, with regard to the Maginot Line – they were not more numerous than in the 1930s. The growing supply of military toys was, rather, a long-term phenomenon, linked to the First World War; these toys were not specific to Vichy. Manon Pignot places heavy emphasis on the continuity between the two conflicts, noting that the children of the First World War had, by the Second, become parents. This means that 'a number of childhood representations formed during the First World War were then projected onto the Second'.[20]

Furthermore, military toys were on the whole less numerous than others: only around ten of them feature in each of the 1930s and 1940s catalogues.[21] Teddy bears, dolls, tea-sets and games of skill were much more present in shops. Archival research reveals a similar tendency: military and Vichyist toys only represent a fifth of the toys made available to children in the wartime period. Of the 111 toys held in the Poissy Toy Museum, only eighteen make explicit reference to military themes, which amounts to just over 16 per cent. At the Musée des Arts Décoratifs, they account for a little under 20 per cent of the toy collection.[22] These observations must of course be qualified by the fact that no archive holds an exhaustive list of the toys available during the Vichy years, and that the toys now on display are by definition objects which have stood the test of time – which begs the question of how much they were used; perhaps military toys got more battered and have not ended up being preserved. Still, drawing on both the catalogues and the archives, the findings suggest that the supply of and demand for military toys did not change significantly during the Vichy years. The evolution is more qualitative, updating the parties represented in line with the new political realities. After the Armistice, Germany could no longer be portrayed as the enemy in manufactured toys and games; although this does not mean that children changed their own play in the same way.

The impact of current affairs is much more tangible in the advertisement pages of the toy catalogues, as well as in children's magazines. Drawing competitions and stamp sales were regularly organized by the Secours National in order, for example, to help French prisoners of war.[23] There was continuity in the moralizing and patriotic message from before and after the fall of France: in December 1939 the Bon Marché Christmas catalogue featured an advert showing lines of tin soldiers behind a doll who was knitting, with the caption 'we knit for them': that is to say, we, young girls, are knitting for our soldiers on the front line.[24] After the Armistice, posters appeared in a similar vein, but now promoting aid for prisoners of war. Children were thus encouraged to participate in the wider project of national defence on a daily basis, under the guise of play. The aim was to create a connection between children and prisoners, a bond whereby each party was responsible for the fate of the other.

Toys can therefore suggest a great deal about the play practices of children, and, by extension about their everyday lives: rather than a militarization of society, what is apparent here is a strong incitation towards both self-sacrifice and participation in the national effort. The aim was to make children understand that they lived in a troubled period, which was, however, not war – which explains the absence of war in the games produced by Vichy's propagandists. For the war had ended with the Armistice, and although France was going through trying times, Marshal Pétain was protecting them. Yet such manufactured toys and games can only suggest part of the story: they cannot tell us how children played with them, or what they thought about them, only what was expected of them by adults.

Beyond manufactured toys: play as a reflection of everyday life

It should not be forgotten that very many children had no access to new toys and games. These became prohibitively expensive during the 1940s, as sales catalogues demonstrate. Dolls, for example, were sold at 30 to 70 francs at the Bon Marché department store in 1939. Two years later, their price had doubled: the cheapest were 77 francs, while the dearest were 140 francs. In 1942, dolls ranged in price from 80 to 232 francs; and by 1943, they cost between 110 and 335 francs.[25] This inflation extended to all toys. Meanwhile, the purchasing power of most families was decreasing dramatically. Alfred Sauvy found that, as early as 1941, expenditure on food could amount to 91 per cent of family income.[26] New toys, in this context, were not a priority, even at Christmas: food, fuel and clothing had to come first. Furthermore, toy manufacturers reduced their output due to factories being requisitioned, often for the German war effort. Materials were more expensive, rarer and of a lower quality. Overall, most children had few toys during this period, and those which existed were often hand-me-downs from parents or elder siblings, dating from an earlier time. Children with toys of their own or new toys were from the most privileged backgrounds. Children's magazines such as *Benjamin* nevertheless proposed affordable activities using only paper, which did give a number of children access to new games, but also allowed the drip-feeding of Vichy's ideals via their pages.

Thus, more often than not, children played without toys. Such toyless activities were those through which they expressed themselves the most, and revealed the fabric of their everyday experiences. In order to access these activities, it is necessary to use sources which are less readily available but also more information-rich. These are often subjective, created by children themselves: drawings, diaries or objects which they made themselves. Such contemporary sources, which need a particular treatment, are complemented by retrospective oral accounts, as the case of Jacqueline T. shows. Indeed, like many others, she remembered that 'if you wanted to play, if you wanted to have games or toys you had to make them yourself, because there was nothing at all'.[27] Oral accounts can thus enrich our understanding of past practices which have left no material trace.

New kinds of play

War, in its armed and direct form, did not last long in metropolitan France: peace was re-established by June 1940, thanks to the Armistice. The difficulties were, of course, by no means over; yet in rural regions, many families remained relatively unaffected. Especially for those in the 'Free' Zone, war seemed very remote, at least until November 1942 when the Germans occupied all of France. As a consequence, apart from those who had survived the painful and traumatic civilian exodus of 1940,[28] children's games appear not to have altered much in the early days. Yet for those not directly affected, the grand adventure of the conflict proved rather appealing, and children's play was increasingly orientated around the events of the current war. Louis Mexandeau has written in his memoirs that:

> in the lives of children, as in those of nations, war is not simply an event, it is *the* event *par excellence*. I experienced the early days of the war as some kind of enchantment: a succession of unexpected events and discoveries, of new emotions and indeterminate fears.[29]

Many of those who were children at the time provide similar accounts of war as a captivating and potentially exciting phenomenon, which unleashed the imagination and allowed for the invention of new games.

In 1939 and across the years which followed, children played more and more 'war' games, and, in their imaginary world of guns and battles, the protagonists were brought up to date in a carefree manner. War was thus present, but in a joyous and light-hearted form. Following the progress of various armies was common, as for Jean-Louis Besson who, with his cousins, unfolded a map on his table-tennis table, and placed on it hand-painted models representing various armies, tanks and planes, adorned with rosettes or swastikas.[30] Jacqueline T. also remembered plotting the progress of the armies in this way: such interest was by no means limited to boys. Everywhere in France, war was a source of inspiration for new games. The 1943 inspection report from Marseille noted that children in the district made more and more reference to war in the playground, pulling in the latest news, or information about the German, Russian or British forces.[31] In some cases, children copied the gestures of the German soldiers who patrolled the streets of their towns and villages:

> The occupying troops have piqued the curiosity of our children, who are more intrigued than afraid; [. . .] they try to parade like soldiers, and to emulate the way in which they speak.[32]

Boys became busy planning attacks, jumping 'face down in the bushes', 'crawling', or parading 'in front of their leader'. They formed troops of volunteers and pretended to be on parade or deep in battle, and nurses also made an appearance.[33]

Play was also shaped by conversations overheard at home, which affected whether the Germans or the Allies were portrayed as 'baddies' or 'goodies'. Existing games were updated, as numerous drawings, songs and dances testify: 'Qui veut jouer à papa-maman, man, man, man' ('who wants to play mummies and daddies – ddies – ddies – ddies') thus became 'Qui veut jouer au bombardement, ment, ment, ment?' ('who wants to play bombing – ing – ing – ing').[34] Yet their games retained a certain innocence even while reflecting the auditory and visual transformation of their environment and the pervasiveness of war.

Nonetheless, shocking experiences such as surviving an air raid or losing a loved one had a very tangible impact on young people's lives, and in such cases the sudden manifestation of the brutality of the conflict tended to shift their relation to war games. This brutality was more felt in the northern part of France: children were much more scared by the sight and sound of a plane flying over, given that they experienced air raids on a more regular and systematic basis.[35] As the Marseille Inspection Report shows, sometimes they ended up so traumatized by such events that they could not integrate them into their games anymore. The report's author thus notes that while children from Marseille got very excited when a plane flew over them, to the point of being almost disappointed not to be the target of an attack, the same sight made refugees from the Occupied Zone extremely anxious.[36] Children's games reflected the evolution of everyday life experiences: games which in the beginning were very popular stopped when the real-life experiences underpinning them proved too vivid, or too painful. With innocence now transformed into knowledge, practices changed, particularly towards the end of the war.

Play practices as a reflection of everyday life

The familial sphere progressively evolved too. With 1.8 million prisoners of war in 1940 and the implementation of the Service de Travail Obligatoire (Forced Labour Service – STO) from 1943 onwards, a number of families found themselves missing fathers or older brothers, which meant that youngsters had to contribute more to household chores. Children's drawings of long queues in front of shops suggest a significant diminution in terms of the variety and the quantity of the food available, all testifying to loss and even hunger.[37] Above all, they suggest a significant reduction of play time: having fun was less and less the order of the day. After school, many were expected to come straight back home and help. Several interviewees recalled being sent to fetch food or firewood. Marie-Noëlle G., who was from a rather privileged background, remembers that her mother sent her and her brother to a friend's house in order to heat up their dinner as she had no fuel left. On their way back her brother suggested that they 'give [it] a try to see whether it's cooked, as otherwise [we'll] have to go back there': the two hungry children ended up eating the lot in the street.[38] Everyday struggles thus reshaped the nature of children's activities. This was particularly noticeable with children from underprivileged backgrounds, but, as Marie-Noëlle's case shows, the middle class was not spared.[39] Age was also an important factor: the eldest were entrusted with the most difficult tasks and had to care for their younger siblings.

Rationing nevertheless became part of a number of play activities, especially in the playground. If boys generally had a predilection for 'war' games, girls' games took on a more economic or domestic dimension, reflecting their role in the private sphere: gender is, of course, a significant variable in the experience of the everyday life under Vichy. Girls played 'shop', but, in an echo of the food shortages they experienced on a daily basis, their shelves were empty. This scene involving several schoolgirls was recounted by the Marseille School Inspector:

> 'I've queued for hours, and I've nothing.' 'Me neither, but I have to go now, my kids are waiting for me. Oh! Poor, poor us!' In a corner of the playground, Françoise makes soap out of clay, sand and water; her 'children' are being really naughty, they always end up getting dirty, so she has no choice but to make them stay in bed. Denise is complaining: her own children constantly tear up their clothes, she spends so much time mending them, and there are no more aprons in the shops. The talkative Marie-Jeanne similarly laments: 'I've bought two [ration] cards this month, I'm broke!' Meanwhile, another girl is about to board a train for the Haute-Loire, where she hopes to buy [ration] cards to sell on the black market.[40]

Children thus reproduced what they saw and heard every day in the familial context, imitating the grown-ups around them. What should also be noted is that the girls were acutely conscious of the difficulties which their families were facing at the time, from lacking the necessary resources to mend children's clothes, to the effects of cold weather, to absence of food and soap. In fact, the black market proved a popular game among school children, which goes to show how vain were the efforts made by adults to keep children away from serious conversations and everyday problems. Children were not dupes: few practices, however illegal or supposedly invisible, escaped them. This also suggests that the

Vichy government's moralizing propaganda, expressed through political toys for example, was perhaps not as successful as hoped: children were less malleable than assumed.

The play world was thus both fictional and imaginative, and reflective of the realities and hardships of everyday life. To accept, face and adapt to the latter, children used games to play through their concerns. Such games were not just ways to make everyday life more bearable, but also a means to understand and interpret it. Children's games could thus be cathartic, and offered a form of resilience amidst difficult and sometimes traumatic living conditions.[41] This proved to be even more the case around D-Day and the difficult months which followed, where the experience of fear and loss became more acute and widespread.

Playing in wartime, but not playing at war: happiness as well as sorrow

While the Occupation was undoubtedly a painful time for many, as is evident from some of the games depicted above, some experiences were better than others. Numerous accounts from people who were children during the wartime years hint at quite happy, if not very happy memories of that period. Children's worlds were not systematically permeated by current affairs. Indeed, there existed many games which had no link whatsoever with war and its impact, as is shown by a series of drawings held at Rouen's Musée National de l'Éducation (National Museum of Education): these drawings depict games or nursery rhymes such as 'Savez-vous planter les choux' ('Do You Know How to Plant the Cabbages?'), 'La Capucine' ('The Capucine Dance'), 'Le furet du bois joli' ('The Ferret in the Lovely Woods'), 'Pigeon vole' ('Flying Pigeon'), 'Au petit chat' ('The Little Cat'), 'A la délivrance' (a type of chasing game), 'A cache cache' (hide-and-seek). None of them echo, directly or indirectly, the war or the regime's propaganda.[42]

Similarly, many homemade toys were unconnected with current affairs. In oral accounts, interviewees seemed almost apologetic for not having any games which seemed to be original or directly linked to the historical context. This was just ordinary life. There was a significant difference, however, between town and country. Food was more accessible in rural areas, and the German presence less tangible. The streets, gardens, parks and fields of their immediate environment provided children from the countryside with many more opportunities to play than the city. Jacqueline T. was struck by the contrast between Paris and the countryside when she was evacuated in 1943, away from the Allies' bombing of the Parisian suburbs: 'it was all so different. Let's say that, in the countryside, life itself was a game, because there were chickens, rabbits, ducks, a garden.'[43] The countryside constituted an immense playground, isolated and protected from conflict and fear. Coming from the city, such a world seemed extraordinary.

We could therefore sketch a 'map of suffering' which would account for the variety of childhood experiences under Vichy, with, on one hand, more privileged areas such as the countryside or the 'Free' Zone (until November 1942), and, on the other, the city, the Occupied Zone, the coastline, and above all the border zones, such as the Nord-Pas-de-Calais (controlled from Brussels) and Alsace and the Moselle (annexed to Germany and subject to a brutal germanization), all of which suffered much more from air raids, deprivation and the German presence.[44]

Conclusion

The sphere of play provides a unique insight into everyday life (of both children and adults) under Vichy, revealing a multitude of experiences, rooted in particular gendered, social and geographical backgrounds. While there were as many experiences as there were children, it is still possible to identify certain trends. I have shown that Vichy's 'political' toys brought current affairs directly into children's worlds, and bore the mark of a strong will to inculcate Vichy's values among this section of the population. The role of toy manufacturers is difficult to assess precisely, as there is a significant lack of archival material in this respect. On the whole, it seems their role was rather minimal for various reasons, ranging from the lack of material resources to the obligation to send toys to Germany and, to some extent, the need to adjust supply to demand.

This is why the analysis of games without toys and of homemade toys provides us a better glimpse into children's worlds. Indeed, while playing, children mimicked their surroundings and expressed their anxieties, in a way which suggests that they were much less malleable than Vichy had thought or hoped. This is certainly down to the fact that they had restricted access to the regime's 'political' games, but also to the fact that the hardships of everyday life impacted on them so much more than the idea of national sacrifice. Speeches exhorting self-sacrifice, whether at school or in the children's press, could make little headway with those already suffering from hunger and cold; the promotion of 'honesty' and moral rectitude existed alongside certain illegal practices which young eyes clearly took in. Such a detachment could only increase as the German Occupation tightened its grip: through 1943 into 1944, children became hungrier and colder, and less free to play, often coping with greater responsibilities at home and the emotional burden of family separation. Such strictures applied particularly to those in urban milieux, those whose fathers were absent, and the elder rather than the younger siblings in a family. But if some grew old before their time, this does not mean that they forgot to play; and it is playing which helped them to face all sorts of difficulties, to laugh, and, in spite of everything, to be happy – or, at least, to try their best.

Translated by Benjamin Bâcle

Notes

1 Archives Nationales (AN), F/17 13364: Report by M. Gait, Inspector of Primary Education in Marseille, 10 December 1943.

2 Childhood can be understood as a social construct, and its boundaries have evolved with time, defined by institutions such as school. Under the Occupation in France, ration coupons divided young people into three categories: J1 (ages 3–6 years), J2 (7–12 years) and, introduced later, J3 (13–21 years). In the 1940s, school was compulsory for children aged between 6 and 14. In this chapter I take childhood to refer to the 6–14 age bracket.

3 N. Stargardt, 'Jeux de guerre, les enfants sous le régime nazi', *Vingtième Siècle, Revue d'histoire*, 89.1 (2006), 61–76; N. Stargardt, *Witnesses of War: Children's Lives Under the Nazis* (New York: Vintage Books, 2005).

4 A. Arleo and J. Delalande, *Cultures enfantines: universalité et diversité* (Rennes: PUR, 2010). The expression can be translated as 'children's culture'.

5 See, for example, L. Dodd, 'Children's citizenly participation in the National Revolution: the instrumentalization of children in Vichy France', *European Review of History: Revue d'Histoire Européenne*, 24.5 (2017), 759–80.

6 In this respect, Vichy's objectives can be compared to those of totalitarian regimes (although there are marked differences in terms of both degree and purpose). See, among others, F. Thuin, *Pétain et la dictature de l'image, Enfance et jeunesse, cinq ans de propagande* (Clermont-de-l'Oise: Éditions Daniel Bordet, 2011), p. 78.

7 This definition can be found in *Jeu, jouet et politique, catalogue d'exposition du 5 mai au 4 juillet 1982* (Poissy: Musée du jouet de Poissy, 1982), p. 24.

8 Regarding politicised dimension of the national charity, the Secours National, see J.-P. Le Crom, *Au secours maréchal! L'instrumentalisation de l'humanitaire (1940–1944)* (Paris: PUF, 2013). See also the chapter by Jean-Pierre Le Crom in this volume.

9 Located at the Librairie Thierry Corcelle, 29, rue de Condé, Paris.

10 G. Ragache, *Les Enfants de la guerre; vivre, survivre, lire et jouer en France (1939–1949)* (Paris: Perrin, 1997), p. 322. See also: J. Proud, *Children and Propaganda: Il Etait une Fois . . . Fiction and Fairy Tale in Vichy France* (Bristol: Intellect, 1999).

11 These masks were designed for adults as well as children. It is likely that they were intended to mock not just to adulate – yet we cannot know precisely their usage in the hands of those who bought them. While department store catalogues feature various faces, it is impossible to estimate how many were sold over this period.

12 This is shown by a study of the department store catalogues (Archives du Musée des Arts Décoratifs de Paris [MADP]), as well by oral history interviews.

13 Musée du jouet de Poissy, 997.55.8.

14 Mémorial de Caen, FC 71, 3: 'Propagande Vichyste'.

15 Available at the Musée National de l'Éducation de Rouen [MNER], 6.5.16.01/1978–02197.

16 C. Capuano, *Vichy et la famille. Réalités et faux-semblants d'une politique publique* (Rennes: Presses universitaires de Rennes, 2009), p. 354.

17 The Ligue contre la mortalité infantile (League Against Infant Mortality) was created in 1902, and became the Comité national de l'enfance in 1922. The aim was to work in partnership with the authorities in order to fight against child mortality, among other things.

18 Available at MNER: 6.5.16.01/1978–02197.

19 See Manon Pignot's works on this subject, especially M. Pignot, 'Petites filles dans la Grande Guerre. Un problème de genre?', *Vingtième Siècle. Revue d'histoire*, 89.1 (2006), pp. 9–16.

20 M. Pignot 'Les enfants', in S. Audoin-Rouzeau and J.-J. Becker (eds), *Encyclopédie de la Grande Guerre* (Paris: Bayard, 2004), p. 1050.

21 MADP, uncatalogued.

22 See C. Mahé, 'Des éclats de rire entre les bombes, les expériences enfantines de la guerre à travers le jeu et les jouets dans la France occupée (1939–1945)', unpublished Master's dissertation, Sciences Po Paris, 2014.

23 See the chapter by Jean-Pierre Le Crom in this volume for more on the activity of the Secours National.

24 MADP: Bon Marché Christmas catalogue, December 1939.

25 MADP, uncatalogued. It should also be noted that the price of the Maginot Line kit was 230 francs in 1939, and the prices of train sets ranged from 100 to 200 francs, while the annual salary of the average worker was 10,520 francs, a little over 875 francs per month.

26 A. Sauvy, *La vie économique des Français de 1939 à 1945* (Paris: Flammarion, 1978).

27 Interview with Jacqueline T., born in 1935 (Mahé, 'Des éclats de rire entre les bombes', p. 152).

28 During the 1940 civilian exodus (often just called the *exode*), between 6 and 8 million French people found themselves on the road. René Clément's 1952 film *Jeux Interdits* suggests the sometimes traumatic experience of death and destruction on the road, in the child protagonist's obsession with a new 'game': populating an animal graveyard. Red Cross statistics show that perhaps 95,000 children were 'lost', separated from their families, during the debacle and the *exode*. Entire newspaper columns were devoted to missing person appeals. See E. Alary, B. Vergez-Chaignon, G. Gauvain, *Les Français au quotidien, 1939–1949* (Paris: Perrin, 2006), p. 350; also H. Diamond, *Fleeing Hitler: France 1940* (Oxford and New York: Oxford University Press, 2007); and N. D. Risser, *France under Fire: German Invasion, Civilian Flight and Family Survival during the Second World War* (Cambridge: Cambridge University Press, 2012).

29 L. Mexandeau, *Nous, nous ne verrons pas la fin. Un enfant dans la guerre (1939–1945)* (Paris: Éditions Le Cherche midi, 2003), p. 325.

30 J.-L. Besson, *Paris Rutabagas* (Paris: Gallimard Jeunesse, 2005), p. 94.

31 AN, F/17 13364: Report by M. Gait, Inspector of Primary Education in Marseille, 10 December 1943.

32 AN, F/17 13364: Report by M. Gait, Inspector of Primary Education in Marseille, 10 December 1943. It is also important to point out that playground games remained gendered: girls played more often at nurses and boys at soldiers.

33 Noted by Mexandeau too. See Mexandeau, *Nous, nous ne verrons pas la fin*, p. 280.

34 AN, F/17 13364: Report by M. Gait, Inspector of Primary Education in Marseille, 10 December 1943.

35 See L. Dodd, *French Children under the Allied Bombs, 1940–45: An Oral History* (Manchester: Manchester University Press, 2016).

36 AN, F/1713364: Report by M. Gait, Inspector of Primary Education in Marseille, 10 December 1943. In her chapter in this volume, Lindsey Dodd shows that children evacuated to rural areas of France often took their traumas with them.

37 A large collection is held at Rouen's Musée National de l'Education. See, for example, MNER: 1979.9330.10: 'Queue sous la pluie' (Queuing under the rain); MNER, 1979.9330.2: 'Queue rue nationale' (Queuing on the rue nationale); MNER, 1979.9330.29: 'Queue d'alimentation' (Queuing for food).

38 Interview with Marie-Noëlle G., born in 1934 (Mahé, 'Des éclats de rire entre les bombes').

39 See Shannon Fogg's chapter in this volume for a discussion of how the middle classes were affected by shortages.

40 AN, F/17 13364: Report by M. Gait, Inspector of Primary Education in Marseille, 10 December 1943.

41 See B. Cyrulnik, and C. Seron (eds), *La Résilience, ou comment renaître de sa souffrance* (Paris: Éditions Fabert, 2004), p. 247.

42 See, for example, MNER, 360100-1979-09387-0005: 'Le furet du bois joli'; MNER, 360100-1979-09391-0003: 'Pigeon vole'; MNER, 360100-1979-09389-0005: 'Au petit chat'; MNER, 360100-1979-09388-0004: 'Le palais royal'. Of course, these drawings were all done under supervision, with the specific instruction to represent playground games; however, nowhere on the page is there a trace of any painful experience. Quite a few of the interviewees mentioned such games during their interviews (Mahé, 'Des éclats de rire entre les bombes').

43 Mahé, 'Des éclats de rire entre les bombes', p. 128.

44 Such geographical factors need to be considered alongside sociological factors, given that children's experiences under the Occupation vary considerably depending on their social backgrounds.

2

Coping in the Classroom: Adapting Schools to Wartime

Matthieu Devigne

A history of the school system under Vichy is first of all a history of what happened in schools themselves – a history of the difficulties and the banalities of a daily life continuously disrupted by the ordeals of war and occupation.[1] Inspector Bellau of the Ardennes education authority remembered coming back from the civilian exodus on 18 July 1940 to 'an indescribable mess': '154 schools had been affected by the war, 32 of which were completely destroyed, while a number of them were occupied, either by the German army or by prisoners; almost all the staff had had to evacuate to the western departments.'[2] Like his colleagues working in other regional education authorities, Bellau immediately set about reopening and keeping open the schools which had been spared destruction or occupation, so that 'primary teaching may continue uninterrupted'. It was only after schools were properly refurnished that the new regime's so-called pedagogical 'realignment' could begin to permeate everyday life in the education sector. But the reform of school practices needs both time and the means to invest in resources – two things that Vichy lacked. In spite of a number of modifications to class organization and curricula, the ongoing changes in everyday life were such that it was doubtful whether a 'revolution' within schools was possible at all. Any innovation was more likely to occur outside of the classroom, through the ceaseless development of charitable initiatives such as food and clothing collections, and canteens. These brought sociability and solidarity to the heart of children's daily lives – vital resources, particularly for those living in cities. Indeed, during these 'dark years', schools proved to be a hub of moral and material resistance, not only for children, but for all the men and women involved in their day-to-day life and organization.

Facing the Occupation

The academic year 1940–1 was particularly complicated in the Ardennes region of north-eastern France. With people coming back from the exodus in waves, school services constantly had to adapt, notably by creating new classes, more often than not headed by inexperienced auxiliaries who only held the *brevet élémentaire* (the lowest level of educational qualification). Such appointments were often the only option for Inspector Bellau: the German authorities, extremely parsimonious in their granting of *laissez-passers*, made it difficult for school staff to move freely around the country. In particular, the Germans mistrusted teachers who had been taken prisoner of war, but were then conditionally released in order to resume their function; their managers were likely to send them south, where they would escape the watchful eye of their erstwhile captors.[3] But the main hindrance to the resumption of teaching stemmed from the requisition of public buildings. School buildings held the advantage of combining sanitary facilities with playgrounds (covered and uncovered) and multiple office spaces for officers; they were, in many ways, perfect ready-made barracks.

The general inspectorate of administrative services, having sent delegates on a special mission to assess the consequences of a particularly chaotic first year in the Nord and the Pas-de-Calais, where the German presence was heavy, reported that:

> Everywhere, education authority inspectors, head teachers and school directors made work their priority, with total abnegation and tireless activity. They harass town councils, appeal to other citizens, negotiate with the Occupier, and now and then, along with their teachers and pupils, act as removal men or carpenters. They have managed, miraculously, to provide their pupils with a normal education, whether it be in a disused factory, a recruitment office, a museum or a dentist's apartment. In the hearts of these skeleton-like cities, amidst all the ruins, behind a heap of rubble and twisted girders, one thus finds quiet teaching spaces, where classes run on time and curricula are scrupulously followed [. . .].[4]

Most annual reports by regional education authority inspectors made similar observations. But these inspectors' reports and complaints, even when supported by local prefects, only rarely managed to convince the local military authorities that something needed to be done. It was only when the Ministry of Education and Marshal Pétain's cabinet intervened that the Germans agreed to release the 530 school buildings to which access had been forbidden since early 1942, but which were standing by unused.[5]

Contrary to its standard practices, the Ministry of Education was now working in an atmosphere of uncertainty. Occupation-related disruptions had blurred the statistical framework which administrators usually adjusted at the start of every academic year.[6] Based on pre-war data and thus unable to account for population displacement linked to war and occupation, current provisions were now obsolete, and so in August 1941, the 'School Map' was updated.[7] The request was made by several education authority inspectors that more positions be opened, and none suppressed; this clarified the situation somewhat for primary education. Under the supervision of the then Minister of National Education and Youth, Jérôme Carcopino, the Ministry asked every education authority inspector to produce a new school map for their department, so that available resources could be better allocated across the country. The initiator – probably Stéphane Jolly, the director of primary education – explicitly recommended that inspectors not yield to the pressure of any local or particular interest; nor should they be lured by 'administrative convenience' in the matter of staff appointments. The only imperative was that no child should be made to walk more than four kilometres to go to school, or three kilometres in mountainous areas.

In spite of all these difficulties, Inspector Bellau was impressed with teachers' attitudes in the Ardennes:

> Morale among staff is excellent: all primary school inspectors are full of praise for the courageous attitude of those teachers who are back at work in the Ardennes. Anyone who has even the vaguest idea of their new working conditions can only agree that they are extremely dedicated: what with schools having been partly or completely occupied or demolished, furniture damaged, teaching resources (often teachers' own work) destroyed or soiled, libraries taken down, books burned, torn or stained, places ransacked […] material life in most establishments is highly precarious. And yet, all of them appear genuinely happy to be back.[8]

Relieved to be back at their posts despite the difficult circumstances, these teachers would be required by the Vichy regime to reorganize a substantial part of the primary education system.

Facing Vichy and its reforms

The 15 August 1941 reform was the most comprehensive of all of the French State's education policies. Carcopino's first aim was to reassert the superiority of secondary education over primary education, by transforming the *écoles primaires supérieures* (the 'upper' primary schools) into modern *collèges*. In addition, the most promising pupils were invited to study for a *diplôme d'études primaires préparatoires* (DEPP – Preparatory Primary Studies Certificate), moving into a second cycle of primary education, which would allow them to go on to high school. As a result, this reform involved a reorganization of primary education. Sport and art education, but also practical subjects – manual work for boys and housework for girls – were thus introduced. But they required material resources which were often lacking, particularly in such times of war and occupation. Such were the logistical problems that by the end of the school year 1941–2, inspectors found that the reform had only been loosely implemented. This led Stéphane Jolly to call his staff to order via an October 1942 circular.[9] Blaming their failure to apply the reform properly on their excessive cautiousness, the director of primary education appealed to his personnel's sense of initiative and resourcefulness in the face of material scarcity: 'Teachers are expected to adapt using their personal observations, recorded on a daily basis, their reflections and their memories.' Vichy, thus, does not appear to have been particularly authoritarian in the enforcement of its pedagogical policies; it was down to the agents on the ground to define the conditions of the reform's application.

General Inspector Pouron was one such agent. While touring the Puy-de-Dôme in 1942, he realized how complex the teachers' situations were as a result of the new ministerial recommendations.[10] What posed the most problems to staff was the division of primary teaching into two cycles, organized around the DEPP. Indeed, in most small, rural schools, the main criterion when it came to organizing classes was that of academic aptitude, rather than age, which meant that pupils of various ages attended the same lessons. In the Puy-de-Dôme countryside, where numbers were often too low to justify a distinction between two cycles, second cycle classes were only ever rarely organized. The only way around that problem was to bring together all the second cycle children from different primary schools in a convenient location. However, town councils were reticent to oblige, and material shortages compounded their reluctance; so much so that in Inspector Pouron's jurisdiction, only the town of Riom had managed to do this. Nonetheless, teachers had been applying the 14 October 1942 circular, according to which no pupil aged twelve or more should be left to languish in the top classes of primary school (*cours élémentaire* and *cours moyen*). It was advised that 'measures [be] taken so that every child, before leaving primary school, may spend a year in the second cycle [of the primary system]'. The General Inspector observed that pupils 'do benefit, in however minimal a way, from the new classes they are made to join', and that as a result, some even went on to prepare for the DEPP. Overall, he declared himself satisfied to see that the schooling of many children had been usefully extended up to the age of fifteen.

Yet forcibly moving those children who had fallen behind into the second cycle of the primary system made the teachers' task more complicated. Up to then, admission into these classes had been dependent on a highly selective process. Pouron deplored that some teachers were struggling to adapt to their new intake, and advised the streaming of these classes to account for discrepancies in ability. Two groups were thus set up in every class in the most important subjects: arithmetic, spelling and writing. To try to prevent such discrepancies in ability arising in the first place, the General Inspector stressed the importance of making pupils work as hard as possible as early as possible, during the elementary or even the preparatory stages of their education. However, this required that pupils come to school on a regular basis, something which was not guaranteed, especially in rural departments such as Cantal, where travelling anywhere was still difficult in the middle of the century. In 1944, Pouron would again observe that:

> Besides the pupils whose attendance is normal and who spend two years in each class, there are a number of others, living in rural areas, sometimes working as shepherds, who only spend 6 months a year at school, and who linger in the *cours moyen* [the top two classes of primary school], if not the *cours élémentaire* [the next two classes down]. And if they are a little slow or intellectually deficient, they tend to quit school at the end of the first cycle.[11]

More generally, rectors and education authority inspectors agreed on the fact that the current circumstances were not making it easy for pupils to concentrate on their studies. Among the things they had to put up with were:

> Insufficient food supplies, bad working conditions (with classes often delivered in inadequate spaces), fathers being absent, mothers unable to look after them because they have to work, time wasted running errands, general anxiety, stress caused by air raid alerts, a lack of qualified teaching staff, a reduced number of teaching hours in primary school. Families are less involved in the supervision of their children's homework; teachers see parents less often.[12]

Gaining the families' trust, however, was not enough to guarantee the success of the whole enterprise. Schools had to be able to make up for the potential indigence or negligence of these families. This is where schools' work outside the classroom became increasingly important from the early 1940s onwards; such work rapidly drew the political attention of the Vichy regime.

Facing children's hunger

From as early as the 1930s, the Ministry of Education saw school canteens as a crucial means to increase school attendance.[13] The war made the development of these canteens even more urgent, as is shown in a memorandum sent by Maximilien Sorre to education authority inspectors in November 1939:

> All of our efforts must focus on subsidising school canteens and allocating maintenance bursaries. [. . .] Current circumstances make it even more necessary not only to develop existing canteens but also to create new ones, particularly in places where such canteens had not been deemed necessary until now.[14]

A year later, the Vichy Secretary of State reiterated the urgent need to develop canteens in order to make them better used by schoolchildren.[15] But the demarcation line and the introduction of rationing had drastically changed the supply conditions. The problem was more pronounced in cities: restrictions operated like a tight belt, and malnutrition was a real risk. In January 1941, the Secretary of State for Supply laid down the conditions of food supply based on the number of ration tickets collected from pupils, and the regional inspector was given the power to issue supply coupons allowing canteens to receive bread, meat, fats, sugar, pasta or dry vegetable supplements.[16] At the same time, the national aid organization, the Secours National, endeavoured to distribute vitamin pills and chocolate-coated bars to all pupils aged six to fifteen in both private and public schools.[17] Eagerly supported by Vichy, the Secours National quickly strengthened its hold on food supplies in the education sector, and in January 1942 became the sole provider of supply coupons to canteens.[18] Each canteen was supervised by the director of the school to which it was attached. This could lead to a heavy workload, particularly in the largest schools. Unless he could recruit qualified staff, he had to manage the supplies himself, as well as take the money handed in by the parents who paid for their children's food, along with subsidy tickets and a vast number of ration tickets.[19]

The telling case of the Bouches-du-Rhône education authority in southern France helps us better understand the important place of food among the everyday concerns of school teachers and administrators. From spring 1940, the canteens of Aix, Arles and Marseille faced a significant surge in the school population as a result of the arrival of a large number of refugees from occupied territories. The urgent question of how to feed those children required a prompt and decisive response on the part of local inspectors, which was only possible if administrative hindrances could be avoided.

Newly transferred to the region, Inspector Fuster was soon impressed with what one of his subordinate inspectors, Coste, had already achieved in the Arles district. Coste had managed to turn what was essentially a means of supplementing existing resources, relying mainly on contributions from families, into a properly organized public service. Reporting on the situation, Fuster presented his colleague's activity as a 'method of organizing food resources which can serve as an example to others'.[20] To start with, the city of Arles only had one canteen, which served only one dish – a thin broth. This canteen was not well used, as families tended to favour packed lunches. As a result, inequalities were made blatant between, for example, workers' children and farmers' children: 'I saw a pupil "completing" his meal with a dozen olives and one salted sardine, while, beside him, a farmer's son was enjoying a substantial portion of rabbit stew.' It was Coste's uneasiness at seeing this malnourished child which spurred him into action:

> It was crucial to act quickly; I could not afford to set up a committee, to compare plans and gather opinions. The summer holidays were only three months away, which meant I could experiment and then study the results in detail, in order to have up and running, after the two-month break, a fully functioning system.

The canteens which Coste launched on 12 May 1940 were able to serve a very substantial soup made with mashed vegetables or pasta as well as another substantial meal. Success was immediate. For two francs, children were given soup, a main course and two sugar cubes. They only had to bring their own bread and a drink. Coupons allocated by the local education authority allowed canteens to put together two different menus per week. For vegetables, discounts had to be negotiated directly with suppliers. In October 1940, school directors, in agreement with the primary inspector, could offer price reductions to disadvantaged families. The difference was paid for by the town council, until the Secours National delivered on its promise to subsidize a thousand meals a month.

School directors were thus burdened with a heavy administrative workload. Every one of them had to constitute a canteen fund for their school, with a reserve of at least 1,000 francs, to be quickly raised through local subscriptions and the sale of tombola tickets. Inspector Coste, meanwhile, set up a central fund to support canteens in deficit, financed by donors. Accounts were updated on a daily basis and statements issued weekly about each deficit, so that the canteens' work could continue uninterrupted. By the summer of 1941, the success of this enterprise had led Coste to consider rationalizing communal food production by investing in the establishment of a central kitchen, able to supply all ten of Arles' canteens. Coste, then, had every reason to be satisfied and optimistic, even more so as 'the results are tangible, particularly in the expert eyes of the doctor, in schools where medical inspections are taking place'.

Meanwhile, Inspector Fuster, in charge of the Marseille area, was lagging behind a little: while the council provided free meals to some categories of children (children of prisoners, widows, unemployed people or from big families), many deprived young people were still denied such help.[21] Fortunately, from the start of the 1940–1 academic year onwards, the American Quakers were complementing the council's efforts to provide free meals to the people most in need.[22] The menus available comprised a soup made of fresh vegetables and pasta, as well as a 'copious' main course. Parents were expected to provide the dessert themselves.

Fuster did think of allowing each school director to organize and supply their own canteen,[23] but for this he would need the authorization of municipal and prefectural authorities, who remained unresponsive to his plea. Henri Gossot, who succeeded him from March 1942, also tried to establish a more integrated catering service in Marseille, but his efforts were met with a similar lack of support, stemming no doubt from the dysfunctional state of the local administrations.[24] Yet, only a few miles away from Marseille, the canteens set up by Inspector Coste in Arles were still performing remarkably well,[25] and had inspired the authorities in Aix-en-Provence to implement a similar system: a central committee comprised of council representatives, the primary school inspector, and school directors, deputy directors and teachers, made it easier to adapt to rationing difficulties and provide the canteens of Aix with much needed food supplies.[26]

> Generally speaking, everywhere except in Marseille, there are school canteens which work to the greatest satisfaction of teachers and families. In Marseille, however, they are notoriously insufficient. No attempt to change the situation – whether on my part or on the part of the town council, which, I cannot deny, has made a real effort – has yielded any tangible result to date.[27]

In the 'Marseille-Sud-Ville' district, the tireless dedication of teachers and canteen workers meant that some canteens did function in a relatively satisfactory manner. Yet the ability of those working on site to maintain standards was seriously impeded by high food and fuel prices. Extreme exhaustion could sometimes lead to exasperation, and staff soon called on both the Secours National and the supply services of academic inspectorate for emergency support.

Two problems remained unsurmountable: the lack of food diversity and its scarcity. Whenever a particular ingredient was lacking, pupils were asked to bring it to school with them; this was the case with green vegetables, until, in 1943, they simply could not be found anymore. Canteens were then left with no choice but to feed pupils with Jerusalem artichokes, sometimes to the point of food poisoning, as in the case of the girls' school on rue Lautard. As far as food scarcity was concerned, the situation was not helped by the carelessness displayed by municipal services, which greatly irritated school directors. Madame Scapula, a nursery school inspector, was thus quoted in Inspector Gossot's report saying:

> It is impossible for directors to control the produce that is brought to their school. The deliverymen working for the council leave everything in the hallway, sometimes whether the director is there or not, and leave before any control can be effected, on the grounds that they are in a hurry, that they must deliver elsewhere, etc.

Davesne, a primary school inspector who also worked in the Eyguières canton of the region, also remarked:

> It seems that the supplying of canteens by Marseille city council is actually a bad idea: the produce is bad quality and the control of deliveries insufficient. Canteens should probably be granted more autonomy, but this would require that they get access to important supplements and be given more efficient means to collect tickets.

According to the academy inspector, it was imperative that the current situation, which was untenable for both staff and children, be resolved soon. This situation seemed to stem from a conflict between the city authorities and the Secours National, with the Secours National reducing its support, being unable to gain any control over local transport and the funding of canteens. 'What is certain', Gossot stated, 'is that our children in public-funded schools only receive a very minimal amount of food aid from the Secours National, in comparison with what the same organization provides to children in Lyon, for example'. On this basis, he asked that district canteens in the Marseille area be made autonomous, and that a committee involving representatives from the city, the Secours

National and the schools be constituted, to rationalize the buying and the distribution of foodstuffs: 'The city of Marseille, which is quite far behind, must double its efforts to make up for the undeniable ineffectiveness of its work to date.'[28]

It seems that, eventually, canteens were granted more autonomy, but also that a central committee was never constituted – leaving the coordination of the 180 Marseille canteens, for the year 1943–4, to the academic inspectorate and its personnel. To deal with this, Gossot drew on the resources intended for social services and schools' extracurricular social work, following a method he had already successfully put to the test in Saint-Étienne during the period 1940–2.[29] A system like this, whereby the Secours National delegated some of its competences to the academic inspectorate, was not, however, exceptional: such an organization also existed in the Seine-Inférieure education authority, as a means to make the services, partly run by the academic staff, more efficient.[30]

It is important to note that such canteens were not only to be found in big cities. Departmental education bulletins, which were still published in a number of regional education authorities during the war, are filled with comments on all the efforts made to feed schools in the countryside. In January 1944, the inspector of the Aude department thus singled out a class in which all pupils were involved in the running of a makeshift canteen, 'peeling vegetables before class, washing the dishes and tidying up after class.'[31] The inspector of the Rhône educational authority, in a 1942 assessment, also praised the schools' staff for managing to serve meals to 41,043 children, in a total of 388 active canteens: 'those substantial meals are unanimously appreciated by parents, who note that, once registered with the canteen, their children no longer lose weight.'[32] The archives are full of such accounts of small victories over the detrimental effects of war on children. Still, however energetic and dedicated the action of the education personnel proved to be, it could barely compensate for the damage done by food shortages and rationing, especially in big cities such as Marseille. The following anecdote, reported by a nursery school inspector in 1943, serves to illustrate both the banality and the pathos of the situation:

> 'What did you have for breakfast before coming to school?' Lucien replies: 'I didn't have any milk, and we have no more bread coupons, so I had a tomato with some salt.' On another day, the same Lucien, who normally has lunch at the canteen, arrived without his lunch basket. When we ask him why, he says: 'my Mummy told me that I can't go to the canteen today; we've got no bread at home' [. . .] little Lucien knows all too young the pressing anxiety of tomorrow's needs.[33]

Resisting the times

The war, the occupation, the Vichy regime: however difficult they may have made everyday life in France, these three factors did not, could not, stop time within the classroom. Of course, teachers and pupils were sometimes forced to move, to do away with part of the curriculum or even to suspend their activities for a brief period of time; but the authorities made full use of existing human and administrative resources so that school could continue without being completely interrupted. More important still, circumstances did not suspend the evolution of the education system in France: relatively sheltered from political and ideological pressure in their respective corners, teachers and other staff members discretely carried on experimenting and reflecting on their practice. It would thus be wrong to see Vichy as a pedagogical 'fallow' period for the French education system: this would be to overlook the extent of the teachers' unceasing efforts to find a compromise between the need to adapt to ministerial injunctions and the individual drive to improve one's own practice and skills.

The primary education reform introduced by the Carcopino law had a strong structural impact on a number of schools, where classes had previously been organized by aptitude rather than by age. The reticence of some teachers to act upon this reform was not unconnected to their growing defiance towards a regime perceived to be less and less likely to last. In his first report after the Liberation, the primary inspector for Rennes would thus state that 'too many teachers saw the reform as owing to a political agenda, and were convinced that it would disappear along with the Vichy regime. This was a serious obstacle for us'.[34] Still, some schools managed to adapt and respond to the authorities' call for innovation. General Inspector Fourrier was, for example, impressed by the level of coordination achieved by the teachers' council of a Haute-Vienne school:

> from the rationalization of the symbols used to grade the homework to that of grammatical terminology and of the various techniques to teach writing, etc. [...] they understand that a school with several classes forms a whole, that no teacher can work independently of the others, and that success resides in the unity of all those who are in charge, in the same institution, of the education of the same children. One could even go further and extend this coordination to other parts of the programme. Why not, for example, draw up the annual list of recitations together?
>
> This would minimise the risk of having the same La Fontaine fable taught to the same pupils in three consecutive year groups – which is something I once witnessed.[35]

These efforts only bore fruit so long as the Occupation or the war did not interfere: requisitions and air raids could lead to the closure of a school or the dispersal of its staff and pupils overnight. When such a situation occurred, teachers mainly focused on finding the right class for the right pupils. A Lyon inspector thus advised one of his teachers, who was in charge of welcoming new arrivals from a recently closed down school: 'make sure to study them attentively, as we need to know whether they can follow this class. Revision exercises in arithmetic and French, over a few days, should give you a fair idea in this respect.'[36]

This is how schools handled war. But the life of schools cannot solely be reduced to pedagogical matters. Schools are also hubs of sociability and resistance against whatever may damage the childhood experiences of their pupils, from everyday anxieties to scarcities of all kinds. Studying the school system during the 'dark years' is an opportunity to explore another dimension of working life within the educational sector; in particular, school canteens emerge as one essential extracurricular task, among many others which proved so vital to children. Inspectors, directors, teachers and all of the men and women working in schools displayed an impressive amount of energy to ensure that children would be fed and both physically and morally safe. These dark years left many of them exhausted, and made the following years, also marked by hardship and deprivation, much more arduous.

Acknowledging these efforts, and imagining the impact they had on everyone involved, helps understand what it must have been to endure and face the challenges of wartime France. Everyday endurance is, after all, another way of resisting – of resisting through a time of countless perils, in order to safeguard the minds and bodies of the youngest, who had the privilege, paradoxically, to be at the heart of public policies, whatever the regime.

Translated by Benjamin Bâcle

Notes

1 This chapter is derived from the author's unpublished PhD thesis: M. Devigne, 'Classe de guerre : une histoire de l'École entre Vichy et République' (Université Paris Sorbonne, 2015).

2 Archives nationales (AN), F/17 13377: Report presented to the Prefect and the Departmental Administrative Commission by the education authority inspector on the state of schools in the Ardennes, 10 May 1940–15 May 1941.

3 AN, F/17 14276: Copy of a letter from the commander of the German forces to the general delegation of the French government in occupied territories, 6 January 1941.

4 AN, F/17 13380: Report from General Inspector Fouret, sent on a special mission with general inspector M. Popineau in the academies of Lille, Nancy and Besançon, 4 June 1941.

5 AN, AJ40/563: Letter from the German Armistice Commission to the president of the French delegation, 27 August 1942. Also AN, AJ40/563: 'Verzeichnis der Schulgebäude die, obgleich nicht mehr belegt, noch beschlagnahmt bleiben', 28 January 1942.

6 The statistics published in the autumn of 1941 were presented as being those of the year 1940/1, when they actually partly reproduced those of the previous years. AN, F17/ 13380: Comparison of the data given on page 166 of the 'Recueil des statistiques scolaires et professionnelles de 1936 à 1942' ('Compendium of school and professional statistics from 1936 to 1942') (Paris: Bureau Universitaire de Statistique), published in 1943, with all of the statistic tables of the year 1940/1.

7 AN, F/17 17543: See 'La Carte scolaire. Situation de l'École publique au 1er décembre 1938' ('The School Map. An Assessment of the State of Public Education as of the 1 December 1938'). Handwritten and unsigned document, probably by Maximilien Sorre.

8 AN, F/17 13377: Report presented to the Prefect and the Departmental Administrative Commission by the regional education authority inspector on the school situation in the Ardennes, 10 May 1940–15 May 1941.

9 AN, F/17 14276: Ministerial circular on the organization of the second cycle in primary schools. Version dated 8 October 1942.

10 Archives départementales du Puy-de-Dôme [ADPD], 208W 30: Report from general inspector Pouron on the implementation of the second cycle, 30 December 1942.

11 AN, F/17 14300: Report assessing the state of primary education in the department of Cantal during the school year 1943/4, 31 October 1944.

12 AN, F/17 13364: Report assessing the level of 11 to 12-year-old pupils in secondary schools and the results of the introduction of the DEPP (based on the Rectors' reports).

13 AN, F/17 14275: Canteens could be supported by council authorities or organized by schools with funds collected from families. From 1938, specific funds were allocated by the Ministry on the basis of appeals launched by education authority inspectors (circular dated 4 February 1938, the modalities of which were reiterated in a circular dated 10 February 1939).

14 AN, F/17 14275: Memorandum by the director of primary education, 13 November 1939.

15 AN, F/17 14275: Circular dated 8 November 1940.

16 AN, F/17 14276: Circular by the Secretary of State for Supply, dated 27 January 1941.

17 AN, F/17 14276: Memorandum to the rectors by A. Terracher, Secretary General for Public instruction, dated 24 January 1941. For more on the Secours National, see the chapter by Jean-Pierre Le Crom in this volume.

18 R. Baudouï, 'La renaissance sociale à l'œuvre dans la reconstruction: du Secours national à l'Entraide française par le Secours social', in C. Franck (ed.), *La France de 1945: résistances, retours, renaissances*, 337–52 (Caen: Presses universitaires de Caen, 1996).

19 See the situation in Lyon as depicted in M. Brison, 'L'école et l'enfant à Lyon: le problème de l'alimentation dans les cantines scolaires', *Revue d'Histoire de la Deuxième Guerre Mondiale*, 125 (1982), 37–71, p. 42.

20 The following examples and quotations are taken from Fuster's report to the Prefect of the Bouches-du-Rhône, 25 February 1942 (Archives départementales des Bouches-du-Rhône [ADBR] 76W 48).

21 ADBR, 76W 48.

22 On the American Quakers' aid to families in Marseille, see the chapter by Shannon L. Fogg in this volume.

23 ADBR, 76W 48: Fuster's report to the Prefect of the Bouches-du-Rhône, 25 February 1942

24 ADBR, 76W 48: Report by the inspector of the Bouches-du-Rhône education authority for the year 1942/3, dated 18 September 1943.

25 See Coste's detailed account, republished in the above report: annexe no. 28, p. 668.

26 ADBR, 76W 48: annexe no. 28, p. 668.

27 ADBR, 76W 48: annexe no. 28, p. 668.

28 ADBR, 76W 48: annexe no. 28, p. 668.

29 ADBR, 76W 48: This is mentioned in the inspector's account of his activities, intended for the general inspector and president of the National Association for School and Post-School Charitable Activities in Primary Education (4 July 1944).

30 AN, F/17 13356: Inspector Famin was pleased with the supply system he had put in place in 1942. The Seine-Inférieure region benefited from its proximity to the place where vegetables were grown. However, finding fat and fruit was as difficult there as in the rest of the country, and the combined efforts of the General Supply Services and the Secours National did not manage to change that. See pages 16 to 25 of the report on charitable activities in the Seine-Inférieure education authority, dated 31 March 1944.

31 Extract from a primary inspector's report, quoted in 'L'alimentation des écoliers', *Bulletin départemental de l'enseignement primaire* (*Departmental Bulletin of Primary Education*) of the Aude department, January 1944.

32 'Nos cantines', *Bulletin départemental de l'enseignement primaire* (*Departmental Bulletin of Primary Education*) of the Rhône department, March 1942, p. 122.

33 AN, F/17 13364: Report by Mademoiselle Radureau, nursery school inspector in Marseille, written between 10 and 17 December 1943.

34 Archives départementales d'Ille-et-Vilaine, 282W 23: Report by the primary school inspector in Rennes for the year 1943/4, 25 November 1944.

35 Extracts from the report by General Inspector Fourrier, 2 March 1944. *Bulletin départemental de l'enseignement primaire* (*Departmental Bulletin of Primary Education*) *de Haute-Loire*, no. 2, April-July 1944.

36 ADBR, 1T 5449: Inspection report of 13 March 1943 by Julia Vaney, teacher in the girls' school on rue Robert, Lyon, 13 March 1943.

3

Reconstructing the Daily Life of a Lyonnaise Family

Isabelle von Bueltzingsloewen

Translated by Lindsey Dodd

Breathing life back into these people posing for the photographer in their Sunday best, Raymond pointed first to his father, Maurice, in a dark suit, kneeling in the front row. The photograph was taken on 7 May 1944 in Avressieux (Savoie) at the Communion of one of Raymond's cousins, Bernard, the son of his paternal uncle Marcel and his aunt Marguerite (figure 3.1). Maurice and his wife Louise had come from Lyon to celebrate this special occasion, reunited once again with their two sons, aged eight and six, who were living at the time with their paternal grandparents in Pont-de-Beauvoisin (Savoie), seven kilometres from Avressieux. As well as his mother and his elder brother Charles, Raymond also pointed out three of his father's siblings: Marcel, Francisque and Andrée. Raymond himself sits on his grandmother Françoise's lap. He commented with surprise that he was holding his father's hand, as though their proximity seemed strange to him.

This fairly ordinary looking photo taken at a family gathering in rural France during the 1940s on the surface betrays little of life at war or under occupation. The serious faces and stiff poses conform to the norms of family photography at the time, reflecting the solemnity of the occasion.[1] It falls to Raymond, then, to shed light on a document which would otherwise be of little of interest to the historian. First, he remarked upon the absence of Robert, his father's youngest brother, who, he explained, was away at the Chantiers de la Jeunesse in Saint-Magne (Landes). He also pointed in the photo to Jean, nephew of an uncle, who lived in Orly but had been evacuated to the countryside by his parents in order to escape the Allied air raids and food supply difficulties in the Paris region. But above all, he situated and interpreted this photograph in relation to an event which turned his life upside down: the death of his father, killed in an air raid shelter at the factory where he worked during the Allied bombing of Lyon on

Figure 3.1 Family photograph in Avressieux, 21 May 1944

26 May 1944. Raymond was certain: his cousin's Bernard's Communion was the last time he ever saw his father. Although he showed no particular emotion as we looked at it together, this snapshot, preserved by his mother in her 'memory box' until she died, holds a strong symbolic charge for Raymond; even more so because it was taken with his father's camera.[2] Having decoded the image, a task which only Raymond can perform, the hidden meaning of this seemingly everyday artefact becomes clear. Indeed, contrary to first appearances, the war and the Occupation are its primary subject.

The aim of this chapter is to examine how the 'dark years' were lived day-to-day by an ordinary Lyonnaise family, which suffered neither persecution nor repression, nor was it uprooted away from familiar locales. It is necessary first to identify the increasingly heavy constraints which weighed upon the family's everyday activities, from shortages of all kinds, to measures taken by the authoritarian Vichy government, to the impact of the policy of collaboration, to the Allied bombing. But more than that, I will bring to light the strategies, more or less developed, which the family employed to adapt to these constraints, drawing on all the resources of their environment – geographical, familial, professional and so on. Such strategies, of course, could but rest on a partial understanding of the circumstances; the full range of possibilities was unknown to the protagonists who, unlike us, did not know how the story would end.

Writing history collaboratively

It was meeting Raymond that inspired me to start thinking at this micro scale about the daily lives of French people during the Vichy years. This was not a chance meeting; it came about through some research I was doing into the victims of the American air raid of 26 May 1944 in Lyon.[3] Raymond is the president of the Association des Anciens d'Olida; the Olida factory, which preserved and cured meat, was where he and his father had both worked, and where his father was killed in 1944. Each year, the Association holds a modest ceremony to commemorate the victims of the bombing, of whom forty-eight were Olida employees who met their end trapped in the factory's bomb shelter, not far from the railway which the United States Army Air Forces had targeted. It was Raymond who, after the factory was knocked down, made sure that the commemorative plaque which had hung next to the former shelter, was conserved and who, on the fiftieth anniversary of the air raid, got the plaque repositioned in a public place; it remains one of the rare commemorative traces of the events of 26 May 1944. Although not politically engaged, Raymond has nonetheless fought hard to ensure that the victims of the Allied bombing have a place in local memory.[4]

Raymond was likewise motivated by a desire to share his experience with others. I understood this most clearly when he decided, surprisingly to my mind, to travel all the way to Saint-Brieuc, some 800 kilometres from Lyon, to meet a man called Claude, with whom I had made contact in the course of my research. Claude's parents had also died when the Olida factory was bombed, yet he and Raymond had never met before, nor was there any specific link that we could establish between Raymond's father and them. That Claude's parents had been alongside Maurice and had died in the same circumstances as him was enough to justify Raymond's expedition to Brittany. It could also be suggested that it was the brutal death of his father on 26 May 1944, rather than any particular interest in genealogy, which had led Raymond to become the 'keeper' of his family's memory, which he has progressively elaborated and enriched, collecting documents and photos from various members, and conducting research in libraries and archives.

Of course, Raymond was just a child during the Occupation.[5] He was born in 1937 and was only seven years old at the end of the war. Like the neuropsychiatrist Boris Cyrulnik, who has written about his experiences as a hidden Jewish child and was born in the same year as Raymond, he nonetheless has very clear memories of events or situations which struck him, particularly those nearer the end of the period.[6] He remembers having seen German soldiers patrolling the platforms at Valence station as he travelled by train to stay with his great-aunt in Murinais (Isère) in summer 1944. He also remembers very precisely having gone to hide in the forest along with other inhabitants of Murinais, and returning home in the early hours of the morning having seen some Forces françaises de l'intérieur (FFI) fighters in action. Chronologically, Raymond's memories are organized around the traumatizing moment of his father's death; he situates all events in relation to 26 May 1944. It is also worth pointing out that Raymond's knowledge of the period and of his family's history comes not just from his own memories, but from a 'family story', nourished and shaped over time. For example, Raymond had often heard it said that his uncle Marcel had transported a 'chef de Résistance' on his motorbike. He describes his own recollections of 26 May 1944 as being mediated by his brother's memories. Two years older than Raymond, Charles had often recounted to Raymond how they watched the American bombers flying overhead to Lyon, how they clapped and cheered to see them; Raymond cannot recall this. On the other hand, he remembers very clearly his mother and his aunt Andrée stepping off the bus in Pont-de-Beauvoisin after his father's funeral, which the boys had not attended. She was wearing, he recalls, a hat, with a black veil.

Most members of Raymond's close family are no longer living; his brother Charles died in 2009. While certain details have been added later by former Olida employees, this family story is really only accessible via Raymond's memories.[7] Or nearly.[8] While he had never considered 'checking' the authenticity of his uncle Marcel's resistance activity, I suggested to him that it might be interesting to find out a little more. Raymond contacted his cousin Jeanine, who sent him Marcel's *carte de combatant volontaire*, awarded to him in 1954, as well as various documents she had conserved after the death of her parents.[9] Such oral sources and family archives – photos as well documents about Maurice kept by Raymond's mother until her death in 1978, and after that by Raymond – have been compared with more classic kinds of historical evidence, such as local press, the *état civil*, censuses, inheritance documents, military records and sources more specifically related to the air raid of 26 May 1944.[10]

Separation: a planned but sorrowful experience

Unlike Claude, whose family fled Alsace to escape its annexation to the Reich and found themselves in Lyon, completely isolated, Raymond and his family were not uprooted geographically. Yet the war years saw the family go through various separations and displacements which contributed to their strategy of adaptation to the new circumstances, and drew heavily on their extended family. Indeed, like many Lyonnaise families, often recently arrived in the city, Maurice and Louise still had strong family connections with the countryside and the little villages of the nearby rural *départements*.[11] While Louise's parents lived in a district of Lyon called the Point-du-Jour which was some way from the centre, she had relatives in the Haute-Loire and in Isère, but she was an only child. Maurice, on the other hand, was one of seven, with four siblings still living by 1940. His parents had lived in Pont-de-Beauvoisin in Savoie since 1909, having moved there from Lyon, where their three eldest children were born.[12]

Louise went to stay with her parents-in-law in Pont-de-Beauvoisin with her two sons when Maurice was mobilized in September 1939. He served as a mechanic in an air force regiment in Barby, near to Chambéry.[13] Just before Raymond was born in 1937, the couple had moved into a three-room social housing flat on the newly-constructed États-Unis estate in Lyon, not too far from the Olida factory where Maurice had worked since at least 1936.[14] Moving in with her parents-in-law, whose house was rather cramped, was perhaps not experienced as an uprooting for Louise, but must have meant a loss of both comfort and autonomy. However, this solution meant that the family could spend longer together when Maurice had leave; and while Maurice's leave card, which is remarkably imprecise, does not state which base he was attached to, Raymond is certain that he was at Barby for the whole of the Phoney War and the Battle for France in 1940.[15] This move to the grandparents' house also caused a further rupture in family life: Louise got a job as a typist at the Cusin furniture factory, leaving her boys with their '*mémé*' (their grandmother).[16]

This chapter in the family's life ended on 20 July 1940 when Maurice was demobilized. But for Raymond, who was not yet three years old, it marked the beginning of an experience of separation from his parents which would last four years. When his parents returned to Lyon with his older brother, and moved back into their flat on Boulevard des États-Unis, Raymond remained with his grandparents in Pont-de-Beauvoisin. He went to school in the village, and made friends with local children. A photo taken in 1942 shows him with other children, all in their Sunday best, carrying a basket of rose petals during the Corpus Christi festivities of 1942. His situation is different again to Claude's: while Claude's parents remained in Lyon having found work at the Olida factory, he was sent to his maternal grandparents in Morbihan in Brittany, far too far to visit.[17] Pont-de-Beauvoisin, on the other hand, was eighty kilometres from Lyon, and Raymond's parents managed to see him relatively often – Raymond believes every fortnight.[18] What we know for certain is that he was brought up by his grandmother until the age of seven, which he certainly understood at the time: a little note survives, which he presented to Françoise along with a needle-case he had made at school for Mother's Day in 1944 (he was not due to see his own mother until the following weekend): 'Dear *Mémé*, I wish you a Happy Mother's Day for Sunday. As my Mummy isn't here, I'm giving you all my kisses because you go to so much trouble for me' (figure 3.2).

To what extent can this family separation be attributed to the context of the war and the Occupation? Responding to this question runs the risk of anachronistic thinking. Not living permanently with one's parents was quite a widespread experience in inter-war France, especially for the younger children of working-class families in which both parents worked. This childcare solution was often used when grandparents – or other members of the extended family – lived nearby.

Would Raymond's family have stayed together had war not arrived and forced this adaptation? Without concrete evidence, the answer can only be conjecture. We know that on her return to Lyon, Louise found work as a secretary for the Patay electrical company, not far from the family home – in contradiction to the principles of the National Revolution which required that a mother of two young children stay at home if her husband was not a prisoner of war.[19] What we do not know is why she made the decision to work: was Maurice's salary insufficient for the family to live on during these years of shortages and high prices? And why were the brothers separated? Raymond stayed in Port-de-Beauvoisin while Charles was sent to Point-du-Jour with his maternal grandparents, much closer to his parents. Perhaps Louise was hesitant to give both of her children into the care of her stepmother, whom she did not know that well, her father having remarried in 1937 after the death of his wife five years before.[20] Perhaps she thought it better to leave little Raymond with his *mémé*, with whom he had just spent a year, and to whom he was very attached.

When I asked him why the family was separated, Raymond replied that his parents wanted their children away from the threat of bombing. While this is unlikely for the years 1940–2 during which there was no real risk (although there may have been an imagined one),[21] from 1943 and particularly in 1944 the Allies' air raids multiplied over French territory.[22] In November 1943, the Prefecture of Lyon set up a voluntary evacuation scheme for children aged between six and fourteen living in zones designated as 'threatened' by the Défense Passive, which controlled air raid precautions across France.[23] The Point-du-Jour

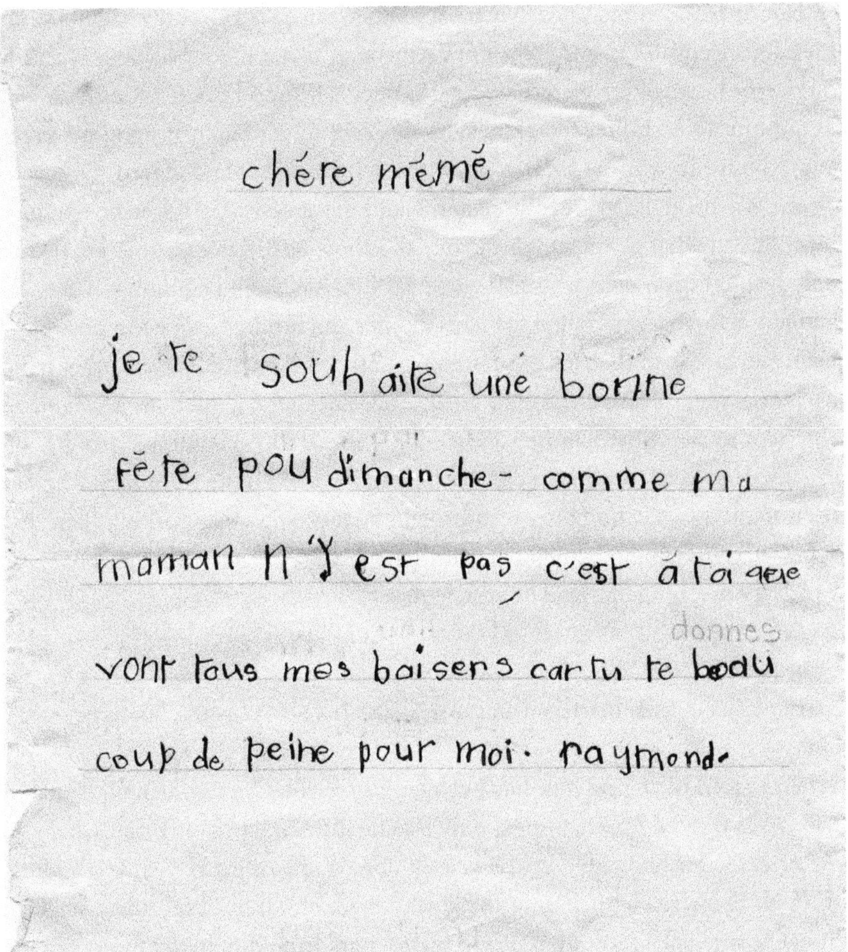

chére mémé

je te souhaite une bonne
fête pou dimanche- comme ma
maman n'y est pas c'est à toi que
vont tous mes baisers car tu te donnes beau
coup de peine pour moi. raymond.

Figure 3.2 Mother's Day card from Raymond to his *mémé*, 1944

district was not at risk, but Maurice and Louise must have believed that Charles would be safer in Savoie. While it is difficult to be precise about dates, Raymond is certain – and a photograph confirms it – that his brother had joined him in Pont-de-Beauvoisin by January 1944 at the latest. Raymond remembers that the boys slept in the same bed, and hid underneath it the vile-tasting Berger deworming tablets that they were supposed to take.

Nor does Raymond know when his mother came to collect the brothers after their father's death. However, he does remember that, not long back in Lyon and on the initiative of his maternal grandmother – his mother's stepmother – who found him to be rather too skinny, he was sent to get fattened up at his great-aunt's house in Murinais. He went without his brother and stayed for several weeks. She owned a grocery store and could more easily lay her hands on food for him. But what he remembers above all is how he did not want to go. He had only just left his *mémé*, who had cared for him since the beginning of the war, and now a further separation from his mother and brother seemed impossible to bear; and on top of that, his great-aunt was a stranger to him. On the other hand, he had a very positive memory of the two brothers' holiday at a *colonie de vacances* in Saint-Symphorien-sur-Coise,[24] about fifty kilometres from Lyon, organized by the Olida factory. It was here that he met Irène Nardonne who had been injured in the bombing of the Olida factory, who was working there as a supervisor. Raymond remembers having shared a room with his brother in which there was a large leather armchair.

A family little affected by shortages

When I asked Raymond if he had been hungry during the war, he replied that he had never wanted for anything – only that he did not like eating rice, which his *mémé* made for him, although he loves it now. While so many people who lived through these years, including those who were children, recall their stabbing hunger pains, such food shortages, it seems, were irrelevant in Raymond's case.[25]

At first, I wondered whether this 'privileged' existence came from the fact that Raymond spent the war outside of Lyon. Yet this explanation is only partially correct. In fact, Raymond's paternal grandparents did not live in the countryside; Pont-de-Beauvoisin was a large village of around 3,000 inhabitants.[26] They had neither a vegetable garden, nor did they keep poultry or rabbits. Furthermore, according to Raymond, they were not 'well off' – a situation he linked to his grandfather Clément's mismanagement of his small transportation business, which had suffered some serious setbacks and which, along with the death of one of the couple's daughters, had been their motivation to leave Lyon in 1909. The 1936 census shows Clément working as a machinist at Chabaud, where he worked until his death at the age of seventy-five in 1952. But, Raymond said, he 'didn't earn that much'. Yet the food restrictions were probably less severe in Pont-de-Beauvoisin than in Lyon where, because shops were not sufficiently supplied with goods, ration tickets could be impossible to exchange for food, and where non-rationed food was hard to find on the open market. Raymond's grandparents also received help from their son Marcel, who lived with his wife Marguerite and two children in Avressieux, where the Communion photo was taken. Marcel was a mechanic at the wire-works in La Bridoire, about twelve kilometres from Avressieux, but the couple also worked Marguerite's grandparents' smallholding, where they had settled in 1927. Marguerite also took in foster children – whom, Raymond says, she treated rather roughly – which brought extra income into the family.

My hypothesis is not the same as Raymond's. According to him, he did not suffer from the shortages because his father was able to provide part of the family with extra food. Described as jovial and generous, always trying to 'sort things out', Maurice left behind him a memory of someone *débrouillard*. Of course, in part this image comes from Raymond's heroic representation of his father, constructed in memory over time. Yet there is also tangible evidence linked to Maurice's professional situation. As a travelling salesman for Olida, the meat company, Maurice had a car which he had bought before the war and of which he was extremely proud. According to Raymond, he carried on using it throughout the war, which suggests that he had a rarely-accorded permit to travel as well as coupons for petrol – or that he had been able to install a gas generator to his vehicle. It was part of Maurice's job to procure all the supplies for the Olida factory at Lyon-Gerland which, as well as preserving meat and making sausages, also preserved vegetables and made jam during the war. Rather than spending all his time persuading shopkeepers to stock Olida products which, during this time of restrictions, did not make good sense, Maurice instead travelled to the nearby countryside to seek out the produce which would maintain Olida's production. From 1943 he signed various contracts with farmers to guarantee a more steady supply to the factory. Raymond had kept a letter written to his father, written by a farmer from Trévoux (Ain) stating that he, plus seven farmers from Saint-Jean-de-Thurigneux (Ain) and one in Ambérieux-en-Dombes (Ain) all agreed to sign a contract with Olida, undertaking to supply 180 tonnes of carrots.[27]

We might also suppose that as he travelled around the countryside Maurice had the opportunity to buy certain supplies for his family directly from the farmers; this practice was part of the so-called 'grey market', at first simply tolerated by the Vichy government and later authorized by the law of 15 March 1942.[28] Among Raymond's collection of documents is a certificate signed by the boss of the Olida factory at Lyon-Gerland, Étienne Fayard, dated 1 October 1943. It states that Maurice was authorized to buy provisions for the factory's Comité social ('social committee'), which had been created by the Charte du travail (Labour Charter) of 4 October 1941.[29] It was therefore likely that the factory had a canteen where its workers could benefit from extra rations provided by the Service du ravitaillement, in particular, a more copious midday meal than their standard rations allowed.[30] The factory may also have had a cooperative shop where products were sold cheaper than on the free market. This important certificate meant that Maurice could travel more freely without being suspected of or arrested for trafficking food and black marketeering.[31]

Through this very specific aspect of his work, therefore, Maurice was able to help his extended family – notably his parents in Pont-de-Beauvoisin and his sister Andrée, a shop assistant, who lived in Lyon with her husband. He had legitimate access to more copious and more diversified kinds of foods than many urban families far better off than his.[32] This corroborates Raymond's memories of his father 'feeding' the family, and he recalls that his parents often came to Pont-de-Beauvoisin armed with food, as well as sending parcels.[33] It is therefore likely that his sudden death on 26 May 1944 had practical consequences in the everyday lives of his close relatives, beyond bereavement. It may also suggest why Raymond was separated from his much-loved *mémé* and sent to his great-aunt in Murinais: although the Liberation began its slow progress several weeks after the bombing of Lyon – and indeed Lyon itself was not liberated until 3 September 1944 – shortages and restrictions worsened and continued for several years to weigh heavily upon all who could not access the black market.

From adaptation to transgression

I asked Raymond several times about his father's 'political profile' before 1940 and during the Vichy years. He always responded that he had no idea, and that he would have liked to have known. Nothing in the family story suggested that Maurice and Louise had any particular political commitments, whether to a party or a trade union. Although the couple had moved in 1936 to the new États-Unis district of Lyon, reputedly a 'red' district, both came from practising Catholic families. They worshipped at the church of Saint-Jacques-des-États-Unis, consecrated in 1933 and placed in the hands of the charismatic priest Father Louis de Galard-Terraube to bring some religion into the lives of this working-class community. A pre-war photograph shows Maurice and Louise posing in front of the church. Their sons, Raymond and Charles, went to secular state schools, but received a Catholic education alongside.

So there is much which remains unknown about Maurice's political opinions: which party did he vote for in the parliamentary election of May 1936, the last one before the war? Did he approve of the foundation of the Vichy regime? What is known, however, is that he joined the Défense Passive, the air raid precautions organization established by the laws of 8 April 1935 and 13 July 1938 (the Law on the Organization of the Nation in Times of War). Perhaps as an aeronautical mechanic he felt a responsibility to participate in the protection of the population during air raids. At the Olida factory he performed his Défense Passive work along with Claude's father Camille, and another colleague Gaston; but Raymond knew nothing of what this work required. The irony of fate was that Maurice, who had no confidence at all in the factory's bomb shelter, died there with more than eighty others,[34] in a shelter considered to be particularly secure by the Défense Passive, while Louise survived, squeezing herself under a parked lorry as the bombs fell, just as her husband had advised.

Although no historical study exists on the subject, it is known that the Défense Passive was a hive of resistance in certain towns. Yet there is no evidence that Maurice was involved in resistance activity, unlike his eldest brother, Marcel. Between February and September 1944, Marcel was a P1[35] agent in an information network under the aegis of the Forces française combattantes (FFC), namely the AJ-AJ network directed by Pierre Duffourc, which was funded and supplied by the Allies.[36] Marcel also led a small group in the FFI, working as a courier, receiving parachute drops and taking part in sabotages.[37] For this work, in which his daughter Jeanine was also active, he received the status of Combattant volontaire de la résistance after the war. Was Maurice aware of what his brother was doing? All we know is that he never took the plunge himself. Yet in early May 1944 it was Maurice who sent false papers to his younger brother Robert, then working at the Chantiers de la jeunesse, in order to help him dodge the forced labour draft, the STO (Service de Travail Obligatoire).[38] According to family memory, Maurice and Robert saw each other briefly at the Bachut tramstop near the États-Unis district on 19 May 1944 before Robert went to ground on a farm in Avressieux. Yet rather than labelling the risky venture of obtaining false papers as an act of resistance[39] it is probably more accurate to see it as an act of family solidarity in a similar vein to Maurice's energetic procurement of extra rations. Maurice sorted out the false papers just as he sorted out the food and the fuel for everyone. Should we therefore consider him as 'accommodating' the demands of the Occupation? Of just making the best of it for himself and for his loved ones? As an *attentiste* who simply waited it out without committing himself?[40] Initially, perhaps. Yet we should also note that when particular events put his family in danger, he chose to disobey.

The sudden loss of the family's rock: the bombardment of 26 May 1944

Thus, until May 1944, Raymond's family remained relatively insulated from the cruelties of war and Occupation, by making use of the resources available to them and adapting to what was nonetheless a difficult situation. Yet Maurice's death on 26 May 1944 marked a tragic rupture. Following the air raid, Louise went to identify her husband's body at the Église Notre-Dame des Anges, temporarily turned into a mortuary; his body remained intact, unlike that of Claude's mother Marie, who was identified only by the key to the sausage drying room where she worked which was found in the tattered remains of her shirt pocket.[41] Maurice was buried in Loyasse cemetery on 29 May 1944, the Monday of Pentecost, along with 394 other victims of the bombing;[42] the rest were buried later. Only four family members could attend the collective service at Saint-Jean cathedral, although Raymond had heard it told in the family that his uncle Francisque managed to get hold of another invitation card which enabled another four to go. Raymond did not know who accompanied his mother – probably her father and her brothers- and sisters-in-law – or with whom she went to her husband's grave the following weekend.[43]

The consequences of Maurice's death were devastating for the family. Louise, a young widow only thirty-two years old, was inconsolable, and would never recover. Charles took his responsibilities as the eldest son to heart and became a model of seriousness. In contrast, Raymond felt himself obliged to play the joyful child. But whenever he had the chance, he tried to escape the morbid atmosphere at home, taking refuge in his church youth club, where he had plenty of friends his own age and lots of activities to take part in. However, for a long time afterwards, he often believed he saw his father in the street even though he could not quite remember what he looked like; in other moments, knowing full well his father was dead, he imagined little scenes where they were reunited once again. He would often meet with Léon, his father's former colleague at Olida, with whom Maurice had plans to go into business with after the war. Léon helped Raymond find his first job at the factory, but all his life felt responsible for Maurice's death: it was Léon who had persuaded Maurice to close his grocery shop in rue des Trois Rois and come to work with him at Olida.

Everyday life remained difficult for the family after the war. Raymond remembers vividly that, without sufficient coal to heat their flat on the Boulevard des États-Unis, it was terribly cold and all three slept in the same bed to keep warm. They ended up moving to a two-room flat in the same district which was easier to heat. Louise and her sons received aid from a number of sources after Maurice's death. Raymond remembers that an American charity sent him and his brother bomber jackets, which they liked very much and wore for many years; today he commented wryly on the bad taste of this gift, given to two children whose fathers were killed American bombers. Like all those who perished under the bombs, Maurice was given the status *mort pour la France* ('fallen in the name of France'), which entitled his mother to a war widow's pension – some of which she had to reimburse after an overpayment – and Charles and Raymond became *pupilles de la nation* ('wards of state', the designation given to war orphans). This meant, for example, that Raymond was exempt from serving in the Algerian war. It also meant that he was given permission to exhume his father and re-bury him in Pont-de-Beauvoisin in 1958.[44]

But above all, Louise benefited from the assistance of Olida, where she went to work not long after the air raid, like many other close family members of the forty-eight employees who were killed in the bomb shelter. The new boss was very sensitive to the tragedy which the factory had suffered, and would sometimes drive Raymond and Charles to the Loyasse cemetery to visit their father's grave. Some years later in 1956 Raymond himself joined the company. While his brother Charles had gone to technical school and found a job as a skilled worker at Thomson, Raymond left school at fourteen-and-a-half to do an apprenticeship with a *charcutier* in Place Bellecour. But after it was completed, he could not find a suitable opening, and Louise persuaded him to apply to Olida. He held various roles at the factory over the years – from gutting to boning to salting to cooking – and even worked as a delivery driver, but finally obtained a job in sales, like his father. It was at the factory that he met his future wife Paulette, an assistant in the accounts department since 1957; they married in 1960 after he had completed twenty-eight months of military service. Along with the entire factory staff, in 1966 he attended the unveiling of a marble plaque upon which were engraved the names of the forty-eight Olida employees who lost their lives on 26 May 1944.

Conclusion

By choosing to reconstitute the everyday lives of a single family during the Occupation, I took the gamble – like many others working on the Second World

War,[45] including some in this book – that changing the scale, which requires the use of particular kinds of sources, would bring to light certain aspects of life which have been until now completely or partially obscured. In other words, I sought to challenge the historiography by showing life in all its complexity. The way in which Raymond's family spent those years allows us to see far more clearly the great diversity of wartime experiences, but also to reconsider some of the categories constructed by historians to label people's behaviour by going beyond the resistance/collaboration dichotomy which characterizes so much writing on the period.

Even though the war certainly disrupted their everyday lives, until 26 May 1944 Raymond's family lived lives which could appear rather privileged in comparison to others' – Claude, for example, had been a refugee and was then separated from his parents (in fact permanently) and sent to Brittany, far away from them. Raymond's privileged existence came first of all from the fact that Maurice, although mobilized as an aeronautical mechanic, did not go to war in 1940. Louise was therefore never in the precarious position of the many thousands of women whose husbands were taken prisoner, often separated for several years, forced to find ways to provide for their children. Furthermore, Maurice's job meant that the family did not suffer from shortages and restrictions, despite the fact they lived in an urban milieu and were by no means wealthy. In touch with their social networks of extended family, factory and parish,[46] Maurice and Louise made good use of the human resources around them to develop strategies adapted to their new living conditions. To protect their children from the threat of aerial bombardment, they chose to send them away, but they were able to send them to relatives rather than to unknown host families[47] or to collective centres (*colonies de vacances* or other hastily organized group lodgings).

These survival strategies were however upset by the fact that the couple had to live and work in a district which was susceptible to the Allied bombardments, which everyone feared. With hindsight, we know that the probability of being killed by the bombs was not high, but Maurice found himself in the wrong place at the wrong time. His sudden death plunged the family into quite serious difficulties. Above all, though, it traumatized Raymond, who suffers from its impact to this day; more so given that, like the many traumas suffered by the civilian population, it went unrecognized for a very long time, and even now struggles to find its place in French public memory of the Second World War.

Translated by Lindsey Dodd

Notes

1 See I. Jonas, 'Verité et mensonge de l'album de photos de famille', *Ethnologie française*, 21 (1991–2), 189–95 and 'L'interprétation des photos de famille par la famille', *Sociologie de l'art*, 1 (2009), 53–70.

2 See J.-H. Déchaux, *Le Souvenir des morts. Essai sur le lien et la filiation* (Paris: Presses universitaires de France, 1997).

3 See I. von Bueltzingsloewen, 'Le bombardement de Lyon du 26 mai 1944: approche micro-historique', in I. von Bueltzingsloewen, L. Douzou, J.-D. Durand, H. Joly and J. Solchany (eds), *Lyon dans la Seconde Guerre mondiale. Villes et métropoles à l'épreuve du conflit* (Rennes: Presses universitaires de Rennes, 2016), 331–52. Two further recent publications which shed light on understandings of lived experiences during this period are P. Laborie and F. Marcot (eds), *Les comportements collectifs en France et dans l'Europe allemande, 1940–1945* (Rennes: Presses universitaires de Rennes, 2015) and J.-M. Guillon, P. Laborie and J. Sainclivier (eds), *Images des comportements sous l'Occupation : mémoires, transmission, idées reçues 1940–1945* (Rennes: Presses universitaires de Rennes, 2015).

4 See I. von Bueltzingsloewen, 'Le bombardement de Lyon du 26 mai 1944: une mémorialisation impossible?', in J. Barzman, C. Bouillot and A. Knapp (eds), *Bombardements 1944. Le Havre, Normandie, France, Europe* (Rouen: Presses universitaires de Rouen et du Havre, 2016), 431–48.

5 The majority of people alive today who lived through the war were still children or teenagers at the end of the war. Historians working on this period need to think carefully about how they use accounts of childhood memories. See L. Dodd, *French Children under the Allied Bombs, 1940–45: An Oral History* (Manchester: Manchester University Press, 2016).

6 See B. Cyrulnik, *Je me souviens* (Paris: Odile Jacob, 2010), and B. Cyrulnik, *Sauve-toi, la vie t'appelle* (Paris: Odile Jacob, 2014).

7 I interviewed Raymond several times at his home; these interviews were supplemented by numerous email exchanges.

8 Out of all his paternal uncles and aunts, only Robert (absent from the Communion photograph), born in 1923, is still alive. One of Maurice's work colleagues, Irène Nardonne-Jacquier, is also still alive. She was 18 years old in 1944 and sustained a serious head injury in the air raid of 26 May 1944. She is still a member of the Association des Anciens d'Olida.

9 These included a thank you letter from the American Strategic Services, dated October 1944.

10 In particular, Lyon's rich holdings of burial and cemetery records conserved at the Archives municipales de Lyon (AML).

11 See J.-L. Pinol, *Les mobilités de la grande ville. Lyon XIXe-XXe siècles* (Paris: FNSP, 1992).

12 Such moves back and forth between town and country were still commonplace in inter-war France.

13 Holding a professional qualification in aeronautical mechanics, Maurice was able to choose to be deployed in April 1939, in accordance with the decree-law of 20 March 1939.

14 Before this, the couple had run a grocery shop on rue des Trois Rois for a short while. One of the Olida sales representatives, Léon, with whom Maurice was friendly, convinced him to apply for a job with Olida.

15 Archives départementales de Savoie (ADS), 1R 319: Card no. 1046.

16 Archives départementales du Rhône (ADR), 6M P667: 1931 Census, for the address 6 impasse Chomel.

17 Claude barely knew his parents, both of whom were killed on 26 May 1944. See the *declaration de succession* after their death in ADR, 3Q32/1890: Lyon, successions, 2e bureau, declaration de succession, no. 1672, 11 September 1945.

18 It is likely that this journey was not always easy, however, particularly after the occupation of Isère and Savoie by the Italians and of the Rhône *département* by the Germans in November 1942.

19 See F. Muel-Dreyfus, *Vichy et l'éternel féminin* (Paris: Le Seuil, 1996); and S. Schweitzer, *Les Femmes ont toujours travaillé* (Paris: Odile Jacob, 2002).

20 Louise's mother died in 1932, before her daughter got married. Her father remarried in 1937 a few weeks after Raymond's birth, to a woman seven years younger than him who had no children and no profession.

21 The Allies did not bomb the 'Free' Zone until after the Germans occupied south of the demarcation line in November 1942.

22 See A. Knapp, *Les Français sous les bombes alliées 1940–1944* (Paris: Tallandier, 2014).

23 The evacuation of children from Lyon became obligatory in the spring of 1944, when schools were closed and ration tickets were no longer issued for those who remained there.

24 Olida had a factory here, in the hilly countryside west of Lyon (the monts du Lyonnais). It appears that this *colonie* also took in the children of Olida's staff from at least May 1944 as a measure to protect them from air raids.

25 See D. Veillon, *Vivre et survivre en France 1939–1947* (Paris: Payot, 1995); R. Gildea, *Marianne in Chains: Daily Life in the Heart of France during the German Occupation* (New York: Picador, 2002); and E. Alary (ed.), *Les Français au quotidien 1939–1949* (Paris: Perrin, 2006).

26 This figure takes in the population of de Pont-de-Beauvoisin in Isère and Pont-de-Beauvoisin in Savoie, which are separated by the river Guiers.

27 The particular foodstuff is not specified in the letter, but the evidence suggests carrots.

28 While the term 'grey market' (*marché gris*) is frequently used by historians, it is unfamiliar to those who lived through the period. When he read the first draft of this

article, Raymond assumed I was suggesting that his father had engaged in the goods trafficking of the black market, and reacted indignantly.

29 These workplace-based committees provided crucial supplements to workers' rations during the war; they were often called *comités patates*, which might translate in British English as 'spud committees'. See J.-P. Le Crom, *Syndicats nous voilà! Vichy et le corporatisme* (Paris: Éditions de l'atelier, 1995).

30 Such additions were not inconsiderable, consisting of weekly extra rations of 250g of pasta, 50g of dried vegetables and a kilo of potatoes each week, plus 200ml of wine per day, 90g extra of meat every eight days and 15g of fats every four days.

31 See P. Sanders, *Histoire du marché noir 1940–1946* (Paris: Perrin, 2001); and F. Grenard, *La France du marché noir 1940–1949* (Paris: Payot, 2008).

32 At his death, Maurice did not have a large enough estate to justify a *déclaration de succession*. See ADR, 3Q32/2319: Lyon, 2e bureau successions, 1944, D, no 21.

33 What were often called 'family parcels' (*colis familiaux*), even though many were not sent between family members, were permitted from October 1941 on condition that they did not contain any rationed goods, and did not exceed 50kg. This was later reduced to 25kg. Such parcels were a vitally important means of obtaining food during the 'dark years', and have been labelled by historians as the 'pink market' (*marché rose*).

34 A large number of *charcutiers* and grocers from across Lyon had gone to the factory on that day to replenish their stock in advance of Pentecost, which is why, alongside the 48 Olida employees, there were so many others.

35 P1 agents did not live clandestinely, but carried on their normal lives alongside their resistance work.

36 The FFC comprised 109,000 male and female members. On 29 October 1944, the American Strategic Services wrote a letter to Marcel.

37 The FFI comprised 260,000 men and women.

38 Robert was 17 years old in 1940, too young to be called up.

39 It is possible that Marcel's brother Francisque, a printer who lived in Lyon, was also involved.

40 These categories are used by the historians Pierre Laborie and Philippe Burrin.

41 According to Raymond, his father always had with him a cork which he planned to bite on if bombed; this was believed to protect the body, or possibly just the dental record, from the blast.

42 In total just over 700 people were killed in this air raid. Claude's mother Marie was buried on 20 June, 25 days after the air raid in the same coffin as the remains of six other Olida employees whose bodies had not survived intact.

43 After the collective funeral ceremony, relatives of the victims were not permitted to go directly to the grave-site. They had to wait until the following Saturday, and needed a *laisser-passer* from the Town Hall.

44 Although accorded the status of 'morts pour la France', these bombing victims did not have their plot in the cemetery in perpetuity. In 1957 the new mayor of Lyon began to put pressure on the families to exhume their relatives.

45 See particularly the contributions to the volume edited by C. Zalc et al. (eds), *Pour une microhistoire de la Shoah* (Paris: Seuil, 2012).

46 To which we could probably also add the apartment block where the family lived, and perhaps even the local district – although Raymond was unable to offer any detail on this.

47 On this subject see Lindsey Dodd's chapter in this volume.

4

The Daily Lives of French Railway Workers

Sylvère Aït Amour
Translated by Lindsey Dodd

The historical association *Rails et Histoire* brings together railway workers, researchers in the humanities and social sciences, heritage professionals and all those interested in trains and railways, past, present and future.[1] In exploring the history and cultural heritage of the railway industry, *Rails et Histoire* aims not to offer an uncritical retrospective on a golden age now passed, but instead to explain how the past has been constructed and how it continues to shape the present. It is not surprising, therefore, that the association's oral history archive has taken a central role in its research activities, shedding light on those parts of the past otherwise silenced, including the experiences of ordinary workers, the reality of railway work on the ground, and the daily lives of all those bound up with the industry. This chapter considers this rich archival collection in relation to one of its major projects undertaken between 2012 and 2014, which gathered a large number of oral testimonies from a range of French railway workers (*cheminots*) active around the mid-twentieth century. After presenting the conditions under which those narratives were collected – which are entangled with the memorial controversies over France's wartime past – it will draw on the words of railway workers themselves to illustrate elements of their work and professional lives during the Vichy years. Rather than propose an argument, the chapter will instead illuminate something of the texture of ordinary people's daily lives, and introduce the reader to this as yet little-used resource.

When the association's first scientific programme was mapped out in the late 1980s (when it operated under the name Association pour l'histoire des chemins de fer (AHICF)), the historian François Caron emphasized the need 'to put an end to the massacre of this collective memory: archival memory is fundamental and irreplaceable, as is oral memory'.[2] Georges Ribeill agreed that it was 'unthinkable to believe you can reconstitute the concrete world of life and work in any kind of realistic way' just by using 'regulations and service orders', and regretted that few published memoirs or oral histories existed.[3] It was in this spirit that the first oral collections were begun in the early 2000s, with the idea of enriching the collective memory of the railways. The advisory board noted the 'primordial role which memory plays in the constitution of a community and of a professional identity' and 'the importance, for the current organisation, of understanding its own collective culture and how that has derived from the past'.[4] Since then, the oral archive has become a priority for the association, continuously expanded, and available for consultation by the academic community as well as the general public. The collection comprises more than 400 interviews, around 1,000 hours of recordings, treating multiple themes, including the activities of different professions within the industry, the history of technology and technical skills, decision-making processes, professional identity, infrastructure, urbanism, leisure, daily life and life in wartime. In fact, the collection encompasses the history of the twentieth century through the twin lenses of personal and professional life.

Daily life and daily work during the Second World War: memories and narratives of railway workers[5]

Between 2012 and 2014, the AHICF ran a collection campaign which focused on the French railways during the Second World War. The objectives of the project were to capture the memory of the employees of the SNCF (the Société nationale des chemins de fer français – the French railway company, founded out of the existing companies in 1938) across the first half of the twentieth century; and, more specifically, to gather data on the daily lives of this two-million strong population (employees and their families) during the Occupation. A large-scale collection project, it was inevitably drawn into the public controversy over the role of the SNCF during this period, and particularly the part it played in the deportation of Jews from France. For the history of the French railways during the Second World War is not a neutral subject. It usually conjures up strong mental images, whether of the deportation trains rolling eastwards towards the death camps, or of the activities of the railway resistance, as exemplified in the well-known film *La Bataille du rail*. This film by René Clément, which won the grand prix at Cannes in 1946, established the idea of the railway resistance firmly in the public consciousness. The AHICF entered into this project fully conscious of these issues, and the expectations that would be raised in terms of what it could deliver.[6]

We launched our appeal for interviewees in January 2012, at a time when the questions raised over the activities of the SNCF were still the object of media attention. In 1991, Kurt Werner Schaechter, a former resistant and son of Austrian Jewish refugees deported from France and who died at Auschwitz and Sobibor, discovered a series of documents which were put forward as evidence that the SNCF received payment for taking prisoners to the camps. These documents were at the heart of a trial against the SNCF, which Schaechter lost. Yet from the 1990s onwards, accusations continued, and led the SNCF to ask historians to investigate, seeking to establish what documentation was available. This shifted the orientation of the AHICF's work towards the Second World War across this period, resulting in several conferences, publications and a study by Christian Bachelier, analysing and detailing the available documentary evidence and state of knowledge about the activity of the SNCF during the Occupation.[7] A year before our appeal for interviewees was launched, the president of the SNCF, Guillaume Pepy, gave a speech in Bobigny officially recognizing the role of the company in the deportation of the Jews of France. He stated that 'the SNCF was a cog in the Nazi extermination machine'.[8] While he also mentioned the resistance of the railway workers, this was overshadowed by the first point. Across the same period, several books appeared which accused the SNCF of complicity and a number of legal proceedings began against the company, in France and from abroad.[9] Such public attention gave rise to a feeling of incomprehension and indeed of indignation among former railway workers who had been in post during the war years; they could not understand these accusations which seemed entirely at odds with what they had lived through.

These issues provide crucial insight into the context in which the narratives for the collection were recorded. On the whole, people volunteered to be interviewed simply because they knew themselves to be among the final survivors of the wartime era and wanted to commit their memories to the historical record. Yet for a good number of others, this controversy proved a motivating factor. They saw a need to respond both to the accusations laid at their door by the SNCF and to the words of Guillaume Pepy, which were construed as a kind of treason. This perspective is clear in the words of Georges Brunel, who was an adolescent during the Occupation.[10] He put forward his motivations for speaking, stating that the controversies had 'knocked him sideways'. He felt that 'the memory of this war has been made wrongly'. He evoked a recent book which, he said, seemed to make the SNCF 'responsible for the deportation of the Jews to Germany'; he also spoke of Guillaume Pepy, who, according to him, had been sent to California by the French government to 'apologise [...] in the name of the wartime railway workers [...] who had sent the Jews to be deported'. George's father was a train driver, and his decision to speak functioned as a defence of his father's memory as well as the railway workers' memory more broadly. Most interviewees were shocked and took the accusations personally, rather than seeing them as against the company. Having lived through those years, many as employees of the SNCF, they had no feeling whatsoever of having collaborated with the occupier, nor of having taken part in the process of deportation; indeed, on the contrary, most of them raised the question of Jewish persecution with great empathy. Furthermore, for the vast majority of interviewees, the SNCF was a fairly distant entity, particularly during the war when they considered that it had fallen into the hands of the Germans, whose will seemed impossible to break. Thus they struggled to understand the media furore and the criticisms being made of them: much was at odds with what they felt they had lived.

The interviewees who stepped forward in response to our appeal were a broad group. The notice asked for 'railway workers, witnesses to the Second World War', and their entourages. Our concern was that we might be too late to interview *témoins directs*, the historical actors themselves. In fact, 63 per cent of the respondents can be classified as *témoins directs*, workers who were in post during the war years. Twenty-eight per cent were their descendants, whether children, grandchildren, nieces or nephews. The remaining 11 per cent was comprised of wives or widows of former railway workers, *témoins indirects* (those present at but not participating in events related to the railways during the war), and a group we called 'victims', whether of repression, persecution, deportation or bombing. All interviewees came forward voluntarily in response to advertisements placed in different publications, most linked to the railways or to the SNCF. These were also displayed in museums and archives, an approach which garnered virtually no responses. Thus it was the case that people who knew of our appeal had access to one of these publications; those outside of the SNCF's broad embrace were unlikely to be reached. This undoubtedly explains the low percentage of *témoins indirects* and victims, who together form only 3.76 per cent of the corpus. For example, Pierre Haddad, who escaped Paris by train and thus escaped deportation as a Jew, and Grégoire Guendjian, a child evacuee saved from certain death by the disobedience of a train driver, only knew of our appeal thanks to their railway-worker neighbours. Without this word-of-mouth dissemination, their precious testimonies would not have been recorded.

Among the people interviewed, elements of a common profile emerge: the majority of the interviewees can be categorized as *primo-témoignants*, that is, those speaking publicly for the first time, and very far removed from the 'professional witnesses' – some of whom are also represented in the collection. Many said they had never been asked to speak of this period before; for some, their desire to remember these difficult years had been liberated by grandchildren's curiosity, often as a result of school projects. In some cases, our appeal seemed to give permission to remember once more, and the authorization they felt they needed to speak and write. Many felt that our collection project was both too late, because of their age, and 'right on time' as only now did they feel ready to speak.

A slice of twentieth-century history

The appeal for interviewees secured the participation of people who had lived through major historical events in French history since the Popular Front; and via the transmission of family memories, gave access to the earlier parts of the twentieth century. We focused our questions on daily life in the first half of the twentieth century, with an accent on the Occupation. We wanted to know how French peopled lived and worked during this period, and how they responded to deprivation, to the German presence, to repression and to the absence of loved ones. After the war, many 'extraordinary' eyewitnesses wrote or told their stories (resistants, deportees, political figures), of significant events and unusual trajectories, but few 'ordinary' people spoke as simple witnesses of daily life.

The chronological limits of the project were thus wide, placing the interviewee and his or her story in a longer history, not just focusing on the difficult and often traumatic years of the Second World War. We were interested what came before and after those 'dark years', from a broad perspective as well as a personal one. The interviewees were asked about family origins, living conditions before the outbreak of war, schooldays, family responses to the evolution of the political situation in the 1930s and 1940s, as well as the creation of the SNCF. Often the key points were moments of significant rupture, such as war, repression, hunger, the Service de Travail Obligatoire (STO – Forced Labour Draft), or imprisonment – but these were also just moments among moments across the course of life: parts of a greater whole.

The analysis of the corpus is only at its beginning, but we can already see that there is no typical *cheminot* experience during the Second World War, but numerous profiles with differences and similarities. Across our interviews, we met railway employees from the biggest cities to the smallest towns; others worked in isolated rural areas, manning level crossings. Some remained in France and in post in 1939 and 1940 in reserved occupations, others were called up to fight, and some became prisoners of war in Germany. Some of those prisoners came back during the course of the war, while others stayed in captivity across the whole conflict. Some opted to work in Germany while others were forced to. We interviewed men, women and young apprentices. Some worked directly alongside the German occupiers, while others said they had only seen Germans fleetingly in 1940 or 1944. French railway workers have often been seen as a homogenous group – an image cultivated through the idea of a widespread kind of resistance as well as the powerful influence of their trade union: they were *les cheminots*. But in reality, this group requires a more nuanced approach: after all, it comprises nearly 500,000 people. So while railway workers' lives cannot all be placed in the same box, and instead should be considered as a mosaic, certain tendencies are visible, emerging from the recorded narratives.

In between wars

The interviewees who were active in their working lives during the period of the Second World War were shaped by events of the 1920s and 1930s. These were years of hope and fear, of economic crisis, of the Spanish Civil War and of the growth of totalitarian regimes across Europe. In the first place, young lives were lived in the shadow of the past: the First World War shaped their early lives, and formed a part of all life trajectories. They spoke about it in their families, they spoke about it at school, at work, in public debates. As Serge Bedu, explained: 'War was always in the background, we heard so much about it [. . .], it was part of our daily lives.'[11] For all those who had lived through it and survived, that conflict left deep physical and psychological wounds. When the Germans invaded in 1940, all the mythology associated with the 'Boche', inherited from the previous war, bubbled up again, carried forward in rumours – and explains, in part, the mass scale of the 1940 civilian exodus.

Yet the Great War was not the only conflict casting its shadow across the interwar years. Janine Boulou, a young typist who started working for the SNCF in 1940, noted that that Spanish republicans fleeing the civil war into France

> were not always that well received because, sadly, those hard times meant that [. . .] the arrival [of] lots of foreigners led to anxieties among people who weren't that well off themselves [. . .]. Although the town councils did do a lot for them. I remember the children that came [. . .], they were given food in the school canteens [. . .], school books, even Wellington boots [. . .]. It was spontaneous, the help. But I must say that things need to be taken in their proper context. It's not always easy to share when you've got so little, and those who had more wouldn't share it.[12]

Not all conflicts were armed, of course. Many of the interviewees were marked by the era of the Popular Front government and could remember 1936, the political struggles, the demonstrations, the gains made by workers; some attended processions with their parents, while others were old enough to go alone. Janine Boulou said that she still recalled 'the enormous excitement' of the Popular Front:

> I was about fourteen years old when the Popular Front came to power. I remember the demonstrations at the Bastille, people's excitement [. . .], flags everywhere. People were crazy with the kind of excitement that I [. . .] didn't see again until the Liberation. My dad knew Pierre Sémard and although I was very young, we went to the meetings.

The reforms of the 1930s also left their mark on professional lives. For railway workers, this was a period of transition as the old railway companies disappeared, replaced by the SNCF in 1938. This newly-formed company was confronted very quickly with war, before any real unification of professional practice or regulations had taken place. The SNCF employed more than half a million men and women, from track-menders to engineers, from drivers to typists, from level-crossing guards to managers – there were hundreds of jobs available, which did not prevent a strong corporate identity from developing, born out of trade union struggles and life in the purpose-built railway workers' housing estates. The interviewees often remarked that the war sped up the unification of formerly separate rail networks, and gave rise to a cohesive new company.

And thus, just two decades after the end of the Great War, France was once again at war. The reserves were called up, the 'phoney war' ensued, then the invasion and the May–June exodus. Maxime Ledru, who joined the SNCF later in 1943 as a young worker, remembered joining the mass of civilians from around Compiègne, fleeing south:

> We left on foot –, with a pram loaded up with our bags, and everyone was on the road. Well, we managed about fifteen kilometres each day, sleeping in, we slept in

> barns –, and then after about –, oh, how far had we gone? Perhaps fifty or sixty kilometres – someone told us that the Germans had stopped, that we could go home [...]

Not long after their return home, relieved, after this first rather chaotic departure, Maxime and his family set off again, this time further and longer:

> There was a train full of refugees from around Compiègne. You could say it was quite organised –, perhaps to the Gare du Nord [in Paris], I'm not quite sure anymore. There were buses put on to take us from one station to another, I suppose it was [the Gare d'] Austeritz, where you left from to get to Dax. Everything was organised. We arrived at Dax and there were coaches waiting for us, and in families, we were placed into reception families. And my family, we were with a clog-maker, in Pouillon, near to, around fifteen kilometres from Dax, fifteen or twenty kilometres. This clog-maker had a big house, and he gave part of it over to us refugees. So we were all there, my brothers, my sisters, and Mum. But we didn't stay long. We left in June. We were evacuated in June. And we came back around the end of September, beginning of October, we came back.[13]

The railways were requisitioned by the French military authorities as of 24 August 1939 in order to organize the movement of troops and equipment. Whole sections of the workforce left Paris, ending up in less exposed towns. Renée Sylvestre, a railway worker descended from a long line of railway workers, recalled that 'the day after [the declaration of war], we were told to leave for Rennes [...]. We all left [...]. In Rennes, we were put to work in the railway workshops'.[14] A quarter of all *cheminots* were thus mobilized for the war effort, and more than half were in reserved occupations, which meant that they were not directly integrated into military units, but were seconded to railway-related work or, more often than not, just continued their normal jobs. Their contribution to the war effort was often made via an increase in their working hours, which frequently reached sixty hours per week. Louis Bleuzet, a driver at the Lens depot, said that: 'when the troops were called up, we were seconded for a month, and weren't part of a fighting unit. [...] We were seconded to Longueau [...]. There, in Longueau, we were seconded on behalf of the army. [...] But I wasn't called up.'[15] For Antoine Guérin, a railway worker in the Somme, 'All the men I was working with, we were supposed to stay put, to not be called up. In 1939, I wasn't working in the office anymore; I was on the tracks, at the marshalling yard at Amiens'.[16] Even if they were called up, they were sometimes kept back from the frontlines and were therefore less exposed to danger. This was often viewed in a dim light by mobilized soldiers; they were seen as having a 'cushy' time of it, sometimes heckled by soldiers leaving for the front.

Home and work during the Occupation

Opinions among the *cheminots* were divided over Marshal Pétain's decision on 17 June 1940 to seek an Armistice. For some, it was the relief of seeing a calamitous war terminated; for others, it signalled hope and the return of mobilized loved ones; and for yet others still, it marked the beginning of a militant engagement, with an immediate refusal to accept this situation. Maurice Gouzon said: 'We said "phew", that's for sure. We said "phew", knowing that we were done for, that we had to finish with it [...] But what came as a shock, for people in the Occupied Zone, was the handshake at Montoire [between Pétain and Hitler, October 1940]. That's when we understood that that old fossil really was an anti-Republican.'[17] On the other hand, for Rose Vincent, a level-crossing guard in the Morvan, later active in the Resistance, the response was more angry: 'In 1940, no, no! We didn't see it as an armistice; we always believed that France would keep fighting. And after the declaration of General de Gaulle, then we could believe it. We always believed it.'[18]

The SNCF thus became one of the essential cogs of the Franco-German collaboration imposed by the Armistice. The French railway network was drafted into the service of the German war economy. All German transport requirements took absolute priority, whether for merchandise, military equipment, troops, prisoners or deportees. To ensure such commands were executed, several thousand German railway workers arrived in France as of June 1940. These were the 'bahnhofs' about whom many of the interviewees spoke, and with whom many had to work. The relations between French and German *cheminots* were generally positive: at the end of the day, they were all *cheminots*, and many of the Germans were there against their will anyway. Jacqueline Berthou's family had to house a German stationmaster at Auray: one Monsieur Mathis, from Leipzig. She described him as a good man, and felt she could say that 'somehow, they [Mathis and her father] got on well together', despite her father's resistance activities. Her father was transferred to Nantes, and Monsieur Mathis soon followed. In 1943 or 1944, Mathis phoned her father, and said: 'Monsieur Berthou, you are a traitor.' Her father thought about fleeing, but Mathis dissuaded him, saying: 'If you leave, I can't help you. If you stay, I can protect you. For me, you're an honest man.' Jacqueline said: 'We never knew whether he knew or not [about her father's resistance activity]. We'll never know.'[19] Serge Ponchon, an apprentice at the beginning of the war, remembered that 'it was a German, a German railway worker who'd give us food to eat. He used to receive food packages from Germany, which got its supplies from France, and so when he'd receive a parcel, he'd share it with us. He was a German *cheminot*. He was a *cheminot*, not a soldier'.[20] Interviewees often made a distinction between those who shared their professional life and concerns, and the soldiers of the occupying army.

Robert Basquin was a young railway worker who, having fled the draft for the STO, was captured and placed in a concentration camp in Spain, before escaping to join the Free French. He remarked upon the cold relations he witnessed between the French and German bosses at the railway depot:

> The German depot manager was always behind the French depot manager. You rarely ever saw him, but he gave his instruction to the French depot manager. [. . .] Whenever they needed locomotives, they just took them straight from the depot, without asking. There were always locomotives. But they had their own locomotives anyway. When they needed armoured trains, military ones, they didn't need us. But if they wanted a normal locomotive, they just took it.[21]

Janine Boulou also spoke of tensions with the Germans:

> One day [. . .] at about 10.30 in the morning, about twenty German policemen, including the Feldgendarmerie, turned up shouting like mad men, 'Tracts, tracts, tracts'. Everyone had to get up, hands behind the neck [. . .], they went through our clothes [. . .], searching through everything, throwing it all over the place, while another one took our names.[22]

Such aggressions, Janine said, made up the *quotidien* of their lives. Thus railway workers' professional lives were disrupted to different degrees, depending on where they lived. While Alsace and Moselle were annexed into the Third Reich, the rest of France was divided into zones with different statuses where the German presence and the severity of demands varied. Around 10,000 *cheminots* went to work in Germany, although the number of departures diminished after October 1943 as the occupiers needed personnel on the ground capable of running the railways. There was therefore a great deal of variety in how railway workers' professional lives were affected by the Occupation; such variation was often dependent upon their particular job, their location and their interpersonal interactions with a range of Germans.

In terms of how their private lives were affected, in some ways this accorded with other parts of the French population whereas in others, railway workers' experiences were unusual. In particular, however, as for the majority of the French population, everyday life for railway workers and their families was marked by difficulties of food supply. Finding enough food to live on resembled an obstacle course in pursuit of necessity, where ingeniousness and resourcefulness became the keys to survival.[23] However, *cheminots* had the benefit of free train travel, which gave those from towns and cities the ability to get to the countryside more easily in order to barter and buy produce. Georges Bellais, a young apprentice during the war emphasized that the 'number one worry' was 'EATING. You had to eat. [. . .] In 1940, lots of people had relatives with small farms. [. . .] We railway workers had a good deal: we could travel every day, for free, no problem, nothing. So we'd go [. . .] to the countryside to look for –, most of all for butter'.[24] He remembered bartering with the peasants, supplying them with seeds, for example, in exchange for food.

Faced with the problems of procuring food, clothing or fuel, the black market developed, accentuating antagonisms and inequalities. Ration tickets appeared from September 1940, and the population was classified according to age and supposed food requirements; from now on, people were no longer just men, women, old, young, bourgeois or working class: they were E, J1, J2, J3, A, V or T (the letters stood for Enfant, Jeune 1 (aged 3–6 years old), Jeune 2 (7–12), Jeune 3 (13–21), Adulte, Vieillard or Travailleur). Among the corpus of interviews, there were numerous J3s, including Robert Calba, for whom it remained difficult to speak of this period. In his eyes, that the black market existed was

> inevitable. From the moment that there were tickets for meat but no meat, tickets for chocolate but no chocolate, tickets for cigarettes –, well, we were allowed four packets of cigarettes a month, four litres of wine a month and, I think, 300 grams of bread per day. With that, you just had to get by. So I could do swaps with the cigarettes, I could try to exchange them for some eggs or a bit of bacon. I did that the whole of the war.[25]

He described it as 'barter', but specified that it was 'paid barter', with the peasants.[26]

More and more severe food rationing was accompanied by problems of fuel supply, exacerbated by the harsh winters and low temperatures of the war years. Coal was always lacking. Hélène Lévêque was a level-crossing guard in Reims. She recalled that 'some train drivers would throw coal down to me. It was greasy [. . .] But I was still happy to have it. I'd collect it up in my washtub, until it was full'.[27] Maxime Ledru had a different experience:

> We had SNCF coke. We had the right to collect up the coke. As the engines were being prepared, their furnaces were cleaned out. All the dirty coke was thrown out into the ditch. [. . .] We were allowed to collect whatever was there. At the end of 1944 there was one engine which was really only used for that purpose: to make coke.[28]

That coke was reserved for the *cheminots*.

Inequalities were both geographical and financial. Indeed, it was better to live in the country or have contacts in the countryside than be stuck in a town. Yet there was no typical experience here either. For town dwellers, there were the advantages which came with the job and the ability to travel more easily. The SNCF sometimes provided communal gardens or allotments for employees where they could grow their own vegetables. On the other hand, rural *cheminots* sometimes suffered quite badly, particularly young people who had been sent to distant posts to replace absent colleagues, far from their families and networks. The problems of the period were not just linked to shortages: there were restrictions on movement, curfews imposed by the German authorities, the censorship of the press and the monitoring of phone calls and letters. Some railway workers had an *Ausweis* because of their work; this German-issued pass meant that they could more easily cross between zones, and were permitted to travel around during the hours of curfew.

Finally, the oral interviews demonstrate that reactions, attitudes and behaviours towards the Vichy regime varied from individual to individual. There were isolated acts of resistance, efforts made to work slowly to impede German production and gestures of solidarity towards those in hiding or those being deported; but there were also denunciations and zealous obedience to orders. The assistance of railway workers was in high demand by the organized Resistance, particularly because of their ability to move around more freely. Nonetheless, engagement in Resistance networks and movements – where they were reasonably numerous – only concerned a minority of the 500,000-strong *cheminot* population.

The violence of liberation

From 1943, and particularly into early 1944 when the so-called 'Transportation Plan' was put into action, the Allies bombed France with increasing strength in preparation for the landings. Railway installations were the key target, from tracks to junctions, workshops and marshalling yards: any part of the network that might paralyse German transport and slow down the movement of troops and military equipment towards the front line.[29] There were heavy casualties among the civilian population and a great deal of destruction. These air raids were prominent in many of the interviews, attached to strong sensory memories not only of sounds, sights and smells but also of emotions, both fears and strong solidarities between those affected.

Janine Lavigne was an accountant at the large complex of marshalling yards, depots and workshops at La Chapelle in the north-east of Paris. When the Allies bombed on 21 April 1944, she said:

> I'd never seen dead bodies before, but there, I saw my first ones [. . .] They took away the injured. [. . .] My father was with us that evening, and all of a sudden we saw all the flares falling, it was like broad daylight. It was incredible. [. . .] The next day, when I went out into the street, I was so shocked, it looked like all the houses were all fused together.[30]

As Wendy Michallat remarks elsewhere in this volume, it was a 'long' liberation. The bombing campaign of spring 1944 was succeeded by the Allied landings in Normandy, starting on 6 June 1944. Some of the interviewees heard about them on the radio. The landings were neither the beginning and by no means the end of the process; heavy air raids continued, along with ground combat, further civilian exoduses, and the gradual liberation of towns and regions. It was only with the surrender of the final 'pockets' of German troops in May 1945 in the towns of Saint-Nazaire, Lorient, La Rochelle and Dunkerque that France was finally free from the occupying forces.

Paul Daviot had joined the SNCF to avoid being drafted into the STO. He had a strong family memory of the Liberation in Calais:

> Saturday. It must have been 30 September '44. My mother had gone to the market, on the place Crèvecoeur, where they used to hold a market, a poor sort of market, just carrots and swedes. By then we didn't have a garden anymore, it had been flooded. The Germans had opened up all the locks, and the town was partly underwater. My mother had gone to the market and, all of a sudden, a man appeared in uniform, in a French uniform, and stood up on the steps of the courthouse, he had a microphone. There were three dozen housewives there, and he started to shout at them: 'People of Calais! You must leave by tomorrow at midday as the town will be razed to the ground. Commandant Mengin.' Then he left. So my mother came home, and she said 'This time, we really have to go, eh.' And the next day, he was right, they started to pelt Calais. At the head of the

> Canadian troops – because it was Canadians who came into Calais – was Commandant Mengin. As a Frenchman, he wanted to liberate his town, a bit like de Gaulle in Paris, if you like.[31]

Nadine Broggi also told the story of the Normandy landings, as experienced by her mother in Bayeux:

> As the crow flies [...], it's about 14 kilometres from the sea. My mother left on her bike because she'd heard the announcements on the radio. [...] When they started to hear the noises, she got on her bike, of course still against the wishes of my grandmother who, poor woman, shouted at her like a wild animal 'Stay here! Stay here!' But Jacqueline, off she went and arrived on the cliff-tops at Arromanches. And there, she always said to me, 'You couldn't see the sea. All you could see were boats. Boats, boats, boats [...]' And she told me that it was the most wonderful moment, the happiest day of her life, even including my birth.[32]

Alongside the tumultuous events of the Liberation came the settling of scores, such as the shaving of women's heads for supposed acts of collaboration. Many of the interviewees had witnessed or participated in various of these activities. The *cheminots* interviewed on the whole suggested that few of their colleagues were touched by the post-war purges, even though *commissions d'épuration* (purge commissions) were established inside the company to investigate wartime activity.

For many families, the end of the war was accompanied by the hope of finally receiving news of family members taken prisoner or deported, and, of course, the joy of seeing loved ones return from their ordeals. Many learned instead of the deaths of their relatives, or lived with uncertainty over the fate of missing people for years. Some of the interviewees spoke of having spent decades in the belief that family members were still alive somewhere, Siberia maybe, or Germany. Roger Tourel was arrested for resistance activities and deported in 1943. His son Jean recounted:

> My mother would go to the station in Nîmes to meet every train of returning prisoners in the hope of seeing my father come back. She often used to take me with her. Those days of waiting around at Nîmes station left their mark on me. When the arrival of a train was announced, people from the charities would hurry over to greet those poor folk who arrived in tatters, starved, wounded, nothing but skin and bones, who didn't know where they'd come from or where they were. Days went by, and the convoys became less and less frequent, and still my father didn't come back. He never came back. After that deep disappointment came the confirmation of his death in Dachau. It was officially announced to us

> that my mother was a widow, and I was an orphan, a *pupille de la nation* ['ward of state', the designation given to war orphans]. I was nine years old.[33]

Jean Tourel has never wanted to know the details of his father's fate, and has shied away from hearing the stories of prisoners who returned from Dachau. He said:

> Even today, I don't want to know more about it. I have this deep hatred inside me, and a thirst for revenge that cannot be satisfied. [...] It takes a generation to forget. Perhaps for my children. How could those grovelling people like the depot manager at Nîmes who denounced my father, or the prison warden who wouldn't let him kiss me goodbye, how could they call themselves men? Did they really deserve those jobs? What did they have inside them instead of a heart?

Railway workers volunteered to man the extra trains bringing the deportees and prisoners home. The priority was the reconstruction of the rail network, so badly affected by bombing and sabotage. Rail traffic needed to get up and running as quickly as possible, in the first instance to take the Allied troops eastwards, and then as an imperative for the economic recovery of the country. Railway workers often spoke of their role in national revival with great pride. Roger Quiquerez had fled Alsace; he spoke of the atmosphere of the post-war as he returned to Neufchâtel:

> I got my job back on the railways again, and we began to rebuild. The Germans had burnt the station down; they'd destroyed the signal box. I spent days upon days re-soldering the cables back together, one by one, to get the signals working again, all of that. [...] There was this incredible feeling of euphoria. We were free! The *Boches* were gone! We'd have worked all day and all night if they asked us![34]

Conclusion

With this project, we hoped to take a snapshot of a certain socio-professional group across the 1930s and 1940s. At the time, the SNCF had around 500,000 employees; if we add their families into the equation, the group represents perhaps over two million people out of a population of around forty million at the time. The collection of these interviews sought to understand not just the past as it was lived, but the past as it has been remembered. As with all historical documents, the content of the interviews was shaped by the context in which they were collected.

The collective participation of the *cheminots* in the Resistance and in the Liberation has been the subject of regular commemorative practices since 1944. The creation of the Resistance-Fer association in December 1944 demonstrates the desire to bring together all those who had participated in the Resistance. This association advocated on behalf of its members to get war medals and pensions, and organized commemoration ceremonies. This group became a determining factor in the construction of the image of an SNCF that was almost unanimously resistant. The making of the film *La Bataille du rail*, supported by the SNCF and achieving great popular success, served to reinforce this representation. Yet by the 1980s, that image had become blurred, particularly with renewed historical interest in France during the Occupation, and in light of the legal proceedings underway against those responsible for the deportation of Jews from France; the SNCF was taken to court in both France and the United States.

It can be difficult to understand events in the past from outside of their context. Oral history archives such as this one have a role to play in expanding our knowledge of context as well as of major events. Very many of the interviewees vigorously emphasized to us the importance of understanding the context in which events took place, in order to have a real understanding of those events. For example, when speaking of the violence which surrounded them during the Liberation era, many insisted that violence and death had been so omnipresent during the Occupation that they no longer paid much attention to it. Not just providing us with context, oral histories give us unparalleled access to the details of everyday life, otherwise inaccessible via documentary materials. As with other studies of the French wartime past which have appeared in recent times, this collection of interviews tends to support the idea that this era must be seen as nuanced; things were not black and white; it was not all Resistance or all collaboration. This is particularly the case when we consider human relations: lots of interviewees spoke of good relations with the Germans with whom they had regular contact, whether with German *cheminots* stationed in France, or even with Germans in Germany where some forced labourers of the STO experienced protection, assistance and positive interaction.

After two years of collection, more than 200 interviews have been recorded, amounting to 400 hours of sound; about 3,000 documents and objects have also been collected.[35] The data is still in a fairly raw form, and not all of the interviews have been formatted, yet it appears to be a remarkably rich source which is just waiting for researchers to make use of it. To get a flavour of the collection, it is worth immersing oneself in these voices from the past, via the website Mémoire orale de l'industrie et des réseaux, or at the offices of *Rails et Histoire* in Paris.

Notes

1 The association's name changed in 2014. The acronym AHICF will be used in this chapter to refer to the association before 2014.

2 F. Caron, 'Histoire économique et chemin de fer', *Revue d'histoire des chemins de fer*, 1 (1989), pp. 19–25. Caron, a specialist in economic and business history, French nineteenth-century history and the history of the railways, was one of the founders of the Association and presided over its academic Advisory Board.

3 G. Ribeill, 'La société cheminote: quelques pistes pour la recherche historique', *Revue d'histoire des chemins de fer*, 1 (1989), pp. 45–54. Ribeill, a sociologist and historian, was also on the Advisory Board of the AHICF.

4 Note presented to the Advisory Board, 16 May 2001.

5 The title of the collection project in French is 'Vie et travail au quotidien pendant la Deuxième Guerre mondiale: mémoire et récits de cheminots'; those of the interviews which are available online at the site Mémoire orale de l'industrie et des réseaux (http://www.memoire-orale.org/liste-entretien.php?col=16&scol=0).

6 Cécile Hochard, who became one of the key interviewers on the project, explored the complexities of this controversial history in 2006 in an article published in the AHICF's journal: C. Hochard, 'Écrire l'histoire des cheminots dans la Résistance. État actuel de l'historiographie', *Revue d'histoire des chemins de fer*, 34 (2006), pp. 27–36 (available online at: http://rhcf.revues.org/529). She also produced a bibliography of sources relating the French railway workers, history and memory of the Second World War, see C. Hochard, 'Les cheminots dans la Résistance: bibliographie thématique', *Revue d'histoire des chemins de fer*, 34 (2006), pp. 115–45 (available online at: http://rhcf.revues.org/540øcto1n8). Other scholarly works include, for example, C. Chevandier, 'Les cheminots, la SNCF et la Seconde Guerre mondiale', in AHICF, *Une entreprise publique dans la guerre. La* SNCF, *1939–1945* (Paris: Presses universitaires de France, 2001), pp. 305–21 (available online at: http://www.ahicf.com/IMG/pdf/33chevandier.pdf); in English, see L. Broch, 'Professionalism in the Final Solution: French railway workers and the Jewish deportations, 1942–4', *Contemporary European History*, 23.3 (2014), 359–80; L. Broch, *Ordinary Workers, Vichy and the Holocaust: French Railwaymen and the Second World War* (Cambridge: Cambridge University Press, 2016); L. Broch, 'The SNCF affair: trains, the Holocaust and divided memories of Vichy France', in *Lessons and Legacies* XII*: New Directions in Holocaust Research and Education* (Evanston: Northwestern University Press, 2017). On the role of the German railways in the Holocaust, see A. Mierzejewski, 'A public enterprise in the service of mass murder: the Deutsche Reichsbahn and the Holocaust', *Holocaust and Genocide Studies*, 15.1 (2001), 33–46. On the film *Le Bataille du rail*, see S. Lindeperg, 'L'Opération cinématographique: Équivoques idéologiques et ambivalences narratives dans *La Bataille du Rail*', *Annales: Histoire, Sciences Sociales*, 51.4 (1996), 759–89.

7 See C. Bachelier, 'La SNCF sous l'Occupation allemande, 1940–1944' (IHTP/CNRS: 1996) (available online at: http://www.ahicf.com/rapport-documentaire-la-sncf-sous-l-occupation-allemande-1940-1944-ihtp-cnrs-par-christian-bachelier,1187.html).

8 T. Fontaine (ed.), *Cheminots victimes de la répression 1940–1945, Mémorial* (Paris: Perrin/SNCF), p. 8.

9 See, for example, F. Laborde, *Tribulations d'une femme d'aujourd'hui: ça va mieux en le disant!* (Paris: Fayard, 2008), or A. Lipietz, *La SNCF et la Shoah: Le procès G. Liepietz contre État et SNCF* (Paris: Les petits matins, 2011).

10 Interview with Georges Brunel (born 1926), recorded by Myriam Fellous-Sigrist (3 April 2012) (available online at: http://www.memoire-orale.org/notice.php?id=188&idth=848&idp=1791).

11 Interview with Serge Bedu (born 1920), recorded by Cécile Hochard (28 May 2013). This interview is not consultable online.

12 Interview with Janine Boulou (born 1922), recorded by Pantéléimon Mavrogiannis (23 October 2013) (available online at: http://www.memoire-orale.org/notice.php?id=211).

13 Interview with Maxime Ledru (born 1926), recorded by Cécile Hochard (14 March 2013) (available online at: http://www.memoire-orale.org/notice.php?id=225).

14 Interview with Renée Sylvestre (born 1916), recorded by Cécile Hochard (14 February 2013). This interview is not consultable online.

15 Interview with Louis Bleuzet (born 1912), recorded by Cécile Hochard (1 October 2012) (available online at: http://www.memoire-orale.org/notice.php?id=191).

16 Interview with André Guérin (born 1919), recorded by Cécile Hochard (10 July 2012) (available online at: http://www.memoire-orale.org/notice.php?id=143).

17 Interview with Maurice Gouzon (born 1921), recorded by Cécile Hochard (6 February 2012) (available online at: http://www.memoire-orale.org/notice.php?id=220).

18 Interview with Rose Vincent (born 1920), recorded by Pantéléimon Mavrogiannis (6 November, 2012) (available online at: http://www.memoire-orale.org/notice.php?id=160).

19 Interview with Jacqueline Bertou (born 1931), recorded by Cécile Hochard (15 April 2013); not available for consultation.

20 Interview with Serge Ponchon (born 1926), recorded by Cécile Hochard (17 April 2012) (available online at: http://www.memoire-orale.org/notice.php?id=154).

21 Interview with Robert Basquin (born 1922), interviewed by Cécile Hochard (15 June 2012) (available at: http://www.memoire-orale.org/notice.php?id=193).

22 Interview with Janine Boulou (born 1922), recorded by Pantéléimon Mavrogiannis (23 October 2013) (available online at: http://www.memoire-orale.org/notice.php?id=211).

23 Many of the chapters in this book deal with issues of food and food supply, highlighting its importance to everyday life. On food and food supply in general, see David Lees's chapter; on resourcefulness and the importance of social networks in the quest for food, see the chapter by Isabelle von Bueltzingsloewen.

24 Interview with Georges Bellais (born 1929), recorded by Cécile Hochard (8 January 2013). This interview is not consultable online.

25 Interview with Robert Calba (born 1921), recorded by Cécile Hochard (13 November 2012). This interview is not consultable online.

26 For further discussion of barter and getting by, the black and so-called 'grey' markets, see the chapter by Isabelle von Bueltzingsloewen in this volume.

27 Interview with Hélène Lévêque (born 1913), interviewed by Cécile Hochard (10 December, 2012) (available at: http://www.memoire-orale.org/notice.php?id=172).

28 Interview with Maxime Ledru (born 1926), recorded by Cécile Hochard (14 March 2013) (available online at: http://www.memoire-orale.org/notice.php?id=225).

29 For a personal experience of bombing during the liberation period, see Wendy Michallat's chapter in this volume, which draws on the diary of student Madeleine Blaess. On the Transportation Plan and bombing more generally, see L. Dodd and A. Knapp, '"How many Frenchmen did you kill?" Allied bombing policy towards France (1940–1945)', *French History*, 22.4 (2008), 469–92.

30 Interview with Janine Lavigne (born 1922), recorded by Cécile Hochard (8 November 2012). This interview is not consultable online.

31 Interview with Paul Daviot (born 1923), recorded by Cécile Hochard (2 May 2012). This interview is not consultable online.

32 Interview with Nadine Broggi (born 1957), recorded by Cécile Hochard (4 May 2012). This interview is not consultable online.

33 Interview with Jean Tourel (born 1936), recorded by Pantéléimon Mavrogiannis (28 August 2013). This interview is not consultable online.

34 Interview with Roger Quiquerez (born 1925), recorded by Pantéléimon Mavrogiannis (7 June 2013). This interview is not consultable online.

35 The documents and objects have been passed to the Service des archives et de la documentation de la SNCF to be digitized and conserved; digital copies are available from *Rails et Histoire*.

5

Helping the Most Needy: The Role of the Secours National

Jean-Pierre Le Crom

During the Second World War in France, everyday life was largely shaped by German demands. The objective of the occupant was to exploit as many resources (whether human, agricultural, mineral or industrial) as possible, in order to sustain the German war effort against the British and, later, the Russians and the Americans. This situation led to a significant drop in the French population's financial and material means, which the Vichy regime tried to address in a number of ways. In the spirit of the National Revolution, the answer could not come from the State, which, according to Maréchal Pétain, was 'overweight and defective';[1] it had to come from families, professionals, communities and organizations (whether philanthropic or charitable).

It is in relation to the question of charitable giving that Pétain would transform and develop the Secours National,[2] which had been founded in August 1914, was active during the First World War, and officially recognized as contributing to the public good in September 1915.[3] Its purpose was to help civilians in their struggle against deprivations brought about by war, through the collection of private donations which were then allocated via various other private organizations, over which it had no control. Fifty million francs were thus reattributed to civilians in need, in the space of the four years of the Great War. It was this organization which the Daladier government decided by decree to revive shortly after the outbreak of the Second World War on 19 October 1939. Bearing the same name, but slightly different in nature, the new Secours National also received subsidies from the State – which would increase substantially over time. It was also now responsible for all the other wartime charities which appealed to the generosity of the public. These charities were only permitted to work on condition that they adhered to the Secours National and pledged to follow its general policies.

Recognizing the scope of the problems stemming from the 1940 defeat, the newly-born Vichy regime decided to resort principally to the Secours National in the implementation of its mutual aid policy. This went on to impact directly upon the everyday life of millions of French people: during the German Occupation, the Secours National considerably expanded its activities, becoming a sort of 'State within the State'. It was eventually closed down in 1949, after having undergone post-war purges of personnel, and renamed Entraide Française in late 1944. This chapter will focus on its activities during the Second World War only. After describing and analysing its ever-growing field of activity during those years, it will go on to show how the État Français repeatedly tried to use it for its own political ends.

To the rescue of the French population

Initially created to coordinate the activities of all other charitable organizations involved in helping the civilian victims of war, the Secours National progressively extended its activity beyond emergency aid to include social care as well. This section will deal first with its supervision of other charities, and then consider the multi-faceted nature of its own activity.

Following the creation of a national system of social insurance in France, and of a benefit system intended for the most deprived, including, among other things, free healthcare and support for the elderly and disabled, by the early twentieth century, the role played by private (often religious) charities had notably diminished. Furthermore their resources, in spite of the relative stability of donations, had also been hit by growing inflation.[4] In response to requests to increase state contributions, the Third Republic had been trying to improve coordination between charities; the Popular Front government was particularly active here, but Finance Minister Henri Sellier failed to deliver any substantial change.[5]

The advent of the Vichy regime changed this situation considerably. Three factors help explain this: first, most charities were receptive to the values put forward by the National Revolution, which made them more favourable to the reforms the new government proposed; second, the nature of the difficulties faced by millions of French people called for a rationalization of emergency help; and third, the regime was, in its early days, deeply influenced by the ideas of Charles Maurras, key thinker of the Action française movement, and in particular his preference for private organizations over public institutions. This new policy was crystallized on the 11 October 1940, by the promulgation of a new law entrusting the Secours National with the supervision of all charitable organizations in France.

This supervision was first and foremost effected through a monopoly over all appeals to public generosity. Before the war, the Comité français de lutte contre la tuberculose (the French Committee for the Struggle against Tuberculosis) or the Petites sœurs des pauvres (the Little Sisters of the Poor, a Catholic charity) could collect donations in churches or launch subscriptions, via the press for example. This was forbidden under the new system: it was now the responsibility of the Secours National to initiate and manage these appeals, as well as to allocate funding to each association, which could no longer rely solely on its own members' contributions and donations.

However, the Secours National only had jurisdiction over providing aid to civilian victims of war. The other organizations which were in charge of aid related to military concerns, and in particular to prisoners of war, were the Committee for the Assistance to Prisoners of War (also known as Comité de Calan), the Service for Prisoners of War, the Légion française des combattants (French Legion of Veterans) and the French Red Cross. This complex and barely comprehensible arrangement would be seen numerous times throughout the war.

In return for its monopoly on all appeals to public generosity, therefore, the Secours National had to decide the allocation of funding to each of the different charitable organizations. By 1 August 1944, it had given a total of 1.6 billion francs to 12,000 such charities. This large sum is partly explained by the fact that the Secours National understood its responsibilities in a fairly generous way. Alongside charities in the strict sense of the term, it also subsidized organizations attached to movements and services whose purpose was not directly linked to charity or aid, such as the kitchens of the Légion française des combattants, working on a mutual aid basis, and even children's summer camps organized by the Légion des volontaires français contre le bolchevisme (the Legion of French Volunteers against Bolshevism, the LVF, better known for sending French soldiers to fight alongside the Nazis on the Eastern Front). In addition, the Secours National was always ready to 'assist the public services, by endeavouring to complement their work'.[6] This it did through occasional funding initiatives, for example, the financial support of people returning from a period in a sanatorium, and even the building and development of prisons.

It should be noted that not all charities called on the Secours National for funding, whether systematically or periodically, and nor did the Secours National grant all requests: out of 7,893 requests made in 1943, 590 were turned down

(7.4 per cent). But the majority of charities soon came to rely solely on its subsidies.[7] Before the war, the Comité français de lutte contre la tuberculose, for example, mainly funded its own activities through the sale of stamps, which brought in some twenty million francs in 1938, and thirteen million in 1939. These campaigns were suppressed from 1940, and the Committee came to be funded by the Secours National – with a little over 12.5 million francs in 1940, and twenty million in 1941.[8]

The Secours National could also request that the State dissolve a charity. Indeed, article 4 of the 4 October 1940 law stipulated that any charity which did not act upon its injunctions could be forbidden to continue by government decree. This device was used to dissolve the Salvation Army,[9] on the official grounds that:

> the activities of this association were too similar to those of the Secours National, and [that] it was important, in the domain of charity and assistance, to ensure that the equitable repartition of the country's resources devoted to the people in need be supported by a unity of inspiration and direction.[10]

The truth was that the Salvation Army, having Protestant roots, was suspected of being opposed to the regime, and even of being Gaullist.[11] In the same way, there were plans to dissolve the French branch of the Quakers, who, being both Protestant and American, were doubly suspicious.[12] But while this dissolution was effectively carried out in the Occupied Zone, Pastor Boegner, president of the French Protestant Federation, successfully asked of René Bousquet and Pierre Laval that they allow Quaker activities to continue in the southern part of the country. The price to pay was a number of changes in the composition of the board of directors.[13] Boegner's protestations may have inspired amendments to a new law of 23 August 1943, which specified that non-compliant charities would first be handed a warning, before being suspended for a maximum of three months by the prefect, and could even be dissolved by a governmental decree on the prefect's request.[14]

The Secours National was not only the 'charity of charities', it was a charity in and of itself. At first its own activity only concerned a few targeted sectors of the population: those who were the direct victims of the war. Yet its action on this front was multi-faceted. The first group of such victims were refugees, whose number reached 2,600,000 during the course of the war. The second were people whose homes had been wholly or partly destroyed – whether by Allied or German bombs, or by ground conflict – many of whom were also refugees. Over the period 1939–45, around four million French people were categorized as 100 per cent bombed out, losing the entirety of their homes and property, while around one million people were considered partially bombed out. Among the ruins, there was much to be done: tending to the injured, burying the dead, feeding, clothing and accommodating the survivors, evacuating children to the countryside. These tasks were tackled by a number of organizations, including the Défense passive (the national air raid precautions organization), the French Red Cross, the Service interministériel de protection contre les événements de guerre (SIPEG – Inter-ministerial Service for the Protection against the Events of War), the COSI (Comité ouvrier de secours immédiat – an aid organization of the collaborationist left), and also collaborationist political parties such as Marcel Déat's Rassemblement national populaire or Jacques Doriot's Parti populaire français. The Secours National's remit was threefold: providing emergency – material, not financial – aid, through the allocation of food, clothes, furniture and temporary accommodation; taking care of refugees – particularly children – by evacuating them to the countryside; and providing food for the youth teams who were assisting bombed-out civilians. In 1943, the Secours National thus distributed to the latter and to refugees 7.92 million food rations, 1.5 million clothes and sheets, 100,000 pieces of furniture, and 600,000 pairs of shoes.[15]

However, the notion of a 'direct victim' quickly came to be interpreted by the Secours National in the largest possible way. Indeed, the Secours soon extended its activities to include what might be termed 'indirect' victims. Among these, some categories were more privileged than others, particularly the elderly, who, in the words of Maréchal Pétain, were 'more affected than all the others by these hard times'. Their situation before the war was already fairly precarious: those who benefitted from a small pension, such as railway workers, postmen or *tabac* employees, could make ends meet with 6,000 to 12,000 francs per year. But for those who had not paid any contributions to the 1910 workers' and peasants' pension system – this amounted to two-thirds of the total of theoretical subscribers – and for those who were subject to social insurances – which were also limited in their application – the situation was far more problematic. These people had to resort to state-funded aid for the elderly: a sum of around 1,800 francs, to which they sometimes could add small annuities accumulated throughout their working life. This, along with homegrown vegetables, fishing (for men) and paid housework (for women), meant that they could just about meet their basic needs. Yet wartime inflation made their situation considerably worse. As a social worker based in the Sarthe during the war explained:

> They began by giving up the superfluous: no more wedding anniversary presents bought in secret, no more fancy dinners to celebrate important days. Then they

> had [to] sell the house in return for an annuity, remove meat from their daily diet, stop buying clothes and start spending less on wood and coal. Those who could still work started looking for menial jobs, such as chopping wood, cleaning and taking in mending.[16]

These material difficulties were more often than not accompanied by a great deal of distress and anxiety. The newly introduced allowance for older waged workers, offered to those aged over 65 years with insufficient resources the sum of 3,600 francs per year (with Parisians receiving an extra 1,600 francs). But this was not enough, especially as it excluded farmers and self-employed people, a large part of the workforce.

One of the Secours National's main initiatives in this respect was to get a young person – often a secondary school or university student – to 'adopt' an elderly person. This might involve the former bringing meals to the latter, staying for a chat, and accompanying them out for a stroll, among other things. This system, first implemented in 1941 in the Seine Department, would eventually reach 18,000 beneficiaries by September 1944.[17] Yet the fact that 16 per cent of the population was aged over 60 or more in 1946 means that the success of this enterprise should be qualified.[18]

Children were another section of the population favoured by the Secours National. It helped them by supplying and assisting school canteens, distributing protein biscuits or vitamin tablets, organizing summer holiday camps and opening specialized care establishments. In December 1943 there were forty-three such institutions, which welcomed either soldiers' children and children of prisoners of war, children of French workers based in Germany, or physically disabled children. They accommodated 4,000 children in total, but 10 per cent of the available spaces were not filled.[19]

The families of prisoners of war were another recipient of the Secours National's aid. As in many other areas, its shared this remit with other organizations. In this particular instance, the other main actor was the Famille du prisonier (the Family of the Prisoner), whose autonomy its president (Madame la générale Huntzinger) defended on the grounds that it employed only volunteers – which was incorrect – and that the families of prisoners of war should not be treated in the same way as the 'needy' people usually associated with the Secours National. The confusion regarding who was in charge of what would only be partly cleared by an April 1941 decision, stating that while the Famille du prisonier was indeed autonomous when it came to intellectual and moral assistance, the material aid it provided was to be monitored nonetheless by the Secours National. Similarly, the latter also supervised the Famille du prisonier's departmental delegates, and its managing director was accountable to a 'super-director'.

The last category benefitting from the Secours National's direct assistance is perhaps more surprising: prisoners and internment camp inmates were not exactly a favoured group, but the infrastructures meant to keep them alive were becoming increasingly inadequate. In internment camps, inmates received only 700 to 900 calories per day, which led to increasing instances of gastroenteritis and hunger oedema. In the camp at Gurs in the Basses-Pyrénées, where Spanish refugees, French Communists and foreign Jews were interned, an average of twelve people died every day during December 1940. Overall, there were 3,000 such deaths in French camps between 1940 and 1944.[20] Things were hardly better in prisons, where numbers increased from 19,000 in 1939 to 50,000 in 1942. In the detention centre of Riom, 120 people died during the first three months of 1942, as opposed to four people per year before the war.[21]

The Secours National began intervening in internment camps from January 1942, alongside the Quakers, the charitable organization of Saint-Vincent-de-Paul and the Red Cross. In relation to food, this brought about daily portions of thick soup, and an additional sixty grams of dried vegetables, twenty grams of pasta, two grams of fat, and either one salted sardine or twenty-five grams of jam or fresh fruit. Out of the 9,000 camp inmates identified by the Secours National in 1943, 2,400 benefitted from its assistance. These were selected by doctors, in agreement with social workers. The Secours National's kitchen worked independently from that of the camp, and was situated in a separate building, which also included a canteen and a storeroom.[22]

Food and clothing aid was thus the Secours National's main and preferred way of providing assistance, whether to refugees, bombed-out people, the elderly, prisoners' families or camp inmates. But in reality this assistance did not stop at any specific category of the French population: from 1940 onwards, it would apply to more and more people, for whom the common denominator was hunger.

From 1 January 1941 to the Liberation, the Secours National served an astonishing 470 million rations in mutual aid canteens (not including those served to bombed-out people), and 405 million more in school canteens. Figures such as these were published on a regular basis, as part of the regime's ongoing propaganda. But when it came to food aid, the Secours National rarely acted alone. School canteens were actually usually managed by town or school councils,[23] and mutual aid canteens by town councils or charitable organizations, such as the Assistants du devoir patriotique, the Salvation Army or the Little Sisters of the Poor, who had traditionally played an active part in the organization of soup kitchens, food banks and the supply of cheap meals.

The role of the Secours National was first to help fund these initiatives as they were set up, often by attributing coupons granting access to primary resources, initially destined for the refurbishment of soup kitchens. It was also to complement the existing food supplies and to provide financial support of up to 30 per cent of the cost for those who could not pay for their meal in its entirety or at all.[24] The Secours National also contributed up to a quarter or a third – depending on the case – of the cost price of school canteen rations.

From 1941 onwards it also organized mothers' tea parties, at which pregnant women, and mothers, their babies and toddlers were given food supplements adapted to their specific needs. The summer holiday camps organized by the Secours National were also motivated by food shortages: it was reported that in 1941, children who went to such camps came back 1.7 kilograms heavier and 1.2 centimetres taller on average. But one of the Secours National's most important operations in this respect was the distribution in schools of vitamin tablets containing vitamins C and B1, and of casein (protein) biscuits. These were made of flour, casein lactose, margarine and sugar, and were reminiscent of the famous 'soldiers' biscuits', although they tasted much better. Depending on how old they were, children were given two, four or six such biscuits.

Finally, the Secours National also played a role in the production of food supplies. It organized or supported family-owned canning factories (112 in 1942) and dehydration centres (6 in 1942), and helped with the cultivation of family-owned vegetable gardens (3 million in 1943, against one million in 1939) by distributing tools, seeds, plants, fertilizers and so on. The produce of these gardens, whose average surface area was about 400 square metres, provided up to 3 per cent of their owners' calorific needs and 6 per cent of their protein needs in 1943; it also provided some financial relief, around 10 francs per square metre according to estimates.[25]

As well as food aid, the Secours National was actively involved in supplying clothing to the French population. Thousands of refugees had lost almost all of their clothes, and the poorest families lacked the means to buy even basic items of clothing or bedding. The prices for these had risen sharply, as German requisitions of primary sources meant that manufacturers had to slow down production. A letter of a woman from Nantes to her prisoner husband illustrates this:

> The boys have nothing to wear. Their shirts are in tatters. Their Communion robes are now four years old and ridiculously short, yet as there's no alternative they still have to wear them. They just don't fit anymore into their green overcoats, which are so shabby! Everything they have is either wearing thin or too small. I spend an awful lot of my time mending. I'm doing it so often that they're becoming a patchwork of different shades of blue. When I was unemployed, I had to sell my textile coupons for food, which means I couldn't buy them the two jackets they needed. I've got a coupon for long-johns – I'll try to get them big and dark so that they last longer, and then I can pass them on to Gustave. I'm going to write to the Secours National as they give second-hand clothes to people in need.[26]

Working with the authorities, the Secours National came up with a system whereby clothes could be salvaged and reused. This was done in three ways: the first option was that which Gustave Pilon, the general secretary of the Secours National, called the 'grey market', as opposed to the better-known 'black market'. This grey market implied buying stock from manufacturers who had not declared it, and who were thus threatened with confiscation. The second way of getting hold of old clothes was to collect them through a public campaign called the *poignée de laine* (the 'handful of wool'). In the early days of the Occupation, these collections were organized with the Comité central d'assistance aux prisonniers de guerre (Central Committee for the Assistance of Prisoners of War – CCAPG). Donors were invited to bring clothes to designated establishments such as prefectures, town halls, schools or Secours National centres; at the same time, primary and secondary school pupils and youth groups were sent out to gather second-hand clothes directly from their owners, using handcarts. While the first collections were rather successful, they were not without incident: for example, a ton of clothes was left for several days in front of the public library in Rodez before it was spotted on the 1 January 1941, soaked in rain water. No action had been taken to store the clothes in a dry place.[27] Moreover, as people learnt to 'make do and mend' what little they had, the quantity of clothes given to the Secours National was diminishing.[28] This is why a third mode of gathering clothes was implemented. On the 11 February 1941, a law was passed which allowed people to buy new clothes without coupons if they gave to the Secours National double the quantity purchased in old but mendable and reusable garments. Six weeks after this system was put into place, the Secours had collected sixteen tons of clothing items.

All these clothes would then be sent to the Secours National sewing workshops, to be mended and sold through its clothing outlets. These sewing workshops provided the Secours with an opportunity to develop aid through work, which was one of its leitmotivs. However, while the number of sewing workshops increased to reach about 800 in 1943, the number of employees – mostly women often working part-time and from home – decreased significantly, from around 50,000 in April 1941 to 17,500 in 1943.

To the rescue of the Vichy regime

The fast-growing development of the Secours National's activities would generate an immense bureaucracy, similar to that of a public institution; however the fact that it formally remained a private organization meant that it was a perfect vehicle for the Vichy regime's propaganda. By providing aid through work, by founding seventy-seven social centres and by establishing housework training centres for 5,000 to 6,000 women and older girls, the Secours National went well beyond the confines of emergency aid and put in place a more lasting and ideologically charged form of social action. This development owed a lot to the ideological thought and activities of the Secours National's director, Robert Garric.

Garric was a Catholic intellectual and man of letters, whose social ideas around national duty were close to those of Marshal Lyautey, and who had created the *Équipes sociales* (social teams) which were both a philanthropic association and a further education institution. In 1939, the Minister of Munitions Raoul Dautry, who became president of the Entraide Française after 1944, called on Garric to head the social services he had just created. There, Garric had worked with Jean Toutée, who became vice-president of the Secours National, Gustave Pilon, who became its general secretary, and Hyacinthe Dubreuil, who also took on managing responsibilities within the organization. Within the Secours National, these men promoted a humane and non-bureaucratic conception of social action, which earned them the nickname of 'Socials', with a capital 'S'. At the 1942 conference of Secours National delegates, it was declared:

> Our job, within the social sector of the Secours National, is to make all forms of aid more humane, more respectful and more compassionate. At no moment should there be any association, in people's minds, between the Secours National and a vast office, a vast anonymous counter behind which bureaucrats would dispense, on a regular basis, in a cold and mechanical and therefore inefficient and dead manner, some kind of assistance.[29]

This group's work and philosophy give us an insight into the development of social services during the Second World War. In each of the departmental delegations of the Secours National was posted a qualified social worker, helped by a number of social auxiliaries who held hospital or district nursing qualifications, along with various unqualified extra care workers. The same system was put in place in departmental sub-delegations, and in some rare cases at cantonal level. A few social workers were also employed as resident workers in social centres. It has been estimated that the number of social workers employed by or 'associated with' the Secours National was 6,023, out of a total of around 9,000 social workers active in wartime France.[30]

The proliferation of the Secours National's activities beyond its initial realm of emergency aid for direct victims of war led to a number of questions about the nature of its attributions and responsibilities. Robert Garric himself asked: 'Will the field of our organization's activities and perspectives thus expand almost indefinitely? Is it not time we tried to enclose our domain, to define and clarify it?'[31] The same day, he also wondered: 'Why do we – the Secours National – take on the duty of teaching about housework? Why are we concerned about juvenile delinquents, or about farming apprentices? And why did we, yesterday, mention nursery schools and other social institutions?' For Garric, the answer was evident: 'the Secours National's work [...] cannot be restricted to emergency aid.'

The significant expansion of the Secours National's activities, which owed much to the wide variety of charities it supervised and to other organizational problems, was met with fierce protestations from inside the Vichy regime itself. Thus in June 1941, the Prefect of the Côte-d'Or department regretted that

> little by little, [the Secours National] is becoming a state within the State, with its cantonal delegates, its regional delegates and its national delegates. This charitable organization's current policies, however legitimate, may well, one of these days, lead to a conflict with the government's own representatives – or even with the government itself.[32]

In his June 1942 monthly report, the Prefect of the Seine pointed out that 'some mayors seem a little unsettled by the growing importance of these big, new charitable organizations', and quoted the mayor of Charenton, for whom 'the Secours National's work, while arguably immensely beneficial to the population, tends to deprive communes of their local charities, turning them instead into its own satellites'. Bureaucratization and the gigantic size of the institution, which were at odds with the spirit of the Vichy regime, were notable targets here: 'people seem to deplore that local, parochial traditions, a natural extension of the family, should be progressively disappearing from the commune.'[33] In 1943, the Prefect of Maine-et-Loire asked the Secours National's departmental delegate to 'stop employing more people and to update him, on a regular basis, on any vacant positions it may have'. This request, however, was deemed by the Minister of the Interior to be incompatible with Pétain's explicit instruction that prefects show support towards the Secours National and not interfere with its operations.[34]

Calls to order kept on coming from the highest echelons of the regime, however, as the problem became increasingly conspicuous. In December 1941, in a stern letter to the president of the Secours National, Pétain's chief of staff Du Moulin de Labarthète thus stated that 'it is not in the Secours National's remit to replace the authorities where food scarcity in cities or rising prices are concerned', and that '[the Secours National] was given to an excessive development of its institutions', which led it to take on 'the scope and the characteristics of a vast collective administration', and 'tended to turn citizens into passive recipients of social assistance'.[35]

Du Moulin de Labarthète's assertion that the Secours National had the characteristics of a 'vast collective administration' begs the question of whether it was, in actual fact, a public or a private institution. When, in July 1941, the Secours provided the municipalities of the Nord and Pas-de-Calais departments with the means to fund the benefits allocated to people in need there, Mr Musin appealed to the government. He stated that 'the 19 October 1939 decree which re-established the Secours National and approved its new statutes confirms, in the wake of the 29 September 1915 decree, that this institution works in the public interest'. But while

> the 4 October 1940 law entrusted the Secours National with the coordination and supervision of charitable organisations, and has given it a monopoly over the management of subsidies and appeals to public generosity, it was not intended to alter the private nature of this institution and its activities; from this, it should be inferred that its representatives' decisions cannot be referred to the *Conseil d'État*.[36]

But this decision should not be taken at face value. The Secours National, in many respects, resembled and acted like a public institution. First because it operated in a bureaucratic way, in Max Weber's sense of the term; it was divided into departments, which were themselves divided into services, just like any administration. It implemented laws and decrees, and generated its own rules, through dated and numbered circulars which were then published in an administrative Bulletin looking suspiciously like the bulletins published by government ministries. It was tightly centralized and hierarchized, and its work was checked by the Court of Audit and the Inspectorate of Finances. A substantial part of its managerial personnel came from the State's Grands Corps, such as the *Conseil d'État*.

Another important question was that of the Secours National's funding. In 1942, its budget was 3,184 billion francs, which represented 3 per cent of the French State's revenue, loans excepted. Over the period between 1939 and 30 June 1946, the sum total of its financial resources was more than 20 billion francs, 55 per cent of which came from subsidies and revenues, while the rest came mainly from public donations, including cash, food and clothing. Its income also included earnings from sources as diverse as the sale of national lottery tickets or of abandoned property, the taxation of public auctions, real estate operations and pari-mutuel betting, the fines for gas and electricity overconsumption, or shared profits from the sale of tobacco coupons or casein biscuits. A notable mainspring was the gains made from the sale of the goods belonging to French citizens deprived of their citizenship rights. A law passed on the 23 July 1940 specifically allocated those earnings to the Secours National. Among the 450 people targeted by this measure – people who had left the national territory between the 10 May and the 30 June 1940 – were Charles de Gaulle, René Cassin, Maurice Thorez and five members of the Rothschild family. The Secours National benefitted from the latter's numerous goods, vineyards (Château-Lafitte, Mouton Rothschild), castles and Parisian buildings, especially 19 to 25 and 26 rue Lafitte, which became its headquarters.

The last aspect to consider is that of the Secours National's employees. These (around 12,000 workers for 40,000 volunteers) were not recruited via examinations or any other selection process, which distinguished them from civil servants. But this needs to be qualified by the facts that a number of ministries, during that period, relied on contractual staff, that social workers held a state certificate, and, above all, that the Secours' workers' wages were aligned with those of their government counterparts.

A propaganda tool

The Secours National's growing power and influence would soon prove attractive to the authorities. As evidenced in a note issued before the October 1940 law, the government was already contemplating two scenarios: either the Secours National should be done away with and replaced by a 'more decidedly political and propagandist' institution directly attached to the State, or it should be reinforced and be made more perennial, but also bear a more visible mark of Pétain's authority. The author of the note was in favour of the latter solution, on the grounds that, 'with some publicity, it would be possible to convince the public that the Secours National was Pétain's own charity'. The main idea was to orchestrate a campaign around the theme of 'the Maréchal taking care of the people's needs'.[37] This plan was implemented during the 1940 Winter Campaign. One of its means of action was via the sale of portraits of Pétain. In the so-called 'Free' Zone, a million such portraits were initially printed, in poster, postcard or vignette forms; then, responding to demand, another million were released. In the Occupied Zone, five million portraits were apparently sold. The operation was a clear success.

It must be noted that the authorities' manipulation of public opinion was tightly controlled during the Winter Campaign. Pétain's appeal to the population had to be published in every single newspaper, on the same day, in the middle of the front page. On the radio, it was to be delivered by a 'sensitive and sincere' speaker, after having been announced in earlier programmes. On each and every day during the following week, newspapers and radio programmes were to reiterate the same message, albeit each time drafted by another 'very talented man, talented enough to be able to channel the essence and the inspiration of the Secours National'. The message itself should be 'ever more objective, more focused on instances of extreme poverty, and with a pressing, anxious, moving and imperious appeal to people's conscience and generosity'. Newspaper editors were expected to 'break down any opposition and show any objections to be irrelevant, especially when these revolved around the idea of "manipulating public opinion"'.[38]

H. R. Kedward has pointed out that humanitarian activities were placed at the forefront of local policies from the very beginning of the Occupation, being deemed apolitical in that they were carried out by left-wing and right-wing municipal authorities alike.[39] This apolitical stance was precisely what allowed Pétain to reiterate the unity of the French nation, to which he had 'given the gift of his person'. This observation certainly applies to the Secours National's first Winter Campaign. Pétain, in this instance, appeared not to be acting as a politician, but to be putting his status and, more importantly, his person, at the service of an apparently neutral social agenda. Within this narrative, it was not the Secours National which worked for Pétain, but Pétain who worked for the Secours National. In reality, the Secours National was being instrumentalized by Vichy. An early 1941 note from Pétain's cabinet made this clear:

> On the other hand, the conditions are ideal for propaganda in favour of the Maréchal via the Secours National and the Entraide d'Hiver [the Parisian branch of the Secours National]. With the Secours National under his authority, and his role in the choice of the Entraide d'Hiver's president, the Head of State can justly claim the moral benefits attached to both organizations' achievements.
>
> In our opinion, in the current situation, the only propaganda which can be exerted freely and efficiently is that in favour of the Maréchal, through the many activities of the Secours National and the Entraide d'Hiver.[40]

From then on and until the Liberation, the image of the Head of State would be associated, in one way or another, with every poster, film or radio report focusing on the Secours National's action:

> almost all of the profits from the sale of objects representing Pétain go to the Secours National: the generosity displayed in buying or donating for that organization invariably involves a reference to the Maréchal (through objects, portraits and other symbols). Each and every one of us shares with the poor not only our cloak (following the example of Martin of Tours), but also the Head of State's warm, enveloping banner.[41]

The Secours National was thus one of the most prominent organizations used by Vichy to manipulate public opinion. Pierre Laborie, in his study of these organizations, notes that 'the sacralization of the cult of the Maréchal leaves no room for improvisation. Everywhere, specialist committees attend to it in the greatest detail, and create ever more emblematic images of the myth'.[42]

It is however important to add, before closing the subject, that the Secours National should not be seen only as a den of Pétainists or collaborationists. Working for it were also a number of authentic resistants, such as Michel Debré, who would go on to become Prime Minister under the Fifth Republic, Léon Chevalme, former secretary general of the Confédération Générale du Travail (CGT) branch of Metallurgists' Federation, Roger and Yvonne Hagnauer, pacifist teachers and revolutionary trade unionists, and many social workers who, in some cases, paid for their engagement with their lives.[43]

Conclusion

As this chapter draws to a close, it is worth reflecting on the idea that while everyday life can of course be studied for its own sake, it is crucial not to lose sight of its political implications. Everyday life in Occupied France was mostly shaped by scarcity – of food, clothes, or shelter. Vichy's way of dealing with this scarcity was to rely on 'natural' communities, such as families, businesses or charitable organizations. The efforts of the latter, under the supervision of the Secours National, to rationalize emergency aid – offered first to civilians directly affected by the war, and then to increasingly larger portions of the population – arguably played a significant role in both alleviating the hardships of a large number French people, and in avoiding a health crisis – although it is difficult to quantify precisely what part it played here. Its recognizable and significant contribution was undeniably why it carried on with its work as the Entraide Française until 1949.

It is quite common to oppose, both when it comes to the Second World War and more generally, everyday life to unequivocal political choices, such as choosing to collaborate with the Germans or joining the Resistance – both of which supposedly only concerned a small number of citizens. Yet this distinction has a rather heuristic dimension. In an earlier work, I have shown that, while the heavily politicized professional terms of Vichy's Charte du Travail (Labour Charter) were met with considerable hostility, its workplace-based social committees – known as 'spud committees' ('Comités patates') by some – were much more successful, on account of the significant role they played in workers' everyday lives.[44] Within the Secours National itself, a number of important figures were also in favour of substituting politics, seen as 'deleterious' since the Third Republic, with the Social, with a capital 'S'.

The study of the role played by charitable organizations or associations under Vichy, however, suggests that such a distinction between the political and the social be qualified. The improvement of everyday life was at the heart of the regime's political agenda, and the development of the Secours National was instrumental to the promotion of Pétain's image. It is uncertain just how much impact this propaganda would have had on a hungry population, but those in charge believed it had some: any reflection on everyday life must take this into account.

Translated by Benjamin Bâcle

Notes

1 Philippe Pétain, 'La politique sociale de l'avenir', *Revue des deux mondes*, 15 September 1940.

2 Secours National can be translated as 'National Aid'.

3 This chapter is drawn from the author's book on humanitarian work during the Second World War, which also covers the activities of other organizations, such as the French Red Cross or the Workers Committee for Emergency Aid (Comité ouvrier de secours immédiat, COSI): J.-P. Le Crom, *Au Secours Maréchal! L'instrumentalisation de l'humanitaire (1940–1944)* (Paris: Presses universitaires de France, 2013). See also J. Kulok, 'Trait d'union: The History of the French Relief Organisation Secours national/Entraide française under the Third Republic, the Vichy Regime and the Early Fourth Republic (1939–1949)' (PhD dissertation, Oxford University, 2003).

4 J.-L. Marais, *Histoire du don en France de 1800 à 1939. Dons et legs charitables, pieux et philanthropiques* (Rennes: Presses universitaires de Rennes, 1999).

5 J. Jouan de Kervénoaël, *Les œuvres privées et l'État. Une formule nouvelle: le Secours national* (Paris: impr. de E. Desfossés, 1941).

6 Archives départementales du Cantal (ADC), 419F 4: Note concerning Secours National policy on grants, 10 January 1944.

7 Centre des archives économiques et financières (CAEF), B 915: Report by the Secours National's financial inspector, 15 March 1944.

8 Archives de la ville de Paris (AVP), 24W 11: Tract from the Comité national de la tuberculose, undated.

9 Decree of 9 January 1943, *Journal officiel de l'État français* (*JO*), 28 January 1943, p. 264.

10 ADC, 419 F 48: Press release from the OFI-Havas agency.

11 ADC, 419F 48: Letter from Marc Boegner, president of the French Protestant Federation, to Robert Garric, chief commissioner of the Secours National, undated.

12 On American Quaker activity in France during this period, see the chapter by Shannon L. Fogg in this volume.

13 *Carnets du pasteur Boegner (1940–1945)*, introduced and annotated by Philippe Boegner (Paris: Fayard, 1992), pp. 233, 238; and ADC, 419F 48: Letter from the president of the Secours Quaker to Robert Garric, 6 February 1943.

14 Law no. 454 of 23 August 1943, *JO*, 11 September 1943.

15 Archives nationales (AN), 2 AG 458: End of year evaluation of Secours National's activities, 1943.

16 ADC, 419F 3: Presentation given by Melle Le Bailly at the Sarthe Departmental Conference of the Entraide Française, 6 February 1947.

17 ADC, 419F 6: Secours social, Report on the organisation of the adoption (*parrainage* – 'godfathering') of the elderly, 1944.

18 ADC, 419F 3: Press conference given by Justin Godard, 19 November 1946.

19 ADC, 419F 7: Executive Committee of the Secours National, 7 December 1943.

20 D. Peschanski, *Vichy 1940–1944. Contrôle et exclusion* (Brussels: Complexe, 1997), p. 93.

21 P. Pédron, *La prison sous Vichy* (Paris: L'atelier, 1993), pp. 52–3.
22 ADC, 419F 55: Secours National Social Workers' Conference, 1943. Speech by Mme Discher on 'The action of the Secours National in camps and prisons', pp. 36–8.
23 On this subject, see Matthieu Devigne's chapter in this volume.
24 ADC, 419F 49: Answers to questionnaires sent in preparation of Secours National Social Workers' Conference, 1943.
25 AVP, 24W 13: Secours National Departmental Delegates' Conference, 1942.
26 G. Douart, *Les civils sous l'Occupation. Nantes dans la guerre* (Maulévrier: éditions Hérault, 1993).
27 AN, F/60 388: Note A/MB, President of the Council (general secretariat), Cdt Ausseur, 2 January 1941.
28 AN, 2 AG 500: Letter from Clément Decomble (Toulouse) to Jean Masson, Winter Campaign of the Secours National in Vichy, 20 November 1941.
29 AVP, 24W 13: Secours National Delegates' Conference, 20–22 June 1942.
30 R.-H. Guerrand, M.-A. Rupp, *Brève histoire du service social en France (1896–1976)* (Toulouse: Privat, 1978), p. 83.
31 AVP, 24W 13: Report from Secours National Delegates' Conference, 20–22 June 1942, p. 2
32 AN, 2 AG 500: Extract from the Prefect of the Côte d'Or's monthly report, June 1941.
33 AN, 2 AG 500: Extract from the Prefect of the Seine's monthly report, February 1942.
34 AN, F/1A 3661: Letter from Ingrand, delegate of the Ministry of the Interior, to the Regional Prefect of Maine-et-Loire, 18 January 1943.
35 AN, 2 AG 500: Letter dated 1 December 1941.
36 *La Gazette du Palais*, 17 November 1943.
37 AN, F/60 389: note undated (but from 1940).
38 ADC 419 F 5: President of the Council (general secretariat), 7 July 1940.
39 H. R. Kedward, *Naissance de la résistance dans la France de Vichy. Idées et motivations (1940–1942)* (Seyssel: Champ vallon, 1989), p. 34.
40 AN, 2 AG 500: Unsigned note (undated, but from 1941).
41 D. Rossignol, *Histoire de la propagande en France de 1940 à 1944. L'utopie Pétain* (Paris: Presses universitaires de France, 1991), p. 89.
42 P. Laborie, *L'opinion française sous Vichy* (Paris: Seuil, 1990) p. 231. On this question, see also L. Gervereau and D. Peschanski, *La propagande sous Vichy* (Nanterre: BDIC, 1990).
43 This question is treated in Chapter 8 of Le Crom, *Au secours Maréchal!*, pp. 237–78.
44 See J.-P. Le Crom, *Syndicats nous voilà! Vichy et le corporatisme* (Paris: Editions de l'atelier, 1995).

6

The American Friends Service Committee and Wartime Aid to Families

Shannon L. Fogg

On 24 March 1941 a representative of the American Friends Service Committee (AFSC) travelled from Marseille to Cassis for her first visit with Madame Alengry. This young mother had been widowed at the age of twenty-four when her husband, a lawyer in Troyes, developed a heart ailment and died suddenly. Madame was left with no income and three young children to support. She entrusted her oldest child, a son named Jacques, to an uncle, and at the time of the German invasion of France, Madame Alengry joined the *exode* with her two youngest children. Eventually making her way to Marseille, she found a position as a secretary and was living temporarily with her daughters in a friend's summer villa in Cassis. Referred to the AFSC by a female doctor working in one of the Quaker-sponsored baby clinics, Madame Alengry's situation perfectly represented the kind of family that the organization hoped to help through its Home Colony programme.[1]

Designed to provide food and financial support to children at home rather than through supplementary rations at school or by placing the children in a group home, the Home Colony programme sought to aid children from 'good middle class homes, where the war has caused the loss of the father or economic difficulties'.[2] The Alengry family, like many others, fitted the bill, struggling to make ends meet in southern France on Madame's meagre wages of 650 francs a month. With its focus on bourgeois families, the Home Colony programme allows us a glimpse into the impact of the Vichy years on those who had previously lived comfortably. Through social workers' reports and publications of the AFSC, we see the disruption of families' daily lives, the sense of shame often associated with aid, the continued importance of social networks and sociability and the role of international agencies in relief work. Examining the Quakers' work in France also highlights the importance of studying the everyday, for it draws our attention to questions of periodization, gender expectations and class in ways that are easily overlooked from other historical perspectives.

Studies focusing on aid often ignore charity during the Second World War, skipping from the interwar years to the postwar period. Others focus on the most destitute or those traditionally associated with charity including the working class or the victims of persecution. The very circumstances of the war encourage us to examine middle-class need, as it was the more affluent (like Madame Alengry) who initially were able to flee the German advance during the exodus and could afford to rent housing or had relationships with people with second homes in safer parts of France.[3] They then faced financial hardships as the war continued, but they were 'unaccustomed to outside help, were often reluctant to accept it, but their needs were pressing, though generally hidden, and they formed a category which was not reached by the more public types of relief'.[4] Looking at middle-class women's experiences thus allows us a glimpse into how the war changed (or did not change) charity. We also see that to find oneself on the receiving, rather than giving, end of charity may have contributed to expressions of shame, which the AFSC believed could be mediated by 'friendly' visits.

The AFSC in France

The Service Committee had its start in the early days of the Great War as English Friends disavowed hatred and called on volunteers for 'a positive work of love'.[5] Men and women volunteered for ambulance work, refugee relief, assistance to aliens and counselling conscientious objectors. After the United States entered the war in 1917, American Friends initiated their own relief measures and created the AFSC in May. By July, one hundred carefully-selected men began to prepare themselves for service in France to tend to 'the spiritual as well as the material needs of the victims of war'.[6] This wartime aid, such as providing food and clothing, caring for refugee children, repairing war-damaged housing and working with other organizations, laid the groundwork for the Quakers' activities in France during the Second World War. Working with the British Friends, the AFSC began providing food to Spanish children affected by the Spanish Civil War, and when thousands of Spanish refugees fleeing Franco's regime crossed into France, the Quakers went with them. Their work soon expanded to include aid to civilians displaced by the German invasion of Western Europe and continued even after the armistice in June 1940.[7] Establishing headquarters in

Marseille, the AFSC's work soon shifted from emergency refugee services to meeting the ongoing needs of children during wartime, focusing primarily on the unoccupied zone. With fifty-six representatives in unoccupied France, the AFSC set about helping people in need of aid.[8]

The Marseille office opened in August 1940, and by that time, the AFSC's blueprint for action was becoming clear. The organization would focus on programmes for feeding and caring for children, emigration advice and help, and material aid to individuals in French internment camps.[9] The food situation was immediately desperate. Early reports indicated that nearly 80 per cent of children were already suffering from under-nourishment and unbalanced diets.[10] Marguerite Czarnecki reported on the situation in Paris in July 1940: 'Something must be done, and quickly: each week I can notice the change in the physical appearance of the children who come with their mother, and I should not be surprised if some of these people committed suicide [. . .] I have been using much more money that I ought to have used, although I only give 10 or 20 Frs. a week to these people, but it is impossible to let them entirely starve.'[11] Margaret Frawley also noted famine-like conditions in Bordeaux the same month: 'There is starvation now and what it will be like later I hate to think. The trouble, you see, is that official services have never really swung into operation and many private organizations with paper plans have now folded their tents and gone home.'[12]

Although it is not explicitly stated, it is clear from the reports that many in need of help were Jews fleeing Nazi persecution and the Service Committee did not make distinctions between various religious groups. The Foreign Service Section explained its position: 'The Refugee Committee extends its services especially to those who do not logically come under the care of any other recognized agency, Catholic, Protestant or Jewish. [. . .] The Committee also seeks to supplement the services of other agencies by developing special projects open to those of all religious faiths.'[13] Much of the scholarly work that has been done on the AFSC has focused on its aid to Jews in France during the war. Donald Lowrie, with the Young Men's Christian Association (YMCA) and head of the Coordination Committee for Relief Work in Internment Camps (the Nîmes Committee), reported that the AFSC served as the 'principal American organization' working within internment camps in southern France.[14] The Quakers established schools inside the barbed wire, provided medical supplies, distributed clothing to internees and delivered supplemental food and materials. In addition, the Quakers worked to liberate inmates and facilitate their emigration.[15] They are also recognized for their role in aiding in the rescue of

Jews in the small village of Le Chambon-sur-Lignon.[16] While this is certainly an important aspect of the AFSC's relief work, it is only part of the story. The AFSC also provided supplemental rations in public schools, distributed vitamins and milk, ran children's homes, established employment offices and rebuilt French villages and farms.[17]

The Home Colony programme

These programmes highlight the wide-ranging nature of Quaker relief work and exemplify the organization's foundational belief that 'poverty has no politics nor country'.[18] However, the AFSC also faced the dilemma of whether 'to help the maximum quantity of war sufferers in a relatively impersonal fashion or to help a lesser number in an intimate, friendly fashion'.[19] The Home Colony programme allowed the AFSC to experiment with personal, private aid as opposed to the large-scale feeding and clothing programmes provided in camps, schools and colonies. While much of the scholarly focus has been on Jewish aid, those helped by the Home Colony programme were 'ordinary' French families. Although some were refugees from other parts of France, most were average civilians who did not face persecution, who had not fled their homes and who were not actively engaged in politics. Many came from previously financially stable families that now faced hardship due to the war. The Home Colony programme began in 1941, and the rationale behind the programme was clear:

> Thousands of French children from homes which have never before known economic hardship are today in great need. Because [. . .] family life is so essential to the morale of both parents and children, it has seemed wiser to give help to these children in their own homes rather than in colonies [collective children's homes]. Weekly packages providing extra food and weekly allocations of money to enable the mother to buy a few extras in the market ease hardships.[20]

Participants in the Home Colony programme received items such as dried beans, sugar, oil, soap and sardines in addition to cash payments.

While the idea may have been simple, selecting families and then convincing them to accept aid was not. In February 1942, the AFSC began to research the Angot family. After visiting the family three times, the investigator reported that Monsieur worked as an accountant, the family had three children who ranged in age from two to thirteen years old, they lived in a six-room apartment, and were also caring for Madame Angot's elderly mother, who was a refugee from

Le Havre. The family was requesting additional food for their children since they could not buy sufficient items and the children were not entitled to meals at the school canteen. The AFSC also visited the school, where they learned that only 28 out of 200 students had access to the canteen and all of them were orphans, children of POWs or war victims. The investigator concluded: 'the Angot family is not in a bad situation' and in his opinion, 'there are a multitude of families like this and one could say that currently a large majority of middle-class French people find themselves in an identical situation'. As a result, the inspector declined to make a recommendation on the family's acceptance into the programme. Rose Thorndike, the head of the Home Colony programme, visited the family in March to inform them 'that the children were not as badly off as many others and that, although we would be glad to take them into the Home Colony temporarily, this was not anything to be counted on for a great length of time'.[21] The Quakers clearly intended to find middle-class families in truly desperate situations, not merely facing general wartime hardships.

Although the Angot family had approached the Quakers for aid, this was not the most common means of identifying participants for the Home Colony programme. In most cases, potential families were referred to the Service Committee by people who knew the family and its difficult circumstances including clergy members, doctors or friends. Members of the AFSC then conducted home visits and interviews, such as those with the Angot family, to determine eligibility. Mothers accepted into the programme were supposed to be 'intelligent, conscientious and capable of good judgment'.[22] Once a family was accepted into the Home Colony programme, family members would later recommend their friends or acquaintances for aid.[23] Thus social networks and building trustworthy relationships were important methods of accessing private aid distribution.

But even with the referral method, many families were reluctant to accept aid. The Auguste family came to the attention of the AFSC 'through a classmate, the daughter of a friend of one our Committee' after one of the daughters became quite ill with pleurisy and her schoolmates feared the family might not be able to handle the increased financial burden related to her treatment. The family was willing to accept food from the Service Committee, but they were averse to taking any financial aid.[24] In another case file, Madame Alengry, whom we met earlier, was described as, 'a proud little person, anxious to show her relatives that she can carry her responsibilities, and she was reluctant to accept even our aid until we made her understand the friendly spirit in which it was offered, and the fact that no one need know that we are helping her officially with money and food'. Appearances were important to middle-class values. The Alengry family, though able to return to their hometown of Troyes, chose to remain in Cassis because they could wear old clothes and go bare-legged. Madame explained that if she were in Troyes, she would have to 'dress according to their "station"' and she would not be able to accept just any job for fear of offending her in-laws. The AFSC volunteer noted, 'This sort of attitude may seem foolish, but such things are a real part of life in a provincial town such as Troyes, and they must be accepted as realities, even at present'.[25] Madame Augé was also concerned about what others would think and asked the Quaker representative to not discuss the family's case because Madame came from a well-known family in Marseille and would not want people to know that she had to rely on support from a charity. The social assistant understood Madame Augé's position and explained that the Service Committee helped families that they considered 'friends' and viewed their aid as moral and material support rather than charity.[26]

Shame and sociability

These examples bring up the dual considerations of shame and sociability. Shame can be defined as a subject's sense of a loss of power or a negative view of the self that can come from others condemning a person or their identity.[27] In the years before the war, charitable aid was generally aimed at the working class and often carried the intention of 'reforming' the character of the poor. For example, the late-nineteenth-century American reformer Josephine Shaw Lowell stated that the poor needed aid 'largely because of their own shortcomings, including drunkenness and idleness'.[28] While the idea of the 'deserving poor' encompassed people who were poor through no fault of their own, such as orphans, widows and the elderly, the stigma associated with charity was engrained in society. Middle-class women had also been actively involved in social work, providing aid and working as volunteers.[29] The AFSC deliberately shaped the Home Colony programme to reach people who 'might not be willing to accept aid of a more public nature' by going into homes rather than asking recipients to visit an office to collect money or supplies. While central distribution would be more efficient, the AFSC feared that it 'might eliminate people who could accuse it of smacking of the hand-out'.[30]

One way, it seems, that people could preserve their sense of self and their former middle-class identity was to continue to follow traditional ideas about hospitality. During home visits, the representatives of the AFSC were often treated as friendly guests, just as they had represented themselves to their clients in need of persuasion or reassurance. Visits with social workers were times to exchange news, observe home management skills, assess children's health and share a drink. For example, Rose Thorndike ran into a mother and her boys on the street in Marseille, and set a date for a visit at their home. The boys, excited about the Simca that Thorndike was driving, were more conversational with her and that excitement carried over to the visit the next day. In her report, Thorndike noted, 'This family is always a joy to visit and to-day there was the additional pleasure of a cup of Coffee'.[31] In another instance, Monsieur Barrière was awakened by a pair of AFSC representatives visiting his home, and was 'much embarrassed not to have coffee or something to offer his guests'. On a subsequent visit to the Barrière home, Rose Thorndike was offered a glass of cider, 'a new experience' for the woman.[32] Even within the context of extreme wartime shortages, it was proper to share precious items with visitors. The Barbaroux family started receiving aid from the AFSC in 1941 after the three children lost their father to an Italian bombing raid on Marseille. Madame made handbags at home for the price of her labour if clients provided her with material. In July 1943, Madame Barbaroux and her daughter Rosette visited Eleanor Cohu, a key AFSC social assistant, at home to deliver the bag Madame had made for the Quaker woman. Cohu noted in her report, 'They stayed a while watching the sun set on the Old Port from my window. Seeing the piano, Rosette said how much she likes to listen to music'. Cohu then played some Mozart and Debussy for the pair. Madame Barbaroux refused to accept any payment for the bag, but gladly accepted an envelope with money that Cohu said was for the children.[33] Turning home visits into social calls, it seems, lessened the impression of charitable aid and created a sense of connection between the aid providers and aid recipients.

In times of extreme penury, sharing food, drinks and small tokens may be seen as a kind of gift exchange. Studies have explored the role of gift giving in relationships, especially as a form of social or economic exchange. Very few, however, examine gift giving during difficult times such as war, totalitarian regimes or slavery.[34] In social exchange models, gifts demonstrate social connections and help maintain reciprocal relationships. While we may interpret the sharing of items between aid recipients and social workers as a reciprocal exchange – hospitality for financial support and increased rations – it may also be useful for understanding how the middle-class recipients dealt with the 'shame' of charity. One study on gift giving suggests that 'a gifting incident could shape people's future identities, especially if it occurred in a context disruptive to the social norms governing everyday life'. The authors argue that many people recognize that following a social norm, such as offering a gift, during a time of great distress and upheaval will 'allow their future selves to gaze back at their present selves with a positive (or at least neutral) self-assessment, so they can "live with" the people they were'.[35] Thus, sitting down for coffee or tea with representatives of the AFSC would allow families to maintain their pride and demonstrate proper middle-class values, even in wartime. Although the context of wartime shortages would seem to encourage selfishness, sharing food demonstrated pre-war social mores and would allow people to return to 'normal' after the Liberation.

While hospitality could present one means of allowing individuals to maintain a sense of identity, relying on the idea of friendship could offer another. Reports on children's situations are full of titbits about individuals' lives and sometimes sound like diary entries about friends calling on friends, clearly falling in line with the AFSC's desire to establish personal relationships. On 30 January 1942, two women from the AFSC visited Madame Agoust and her family. While Hélène, Madame's fourteen-year-old daughter was the aid recipient, the entire family was involved in the social interactions with the Quakers. The handwritten report captures the meeting:

> Hélène and her grandmother and grandfather were just about to have a cup of tea. They invited us to share some with them and we sat around the table and drank the tea out of pretty china cups. The room was so nice and warm from the stove in the corner that I even took off my coat. Grandpa and grandma gave us quite a talk about their former prosperity, his apprenticeship in Paris in his youth, etc. He is quite an endearing looking old gentleman with a bald head and a bushy white mustache, through which he strained his tea with a practiced air. We were there for almost an hour and Hélène scarcely spoke during the entire time, nor did her expression ever change – not even when the bar of chocolate came into view. When RDT [Rose Thorndike] was spooning out her portion of confiture into a pot she said 'C'est trop,' – which seemed like almost too high a degree of politeness for a child. She is a beautiful girl with rather classic looking features – but really far too grave and serious. I didn't get the impression that her lack of animation was due to listlessness, but she did seem rather wooden and perhaps over-restrained. She gives an impression which it is difficult to express. I should like very much to see how she behaves with other girls of her own age.[36]

While this passage notes the conversation, the tea cups and Grandpa's moustache, we also see an evaluation of Hélène's health and manner.

The importance of establishing friendships was noted in the regular bulletins from France. To aid workers, these relationships were about more than just overcoming feelings of shame about charity. A bulletin from France in 1942 described the bi-weekly visits as key in building international relations: 'Such visits become much more than cursory trips to deliver supplies, for the friendly contact is a continuing demonstration of American interest.'[37] A French teacher, in explaining the donations and work of the Americans, stated, 'You understand, [...] this is not almsgiving, this is true brotherly love'.[38] A report that described the Home Colony service in December 1942 noted that the programme could be expanded and highlighted the 'qualities of personal visitation and fellowship which French families will value at this difficult time'. The importance of the work went beyond personal fellowship. As one report stated, 'To the workers in the Quaker service in France, it has been increasingly evident that an American relief organization which functions at this critical time does more than give material assistance. It is a hand of friendship, a faith in the spiritual and democratic values of France, which, as an expression of the good will of this democratic nation, gives France renewed confidence in the democratic way'.[39] In the view of the AFSC, friendship was key to relations on both an individual and international level.

Scholars have demonstrated the 'long-standing importance accorded to friendship as a relationship fundamental both to social and individual wellbeing'. Friendship is seen as an important indicator of social integration and as vital for both physical and mental health.[40] For the Quakers, friendship represented a spirit of helpfulness, fellowship and brotherly love for all people. The best way to alleviate distress, according to the AFSC, was through individual relationships in personal, intimate settings. We must then consider the role of friendship in the extraordinary circumstances of daily life during the Second World War. Friendly bonds were ruptured by the mass movement of the population, the introduction of discriminatory legal measures and the fear engendered by occupation. Friendship also has an important gendered dimension. While acknowledging women's capacity for friendship throughout history, Mark Peel calls the twentieth century 'the age of female friendship, or perhaps the age when friendship became female'. Peel argues that the meanings and possibilities of women's friendships changed in this period and included ideas of friendship as 'a bulwark against oppression [...] and as a model for a better world'.[41] Such a characterization is important when we explore the Quakers' Home Colony programme as it was primarily female volunteers interacting with French mothers with the goal of improving children's lives. Drawing on stereotypes, one relief worker described women's important role in aid in a pamphlet from 1945: 'Woman's whole experience throughout the ages has made her more adaptable than men – more ready for the thousand and one interruptions, make-do-and-mends and improvisations which emergency work involves but which exasperates a capable man'.[42] Thus, women drawing on their skills as women, were believed to be vital for the success of relief work.[43]

The idea of befriending aid recipients was not new in charity and welfare work, although the practice of 'friendly visiting' usually implied 'the transformation, improvement or assimilation of the immigrant, the colonial subject, the social inferior or the hapless victim'.[44] The Quaker women helping French middle-class women who found themselves in a difficult position due to the circumstances of war were, we can argue, in a somewhat privileged position. However, the Service Committee often emphasized the hardships that faced everyone in France – the aided and the aiders alike. Before the war, these women would have been social equals and the idea of charitable friendly visits during the Second World War deserves further exploration within the context of social work and international aid more generally.

The international nature of Quaker aid must also be emphasized. Before the war, the British Friends Service Council worked in conjunction with the AFSC to provide relief services for Spanish refugees in France. With the outbreak of hostilities, the British left France, but Quaker work continued with support from individuals of all nationalities including Danes, Dutch, Norwegians and Irish in addition to the Americans and the French.[45] The fact that the Quakers had provided extensive aid in interwar Germany helped facilitate their work under Nazi occupation, and both financial and material support came from many sources.[46] All of the AFSC's expenses in France were covered by money from the Secours National, the official French aid organization, which allowed the Quakers to use all the funds they raised abroad to purchase food and clothing to import.[47] Using funds from churches, philanthropic groups and individuals, the AFSC purchased food from Switzerland, Portugal and North Africa.[48]

Studying the aid provided by the Home Colony programme also encourages us to re-examine the periodization of the war. As we have seen, the Quakers began their work in France before the war with Spanish refugees and did not institute the Home Colony programme until 1941. Within the social workers' reports there are no significant changes associated with the military or political course of the war in ways that we might typically expect. For example, there is no mention of the German Occupation of the Southern Zone in November 1942 within the reports from home visits. With the elimination of the 'Free' Zone, American Quakers were forced to leave France, although Eleanor Cohu, as an American with French citizenship due to marriage, remained in Marseille and continued to work with Secours Quaker, the French branch of the organization. The only indication that things had changed was that the visit summaries changed from being written in English to being written in French. There is also no mention of the Allied landings or the Liberation of France. Aid continued being provided through the Home Colony programme in the same manner into 1947. In fact, the bombing of Marseille and the destruction of the Old Port increased the need for aid towards the war's end. Eleanor Cohu reported from Marseille in August 1944, 'Secours Quaker staff all well, carrying on work with much reduced possibilities. Following activities still functioning: Medical suralimentation center for 300 undernourished children, shortly to be expanded to 450; work room; program for pretubercular children; greatly reduced distributions to baby dispensaries; monthly distributions to 250 home colony children. Our food reserves will be exhausted by end of September'.[49] The Quakers also distributed milk and hot meals in Marseille following bombings and provided more than 4,000 rations per day during the week of the city's liberation.[50] As one aid worker explained, 'with the liberation all the people who were hidden came out in the open air and we had a perpetual stream of demands of food, clothes and money from people who suddenly again had to stand on their own feet and earn their own living and were lost by it'.[51]

In March 1946, Madame Agoust visited the Quaker offices in Marseille, accompanied by her daughter Hélène. The girl who had been described as 'grave', 'serious' and 'over-restrained' appeared healthy and happy and was preparing to re-start her studies in Aix. The report notes, 'Madame Agoust thanked us for our moral and material aid; aid that greatly supported her in the difficult moments. It was Hélène especially who knew to express her gratitude with simplicity and kindness'.[52] During the Second World War, the AFSC provided moral and material support to hundreds of children like Hélène and their families by extension. Examining the programme opens up new avenues to explore in the history of everyday life in France during the Vichy years including the role of friendly relations, shame and sociability among the middle class and international aid workers.

Notes

1 The files of the Alengry family are found in Archives of the American Friends Service Committee [AAFSC], Philadelphia. See AAFSC, Committee Records Relating to Humanitarian Work in France, 1933–1950, Series VIII – Marseille Office, reports (box 58, folder 37).

2 American Friends Service Committee (AFSC), *Bulletin on Relief in France*, 38, 10 January 1942, p. 3.

3 See H. Diamond, *Fleeing Hitler: France 1940* (Oxford and New York: Oxford University Press, 2007), pp. 23–4.

4 American Friends Service Committee, 'Activities in France (Baden-Baden Report) to November, 1942', 13 June 1943, p. 19 (available online at www.afsc.org/document/activities-france-baden-baden-report–1942).

5 *Under the Red and Black Star: A Brief Account of the American Friends Service Committee* (Philadelphia: The American Friends Service Committee, 1949), p. 3.

6 *Under the Red and Black Star*, 4. See also, D. E. Trueblood, *The People Called Quakers* (New York: Harper & Row Publishers, 1966).

7 A brief overview of the Quakers' work in France is found in its Annual Report for 1940. See AFSC, *Annual Report 1940*, pp. 9–13. For an account focusing on aid to Spanish Refugees, see H. E. Kershner, *Quaker Service in Modern War: Spain and France, 1939–1940* (New York: Prentice-Hall, 1950). See also C. E. Pickett, *For More than Bread: An Autobiographical Account of Twenty-Two Years' Work with the American Friends Service Committee* (Boston: Little, Brown and Company, 1953).

8 AFSC, 'France and the American Friends Service Committee', *Bulletin on Relief in France*, 13, 2 December 1940, p. 1. The number of people associated with the AFSC changed over time. In 1942, there were fifteen Americans and 150 Europeans on the Committee in France. See *American Friends Service Committee in France* (1942), p. 15 (available online at https://www.afsc.org/sites/afsc.civicactions.net/files/documents/1942 Letters to Quakers from School Children–Southern France.pdf).

9 M. Frawley, 'Summary', *Bulletin on Relief in France*, 6, 18 September 1940, p. 3. The bulletin suggested providing food and clothing to internees at Vernet, Reucros and Gurs.

10 M. Frawley, 'Summary', *Bulletin on Relief in France*, 6, 18 September 1940, p. 3.

11 M. Czarnecki. 'Reports from France', *Bulletin on Relief in France*, 4, 15 July 1940, p. 1. Czarnecki, though not using the word 'Jews', was describing the situation for ex-German and ex-Austrian refugees, mainly women, children and the elderly. She contacted the American Joint Distribution Committee in Bordeaux about their situation but had not received a response. For more on Czarnecki, see 'Hommage à Marguerite Czarnecki (née en 1905): témoignages sur ce que peut "être" et "faire" une femme quaker' (Paris: Centre Quaker International, 1988). Held at the Library of the Society of Friends, London (LSFL).

12 M. Frawley, 'From Bordeaux', *Bulletin on Relief in France*, 4, 15 July 1940, p. 2. For a brief overview of the material effects of war on children see S. Fishman, *The Battle for Children: World War II, Youth Crime, and Juvenile Justice in Twentieth-Century France* (Cambridge, MA and London: Harvard University Press, 2002), pp. 52–9.

13 AFSC, *Annual Report 1940*, p. 3.

14 D. A. Lowrie, *The Hunted Children* (New York: W.W. Norton & Company, 1963), p. 52.

15 *American Friends Service Committee in France* (1942), pp. 9–11, 13 (available online at https://www.afsc.org/sites/afsc.civicactions.net/files/documents/1942 Letters to Quakers from School Children – Southern France.pdf).

16 The classic work on Le Chambon is P. P. Hallie, *Lest Innocent Blood Be Shed: The Story of Le Chambon and How Goodness Happened There* (New York: Harper & Row, 1979). More recent accounts include P. Henry, *We Only Know Men: The Rescue of Jews in France during the Holocaust* (Washington, DC: The Catholic University of America Press, 2007) and C. Moorehead, *Village of Secrets: Defying the Nazis in Vichy France* (New York: HarperCollins, 2014).

17 For descriptions of the various wartime projects, see *American Friends Service Committee in France* (1942) (available online at https://www.afsc.org/sites/afsc.civicactions.net/files/documents/1942 Letters to Quakers from School Children – Southern France.pdf). More than half of AFSC's aid went to needy French people. See D. F. Ryan, *The Holocaust and the Jews of Marseille: The Enforcement of Anti-Semitic Policies in Vichy France* (Urbana and Chicago: University of Illinois Press, 1996), p. 151. On a more general level, scholarly work on wartime aid in France has also focused on aid provided to Jews while studies on general aid for the French are less numerous. See, for example, Y. Bauer, *American Jewry and the Holocaust: The American Jewish Joint Distribution Committee, 1939–1945* (Detroit: Wayne State University Press, 1981), L. H. Faure, *Un 'plan Marshall juif:' La présence juive américaine en France après la Shoah, 1944–1954* (Paris: Armand Colin, 2013) and I. Goldsztejn, 'Le rôle de l'American Joint dans la reconstruction de la communauté', *Archives Juives*, 28.1 (1995), pp. 23–37. J.-P. Le Crom provides an overview of French aid in *Au secours, Maréchal! L'instrumentalisation de l'humanitaire (1940–1944)* (Paris: Presses universitaires de France, 2013); see also his chapter in this volume.

18 LSFL: H. van Etten, 'Le Secours Quaker: Rapport 1944' (Paris: Society of Friends, 1944), p. 11.

19 AFSC, 'Activities in France (Baden-Baden Report) to November, 1942', 13 June 1943, p. 2 (available online at www.afsc.org/document/activities-france-baden-baden-report-1942).

20 'Care of Children', *Bulletin on Relief in France*, 43, 18 May 1942, p. 2. Sarah Fishman establishes French concerns about 'broken' families and the rise of juvenile delinquency in *The Battle for Children*.

21 See documents related to the Angot family in AAFSC, Committee Records Relating to Humanitarian Work in France, 1933–1950, Series VIII – Marseille Office, reports (box 58, folder 37). Ironically, the Angots would continue to receive aid until March 1946 despite earlier attempts to cut it off. The idea of 'social diagnosis' or investigating a family situation was well-established in social work by this time.

See J. Pierson, *Understanding Social Work: History and Context* (Berkshire: McGraw Hill Education, 2012), pp. 53–4.

22 *American Friends Service Committee in France* (1942), p. 8.

23 See, for example, the Baccuet family's case files in AAFSC: Committee Records Relating to Humanitarian Work in France, 1933–1950, Series VIII – Marseille Office, reports (box 58, folder 38). Madame recommended a widow in November 1943 and another one in October 1944.

24 AAFSC, Committee Records Relating to Humanitarian Work in France, 1933–1950, Series VIII – Marseille Office, reports (box 58, folder 37), case file for Auguste family.

25 AAFSC, Committee Records Relating to Humanitarian Work in France, 1933–1950, Series VIII – Marseille Office, reports (box 58, folder 37), case file for Alengry family. By not returning to her hometown, Madame Alengry was also not eligible for state aid. On refugees and allocations see N. D. Risser, *France under Fire: German Invasion, Civilian Flight, and Family Survival during World War II* (Cambridge and New York: Cambridge University Press, 2012).

26 AAFSC, Committee Records Relating to Humanitarian Work in France, 1933–1950, Series VIII – Marseille Office, reports (box 58, folder 37), case file for Auguste family.

27 R. Kitchen, *A Legacy of Shame: French Narratives of War and Occupation* (Oxford: Peter Lang, 2013), pp. 21–3. See also B. Williams, *Shame and Necessity* (Berkeley: University of California Press, 1993).

28 Quoted in C. N. Dulmus and K. M. Sowers (eds), *The Profession of Social Work: Guided by History, Led by Evidence* (Hoboken, NJ: John Wiley & Sons, 2012), p. 12. Dulmus and Sowers provide an overview of the evolution of social work in Chapter 1. For the attention placed on the working class in France see Fishman, *The Battle for Children* and L. L. Downs, *Childhood in the Promised Land: Working-Class Movements and the* Colonies de Vacances *in France, 1880–1960* (Durham NC and London: Duke University Press, 2002).

29 Pierson, *Understanding Social Work*, pp. 57–9. See also B. G. Smith, *Ladies of the Leisure Class: The Bourgeoises of Northern France in the Nineteenth Century* (Princeton, New Jersey: Princeton University Press, 1981), especially chapter 6. Sarah Fishman states that 'the majority of social workers in France in the 1940s were single, middle-class women' (*The Battle for Children*, p. 96).

30 AFSC, 'Activities in France (Baden-Baden Report) to November, 1942', 13 June 1943, pp. 18–19 (available online at www.afsc.org/document/activities-france-baden-baden-report-1942).

31 AAFSC, Committee Records Relating to Humanitarian Work in France, 1933–1950, Series VIII – Marseille Office, reports (box 58, folder 38), case file for Baccuet family, report dated 3 April 1942.

32 AAFSC, Committee Records Relating to Humanitarian Work in France, 1933–1950, Series VIII – Marseille Office, reports (box 58, folder 38), case file for Barrière family, reports dated 4 March 1942 and 10 June 1942.

33 AAFSC, Committee Records Relating to Humanitarian Work in France, 1933–1950, Series VIII – Marseille Office, reports (box 58, folder 38), case file for Barbaroux family, report dated 3 July 1943.

34 J. G. Klein, T. M. Lowery and C. C. Otnes, 'Identity-based motivations and anticipated reckoning: contributions to gift-giving theory from an identity-stripping context', *Journal of Consumer Psychology*, 25.3 (2015), 431–48, p. 432. On social exchange, see J. A. Ruth, C. C. Otnes and F. F. Brunel, 'Gift receipt and the reformulation of interpersonal relationships', *Journal of Consumer Research*, 25.4 (1999), 385–402.

35 Klein, Lowery and Otnes, 'Identity-based motivations and anticipated reckoning', p. 432. The authors examine gift exchange in Nazi concentration camps as a form of an extreme identity-stripping context. They consider food exchanges as a form of gift giving.

36 AAFSC, Committee Records Relating to Humanitarian Work in France, 1933–1950, Series VIII – Marseille Office, reports (box 58, folder 38), case file for Agoust family.

37 AFSC, *Bulletin on Relief in France*, 46, 16 October 1942, p. 2.

38 AFSC, *Bulletin on Relief in France*, 30, 10 May 1941, p. 3. This echoes mainstream ideas about social work prevalent in the US at the turn of the twentieth century. See M. Peel, 'New worlds of friendship: the early twentieth century', in B. Caine (ed.), *Friendship: A History* (London and Oakville: Equinox, 2009), pp. 282–90.

39 AFSC, 'Dividends in Democracy', *Bulletin on Relief in France,* 13, 2 December 1940, p. 2. The 'friendly' relations are mentioned at length in *American Friends Service Committee in France* (available online at https://www.afsc.org/sites/afsc.civicactions.net/files/documents/1942 Letters to Quakers from School Children – Southern France.pdf).

40 'Introduction' in Caine (ed.), *Friendship,* p. ix.

41 Peel, 'New worlds of friendship', p. 281.

42 LSFL, box 670/36: F. M. Wilson, 'Advice to Relief Workers Based on Personal Experience in the Field' (1945), p. 9.

43 LSFL, Lucy Backhouse Papers, TEMP MS 637, folder 13: Friends Service Committee – Europe Committee. European News Sheet (December 1940), p. 3.

44 Peel, 'New worlds of friendship', p. 284. Peel uses the example of early twentieth-century reformers in the United States as well as colonial relationships. He also discusses the friendships made between soldiers during the war, but does not discuss women's friendships on the home front.

45 R. C. Wilson, *Quaker Relief: An Account of the Relief Work of the Society of Friends 1940–1948* (London: George Allen and Unwin Ltd, 1952). See also LSFL: H. E. Kershner, 'AFSC in France' (1941), pp. 3–4.

46 Moorehead, *Village of Secrets*, p. 124 and Ryan, *The Holocaust and the Jews of Marseille*, p. 155.

47 Kershner, 'AFSC in France', p. 4.

48 AFSC, *Annual Report 1940*, p. 13.

49 LSFL, Lucy Backhouse Papers, TEMP MS 637, folder 13: Friends Service Committee – Europe Committee, October/December 1944. A report from the Quakers in Toulouse and Perpignan also elaborates on the growth of the Home Colony programme after the war. Those aided changed from war victims to children whose fathers were arrested during the Liberation. See H. Friedlander and S. Milton (eds), *Archives of the Holocaust: An International Collection of Selected Documents*, vol. 2, part 2: American Friends Service Committee 1940–1945, ed. Jack Sutters (New York and London: Garland, 1990), pp. 516–17.

50 LSFL, 'L'action du Secours Quaker' (Paris: Canadian Friends Service Committee, [1945?]).

51 Report from Quakers in Toulouse and Perpignan in *Archives of the Holocaust*, p. 517.

52 AAFSC, Committee Records Relating to Humanitarian Work in France, 1933–1950, Series VIII – Marseille Office, reports (box 58, folder 38), case file for Agoust family.

7

Urban Lives, Rural Lives and Children's Evacuation

Lindsey Dodd

In late March 1943, Monsieur Jacques-Henry, Prefect of the Creuse, travelled to Paris to discuss the evacuation of Parisian children to his department because of the food supply difficulties in the capital.[1] While he was there, on 4 April, the United States Army Air Forces bombed the Renault factories in the western Parisian suburb of Boulogne-Billancourt killing around 340 civilians there, injuring 500 more and leaving over 8,000 homeless.[2] The Prefect wrote immediately to his colleagues at home:

> You cannot imagine the horror of the scenes I have witnessed. An imperative and immediate duty has arisen. I have asked that the entire school-age population of Boulogne-Billancourt, about 6,000 children, be sent to the Creuse. Knowing the typical generosity of the people of the Creuse, I can say without hesitation that they will be welcomed into families and will thus find homes to replace those from which they have been forced.[3]

This was not the first time the Paris suburbs had been bombed. In March 1942 the RAF targeted Renault with similarly deadly results; the area had also been bombed by the Germans during the invasion of 1940. Yet the threat of Allied air raids was increasing and the death toll among civilians mounting. The Paris region was by no means the worst affected by air raids, although it suffered frequent alerts which disrupted sleep and increased anxiety among residents. The air raid of 4 April 1943 thus provoked a new initiative in child-saving: not only were youngsters becoming increasingly ill from undernourishment, they were now threatened by bombs. One in six of those killed in the first two Allied raids on Boulogne-Billancourt (of four in total) was under fifteen years old.[4]

There has been very little historical interest in the evacuation of French children during the Second World War. In a recent study on schools in

Saint-Nazaire, Matthieu Devigne cites only Laura Lee Downs.[5] Since 2005, Downs has convincingly used a Franco-British comparative analysis of children's wartime evacuation to explore the differences in theories and practices of childrearing in those two countries. Her point of departure is the absence of child evacuation in popular memory of the period in France in contrast to its central place in the British narrative, not only of war but of the birth of the post-war Welfare State. She concludes that this sharp difference is down to the differences in how 'relationships among family, state and society were understood in a liberal democracy versus a republican one at the end of the 1930s, and then inside the authoritarian successor to that republican order'.[6] In Britain, children were positioned inside the notionally apolitical family sphere, thus evacuating them under the care of the State provoked an ideological rupture, and fed growing psychoanalytical concerns over the separation of working-class children from the family milieu, and particularly from their mothers. In France, children were, in contrast, positioned 'along the public-private frontier', seen as 'public beings with a life outside their families';[7] evacuating them to rural families posed no rupture with past practice given the long tradition of the *colonies de vacances* and the raising of urban orphans in the countryside. Indeed, far from creating emotional damage, placing a child into a rural familial structure where s/he benefited from paternal authority, maternal affection and a set of siblings, was, French experts maintained, 'to the child's great benefit';[8] Downs more recently added: 'The underlying presumption is clear: families other than the family of origin are entirely equipped to meet the emotional and psychological needs of those children placed therein.'[9] She thus shows French wartime evacuation as part of a longer tradition of childrearing theories and practices of temporary rural migration for the purpose of supporting healthy physical growth and the republican-style socialization of children. The main difference now, Downs remarks, was that now 'it occurred under the shadow of war'.[10]

Since she first put forward these ideas in 2005, her conclusions have remained constant and illuminating about different conceptions of state–family–child relations: it seems that 'the French' – in contrast to 'the British' – 'understood evacuation neither as a matter of social confrontation [between working-class urban children and wealthier rural people] nor as a moment of deep psychological risk for the child.'[11] For this reason, it is 'not remembered as an event of any collective or national significance' in France.[12] In this chapter, I will build on Downs's work by shifting the focus to the lived encounters of everyday life, and suggesting the importance of the shadows which war cast on this new rural influx. In a first section, I will discuss the confrontations which occurred when urban children arrived in rural homes, and then, in a second section, consider the psychological risks that evacuee children ran and had to manage. In archival documentation and oral history I find evidence both of social confrontation (as well as resolution) and of psychological disturbance (as well as adaptation).

Whenever our gaze moves from the collective to the particularities of individual experience, making generalizations becomes more difficult; historical writing becomes perhaps less satisfying but more reflective of the multiplicity of human perspectives. Shifting from discourse, elaborated in official texts by experts, to ordinary people's lived experiences creates a number of methodological uncertainties. Archival evidence that gives insight into everyday life is messy; often partial and fragmented, it demands of us the recognition that the written words we uncover are only the tip of an experiential iceberg – of uncharted moments, of unstated motivations, of emotional nuances – which can never be fully apprehended. As I will suggest in a third section, locating the messy complexity of the past depends on the sources we use: that archives in the reception localities tell us a different story to those in the sending localities, and that oral history narratives may construct evacuation as an event of great personal, if not national, significance.

The first convoy of 1,200 child evacuees arrived in the town of Guéret in the Creuse on 24 April 1943, just twenty days after the second air raid on Renault. All were from Boulogne-Billancourt. Responding to appeals in the press which offered 15 francs per child per day and free medical care, local people volunteered to house them.[13] During May, thousands more arrived, not just from Boulogne-Billancourt but from other industrial Parisian suburbs: Asnières, Courbevoie, Colombes, Clamart, Gennevilliers, Ivry, Puteux, Suresnes. Yet more evacuees turned up in the spring of the 1944 as the Allies' bombing campaign intensified. In total, the Creuse took in around 8,500 children from the Paris region, a proportion of whom were from Boulogne-Billancourt;[14] the department also sheltered a similar number of adult refugees from various places. This may seem small compared to the 300,000 refugees who swamped the Creuse during the 1940 exodus, but most of those people went home fairly soon after the defeat.[15] Many of the unaccompanied child evacuees stayed for two years, sometimes more.[16] The evacuation of these children was a joint venture, operating collaboratively between the Ministries of the Interior and of Education, and at a local level through the Prefecture of the Seine – its Economic and Social Affairs division and, in practice, its primary school inspection team – and the Prefectures of the reception departments. The Creuse was the first reception department to be drafted in, and acted as a model for the others.[17] The choice of reception departments was regulated by the German authorities; indeed, the Seine and its municipalities would have preferred to make use of regions where long-standing partnerships through the pre-war *colonies de vacances* movement existed.[18] Having to conform to German demands, however, meant that new relationships were formed. It is estimated that the State participated in the evacuation of around 215,000 children from the most war-torn parts of France.[19] What should be remembered is that many more children were sent, for reasons of health, care and or safety, by their parents to relatives in the countryside without the involvement of the state.

Social confrontations

Downs explains that the evacuation of children in wartime France formed part of a continuity with past practice, particularly that of the *colonies de vacances* which had billeted children in rural families for many years. In contrast to the more novel situation in Britain, France did not face any 'comparable threat of cross-class friction'; indeed, there were plenty of experienced peasant families willing to open their doors to urban evacuees. Yet the circumstances of the war had broken down the familiar practices of the pre-war *colonies.* First, evacuated children were lodged in family placements; yet as Downs states elsewhere, family placements were much less common in *colonies* by the mid–1930s, and their popularity was dwindling rapidly; during the war, she writes, they were something of a 'last resort'.[20] Thus living with a strange family would have been unusual for very many children. Furthermore, children born after 1934 would have been less likely to have experienced a *colonie*: the *colonies de vacances* did not cease during the Occupation, but due to requisitioning and restrictions on movement, places were far more limited. Third, this was no longer a summer holiday. Children left for an indeterminate period of time, often spanning the winter. Fourth, many families had been broken up by war and so the stability of the home environment was already undermined. Fifth, the disruption of the 1940 exodus and negative experiences of the lukewarm rural hospitality offered to some refugees made parents extremely reluctant to part with their children. And finally, this evacuation took place under the shadow of bombing, which cannot be ignored. For those who had undergone a direct attack, or had witnessed the ugly chaos of the aftermath, psychological traces remained. Even those who had not been directly bombed had spent night after night in bomb shelters, sleep disturbed by sirens.[21] The child who departed Austerlitz station for Guéret in 1943 or 1944 did so in very different circumstances to the one who left for a summer *colonie* ten years before.

In advance of the 1943 evacuation, volunteer host families were sought via the press. By looking at people's motivations for lodging children, it appears that this may well not have been a familiar practice. It was also tainted by the conditions of war. Several intercepted phone calls attest that taking in an evacuee was motivated by national solidarity at a time of unusual hardship, rather than by past behaviours: as one woman explained, 'they're French too, poor kids'.[22] Compassion was also evident: 'We'll be taking one [. . .] You've got pity those who haven't got enough to eat.'[23] But these were not the only sentiments around: one caller remarked that 'the state is telling us to take these children in', while another complained that 'we're being morally obliged to take a child from the Paris region [. . .] which I'm not happy about'.[24] Monsieur Killian, a cantonal inspector supervising a group of evacuated children, noted that some chose to lodge an evacuee 'to avoid having to take an elderly person', and others did it 'for financial gain'.[25] He complained vigorously about the latter: 'I am convinced that in time there will be an outcry over the scandalous exploitation of the youngsters from our towns': certain farmers, he wrote, now had a 'young Parisian servant', whom they did not pay and indeed received a state allowance for.[26] He also noted, however, that other families had set up savings accounts for their evacuee, paying into it either their state allowance or some recompense for labour. Many families were motivated by a need for helping hands, labour being in short supply. In fact they had been told not to treat the children as 'holidaymakers': children should 'help around the house and in the fields, in a manner appropriate to their strength'.[27] These diverse motivations suggest an underlying tension as urban confronted rural; we also learn of the shades of opinion which prompted unknowable differences in children's treatment, making generalization at the level of everyday experience difficult.

It also appears that urban children's poverty, exacerbated by the restrictions of war, was a surprise to the families who lodged them. At official levels, of course, it was all too familiar, and social services in towns had long been working to counter it. Poor children's ill-health had inspired the *colonies de vacances* movement and, during the interwar years, reforming mayors in the Parisian suburbs invested in progressive public health services.[28] But by autumn 1942, the neediest children in Paris were in a 'wretched physical condition';[29] some of those very sickly children arrived in the Creuse the following spring. Existing physical infirmities were compounded by war conditions in the Paris region, leading to undernourishment and sometimes neglect; reports of 'mental debility', fits and incontinence emerged. Of one eleven-year-old, it was noted that he was 'afflicted with infant paralysis, physically very weak. He can barely dress himself and struggles to clean himself'.[30] While these problems were not the norm, they indicate the severity of some cases with which medical staff and foster families had to deal. People in the Creuse were shocked. One woman told a friend that her evacuees were 'terrifyingly skinny', while another reported 'but, well! It's abject poverty [...] We had to wash them, delouse them, find clothes for them – they didn't even have nightdresses'.[31] One little girl had arrived 'wearing no knickers, just a dirty dress'.[32] Many of the children's families could not muster even a change of clothes, or were unwilling to part with their limited resources. And for 'some lousy ones [and] several incontinents', perhaps the neediest of all, the future was unsettled: families refused to take them, and they were placed collectively in a centre at Grancher.[33] Yet while rural people grumbled about the shortage of clothing, there was none of the censorious newspaper reporting – dirty, lazy, flea-ridden, thieving, feckless, vulgar and not toilet-trained – which quickly followed children's arrival in English and Welsh reception areas.[34]

While class did not emerge as a point of social confrontation in the striking way that it did in Britain, the judgements of rural people about working-class character demonstrate an imperfect 'harmony between [...] two worlds' only recently separated by urban migration.[35] In Britain, children's unsuccessful adaptation was frequently (but not always) interpreted in behaviouralist terms: poverty and deprivation were blamed on bad parenting (mothering in particular), rather than on structural factors such as unemployment or inadequate housing.[36] In the French evacuation, however, little top-down criticism of parenting appeared: welfare reformers had already recognized that structural factors were inherent in urban children's poverty. But at the level of everyday interaction, attitudes point to certain prejudices. A woman told a friend 'they're going to drive me crazy [...] they're real little urchins. What do you expect, they're the children of Parisians, and of workers'.[37] Complaining about the poor state of the new arrivals, her friend said 'the parents couldn't care less, could they'; 'certainly not' was the reply. A mayoral employee despaired: 'I don't know where I'm going to place them, they're workers' children.'[38] The children's status marked them as 'other'– not as universal republican citizens – and surfaced amidst concerns about character and assimilation. Yet in other situations there was recognition that adverse conditions at home had impacted on difficult children's behaviour and development, rather than inherent character flaws: the Protestant Maison d'Accueil Chrétienne pour enfants reported in neutral language on the work situation of evacuated children's parents, the typical absence of fathers, the children's poor school attendance, and the overcrowdedness of their homes.[39] Overall, it seemed that rural people tried to comprehend the hardships of urban lives. Indeed, condemnation was reserved for their neighbours: one letter writer in the Creuse commented sarcastically that 'our big landowners who are all millionaires at the moment don't want to know', while a mayoral employee stated that 'it's with the small farmers that I've managed to place them'.[40] Anger was directed at selfish locals not at negligent urban parents.

Yet the fact that many evacuated children ended up with poorer families created its own problems: criticism flowed not only from countryside to town, but from town to countryside too. During a medical visit in summer 1943, Dr Bezançon from Boulogne-Billancourt noted that 'the hygiene of houses is usually adequate but in a certain number of cases it is barely so: very small dwellings, poorly ventilated, sometimes cleanliness and bedding leaves something to be desired'.[41] On occasion this resulted in the urban authorities exerting pressure: the mayor of Boulogne-Billancourt insisted that siblings Michel and Lydia T. be moved: 'the children must sleep in a bed and not on a straw mattress on the ground [. . .] The bodily cleanliness of the children must be attended to daily and not weekly.' Despite protests from local inspector Monsieur Huré that these children were housed with 'good women who look after the children in their care very well', different standards of everyday hygiene existed.[42] In the majority of cases, living conditions were deemed acceptable; many evacuees shared rooms with other children, or with grandparents, the foster parents themselves, and sometimes with family servants. These children would have been used to sharing spaces with others, but not with strangers, and indeed, large bedrooms in the stillness of dark country nights could surely be disconcerting.

Psychological risks

The rationale behind evacuating urban children was food supply: it was only after the air raid of 4 April 1943 that bombing created a greater sense of urgency. But the danger posed by food shortages in the capital remained a strong impetus, and children's physical health was the main means of persuading parents to part with them. The attention given to physical health, growth and development overshadowed any concerns about psychological disturbances and, as Downs emphasizes, anxieties over the psychological risks of family separation '*never even came up*' [her italics] in official discussions about evacuation.[43] The reports which she uses are drawn from the archives of urban municipalities and indicate the genuine success of placing undernourished children in close contact to food and fresh air. Such reports were designed – as she acknowledges – to reassure parents that their children were doing well. Dr Bezançon reported that in the Creuse 'the majority of the children are putting on weight, some very visibly'.[44] The Maison d'Accueil Chrétienne pour enfants noted that four evacuees had put on two kilos in a month, and four about a kilo; in the Lot, an average weight gain of six kilos in five months was reported, and three centimetres in height.[45] Qualitative evidence comes from the children's foster parents and their teachers: young Adrienne B. was reported as 'looking splendid, with chubby, rosy cheeks. She eats well, is always outside walking with Mme G. or playing in the fields'.[46] Such improvement was indeed the intention of the evacuation, and in this sense it worked preventatively to lessen the physical impact of the harsher years of 1944 and 1945.

The fact that anxieties about psychological risk were absent does not mean that they did not exist. Those in charge of the evacuation certainly promoted urban children's successful adaptation to their new environment, and there is no reason to doubt that for many this was the case. Inspectors reported 'more and more affectionate relationships with foster families',[47] and the fact that children were 'thinking sadly about their return home and would much rather stay in the Creuse' was taken as evidence of positive adaptation.[48] Letters written by children were published to demonstrate how well foster families had substituted biological families. A thirteen-year-old girl thanked the family looking after her little brother: 'he sees himself as part of your family now. Thank you for having understood so well how to replace my Mum and Dad'.[49] Another evacuee wrote in praise of the love shown by foster mothers 'who take the place of our own mums who are so far away from us'.[50] But alongside these statements, the sadness of separation is also evident in unpublished reports. Of little Jacques S. it was noted that 'his sensitive nature shows in the homesickness he suffers so often, far from his parents'; Guy M. longed for his sister who was not billeted in the same family;[51] and among those who wished to stay in the Creuse, it was noted that what they *really* wanted to do was to 'to go home, fetch their mums and bring them back here straight away'.[52] The anxieties of separation flowed in other directions too: biological mothers were distressed that their children did not want to come home,[53] and the affection invested by foster parents made the child's eventual departure a heart-breaking prospect.[54] Family separation was not viewed as a long-term psychological risk to children, but many experienced it as a psychological disturbance in the moment.

In Britain, alongside the more well-known psychoanalytical discourse on the family, a legion of child psychologists were conducting research into the impact of exposure to bombing on the very young.[55] In contrast, French paediatricians remained far more concerned with children's physical health, but there was recognition nonetheless that evacuees arrived in the countryside 'damaged, from neighbourhoods devastated by the horrors of war'.[56] While the Vichy press made use of their trauma to criticize the Allies,[57] the psychological or 'nervous' damage resulting from air raid exposure was also commented upon by medical practitioners. In 1943, paediatricians Mercier and Despert cited contemporary observational evidence from France that evacuated children frequently 'cried pitifully, asking for their mothers until they fell asleep from exhaustion'; adjustment to their new homes 'was only apparent, and [they] showed indications of deep-seated trauma'. They described how these children 'never smiled and the foster mothers invariably noted their lack of gaiety and enthusiasm'.[58] There is no evidence, though, that advice was given to foster families or to the schoolteachers who accompanied the evacuees about how to deal with the psychological disturbances that impinged upon children's emotional adaptation. As ever, faith was placed in the curative powers of the French countryside. It was through 'calmness and affection', food, sleep and exercise that anxieties would be resolved, rather than specialist care.[59]

The phenomenon of bedwetting may tell us something of children's anxiety – an anxiety which sometimes receded as they settled in. During the British evacuation, the prevalence of enuresis split opinion, conservative social reformers attributing it to poor parenting and psychologists recognizing that it 'may result from a sense of insecurity'.[60] For French foster parents struggling to dry bedlinen on a daily basis, particularly into the winter (which suggests the duration of the problem), bedwetting was a real headache. Some bedwetters were removed from the family environment thought to be of such benefit to them, and placed in medical centres; sending them back to Paris was also proposed.[61] It was recognized that many of those sent to medical centres had particularly broken family lives: out of twenty children sent to Lourdes in early 1944, most had parents who were dead or absent, or they were homeless or had been abandoned.[62] It was noted of the bedwetters that 'several weren't incontinent at first': the problem had developed since they arrived.[63] Although some children were removed from family care, other rural families were committed to helping them; a report on Danièle B. notes that '[Mme M.] is more and more attached to the child and happy to keep her despite her limited means [. . .] she is trying to cure her bedwetting problem'.[64] Of Marcel C., it was reported that he was 'being monitored for his bedwetting – progress. The child is cared for extremely well, and they praise his good character'.[65] Bedwetting children in France happily received none of the public stigmatization that their British counterparts faced; but this widespread experience cannot be ignored as it testifies to a distressing and potentially humiliating episode, especially for older children, which was undergone by many. It also suggests that accounts of a smooth transposition from town to country do not tell the full story.

Locating the messiness of everyday life

Family–state–child relations are useful to conceptualize away from the realities lived by children and their families 'on the ground', as they force us to question our assumptions about what is 'normal', and what is 'expected' when a child is removed from his or her family. While the weight of international research from both the Second World War and more recent conflicts must challenge the idea that easy adaptation is the norm for lone child evacuees and refugees, grappling with individual cases will always expose the limits of generalization. It certainly seems that the children of the 1943–5 evacuation in France largely coped well in their new environments and this may well have been because of long-standing urban–rural interactions and the consequent absence of official anxiety and press hysteria. But it would be complacent to assume that an absence of 'horror stories' in the archives of the urban municipalities means that children were necessarily well adapted, foster families were caring and experienced, and biological families were substitutable.[66] The evidence is elsewhere, and shows us that alongside happy *petits réfugiés* living in harmony with rural playmates there also existed social confrontation, psychological disturbance and lasting, everyday distress which written records can only hint at. A few examples must suffice here.

In April 1944 a ten-year-old girl was admitted to hospital. She was diagnosed with gonorrhoea. For the authorities in the Creuse, the pressing problem was how to keep her 'extremely violent' biological father away from the foster father, whom she alleged had raped her. A recently released prisoner of war, the girl's father was sure to murder the other man once he knew that his daughter had been 'damaged for life'.[67] Were these the trusted networks of family placements into which urban children were placed, or hastily assembled new ones, drafted in under the pressure of war and inadequately vetted? In November 1944, the police opened an inquiry into reports of physical abuse against a twelve-year-old evacuee called Roger who, it was claimed, had been beaten, kicked and slapped by the farmer and his wife with whom he and another boy, aged seven, were billeted. When questioned, Roger admitted 'frankly and spontaneously that he had never been beaten and if he had been punished from time to time it was because he thoroughly deserved it'.[68] A verdict of malicious denunciation – not uncommon in wartime France – was returned, the children used as pawns in a neighbours' dispute. Only ten years old, Raymonde had been put to work, her mother complained, as a 'farm hand'. To 'cure' her fear of animals, her foster father locked her in the cowshed until her screams alerted the neighbours. She had lost two kilos since arriving in the Creuse, and was anaemic: hardly an advertisement for rural recuperation.[69] Young Fernand arrived in the Creuse at the age of thirteen; by 1945 he was on his fourth foster family. He had a habit of disappearing for days on end, and his foster parents, who had recently picked him up from the roadside 'so drunk that they had to put him in a wheelbarrow', were at the end of their tether. Fernand stole, he threatened to burn down the house and had assaulted a neighbour with a knife.[70] Was he just 'acting out', or should we see in his behaviour the evidence of something else about which the archives are silent? Such individual cases may be isolated examples, but they illustrate the complex lived realities of multiple lives adapting to new everyday circumstances.

Archival sources, particularly official ones, provide snapshots of the past which are frequently inadequate to reveal the messiness of everyday life. Oral history opens other doors, and allows us not only to ask the historical 'sources' the questions we seek to answer, but to encourage their participation in interpreting their own lives. As such, oral history is a powerful tool for understanding everyday experiences because it allows access to emotional and sensory information, and its retrospective quality gives insight into the enduring legacy of past events. For Yvette Chapalain, evacuated from the town of Brest into the Finistère countryside, evacuation remained a distressing experience to recount.[71] While her story differs to those of the Creuse evacuees as she was sent to a rural boarding school and not billeted with a family, her account suggests both confrontation and distress.

> I've got some bad memories of those years which still upset me a bit. It was just that we didn't have any choice, but were sent away to these other schools where we weren't made very welcome by the other children, the children who lived there. We were 'the refugees'. [. . .] They had good bread, pancakes, things like that [. . .] We didn't find much affection there. No, no, frankly, no. We were imposed upon them. That's it. We were in the way.

Later on, when asked to reflect more generally on children's experiences of war, her response returned again to her own evacuation:

> *What does war mean to a child?*
> Destruction. Firstly, because they separated children from their parents. [...] Being separated from your childhood friends, because I didn't have my school-friends with me. So yes. A feeling of destruction. Certainly. A child needs to be with its family [...] There were no more goodnights, at bedtime. My mother wasn't with us at bedtime. Tears, tears, thinking about home.

Unlike archival evidence oral history is not a snapshot of the past: it is the product of layers of memory processes, both individual and collective, over time and in the interview. Nonetheless, experiences such as Yvette's suggest that removing children from secure family environments, particularly in times of conflict and uncertainty, may not always benefit the child.

Conclusion

In the darkest days of war, many rural people nurtured physically and emotionally the human resources of the nation's future.[72] It was not quite the case, then, that the peasants grew fat while the cities starved: many urban children grew fatter and suffered less than they might have done because they were evacuated.

The two-way interaction between town and country seemed to bode well for a national future less riven by division. Monsieur Pecque of the evacuee reception service in the Creuse stated confidently in 1944 that 'the closeness between city kids and country folk is a fact'.[73] Social confrontations were met and managed within in the encounters of daily life, of problem-solving and care-giving. Yet behind the weight gain and rosy cheeks lies a set of questions about family separation: the breaking of bonds which did not worry French officials seemed to worry many children, and the shadow of war could be long and dark. While anxieties over family separation may have never come up in contemporary discussion, much remains unknown at the level of personal experience.

Olivier Wieviorka has written that for the French population, the period 1940–4 'was everything but a warrior experience' (*experience guerrière*):[74] but war is not only about frontline action, and children's evacuation demonstrates its encroachment deep into civilian life, and into regions usually considered little affected by these years of upheaval. Downs rightly points out that other events have superseded it: *exode*, occupation, penury, collaboration, resistance, persecution, deportation. It is indeed the case that these provide the dominant motifs in scholarly research and in public memory of the period. Children in general have found little place in historical accounts: their experiences are a 'bad fit' with analyses which are frequently top-down, and bound up with blame and accusation.[75] By shifting our gaze from the top to the bottom, we see more clearly how children's lives during this period – and evacuation in particular – fit into a story of everyday life in *wartime* France, but less well into a narrative of occupation, collaboration and resistance. A historiography which persists in working only inside its own established frameworks will continue to miss the everyday realities of French lives in a period of world war.

Notes

1 Archives départementales de la Creuse (ADC), 288W 43.1: Minutes of conference of 7 April 1943 (Prefecture of the Seine) concerning evacuation of Parisian school population. The meeting was chaired by the Prefect of the Seine and attended by the Prefects of the Creuse, Haute-Saône and Yonne, as well representatives from the Refugee Service, Education Ministry and the Inter-ministerial Service for Protection against the Events of War (SIPEG).

2 C. Baldoli and A. Knapp, *Forgotten Blitzes: France and Italy under Allied Air Attack* (London: Continuum, 2012), p. 94.

3 ADC, 987W 110: Prefect of the Creuse to Mayors, Sub-Prefects, Archbishops etc of the Creuse, 12 April 1943.

4 Archives Municipales de Boulogne-Billancourt [AMBB], 6H 19: Prefect of the Seine to Mayor of Boulogne-Billancourt, 18 September 1943.

5 M. Devigne, '"Les enfants d'abord!" Le repli des écoles loin des dangers de la guerre en France (1939–1944)', in J.-F. Condette (ed.), *Les Écoles dans la guerre: acteurs et institutions éducatives dans les tourmentes guerrières (XVIIe-XXe siècles)* (Lille: Presses universitaires du Septentrion, 2014), 379–98. Downs has published three articles on this subject. See 'Milieu social or milieu familial? Theories and practices of childrearing among the popular classes in twentieth-century France and Britain: the case of evacuation (1939–45)', *Family and Community History*, 8.1 (2005), 49–65; 'Les évacuations d'enfants en France et en Grande-Bretagne (1939–1940). Enfance en guerre,' *Annales. Histoire, Sciences Sociales,* 66.2 (2011), 413–48; and most recently 'Au revoir les enfants. Wartime evacuation and the politics of childhood in France and Britain', *History Workshop Journal*, 82.1 (2016), 121–50.

6 Downs, 'Au revoir les enfants', p. 142.

7 Downs, 'Au revoir les enfants', p. 145.

8 Downs, 'Milieu social or milieu familial?', p. 56.

9 Downs, 'Au revoir les enfants', p. 132.
10 Downs, 'Milieu social or milieu familial?', p. 57.
11 Downs, 'Au revoir les enfants', p. 134.
12 Downs, 'Au revoir les enfants', p. 124.
13 ADC, 288W 43.1: Note from Colonel Michon, 12 April 1943.
14 ADC, 288W 43.1: Note from Colonel Michon anticipates 5,000 children to be sent to the Creuse, 12 April 1943; a note in ADC, 288W 43.1 cites 8,585 Parisian refugee children in June 1944 (18 June 1945). Precise numbers are difficult to pin down. Around 3,000 children were evacuated by state services from Boulogne-Billancourt, it seems, perhaps half of them to the Creuse. (Data collated from across AMBB, 6H 17, 6H 18 and 6H 19.)
15 AMBB, 6H 19: Prefect of Seine to all mayors, 13 July 1943; C. Bellot-Antony, 'La vie quotidienne en Creuse durant la Seconde Guerre Mondiale (1939–1945)' (unpublished Masters dissertation, Université Clermont-Ferrand II, 1993), p. 21.
16 ADC, 288W 43 1: Note listing numbers of evacuees from Paris region 30 June 1944–4 June 1945, 18 June 1945.
17 ADC, 288W 43.1: Minutes of conference of 7 April 1943.
18 ADC, 288W 43.1: Minutes of conference of 7 April 1943. For discussion of prior evacuations of children from Boulogne-Billancourt, see L. Dodd, *French Children under the Allied Bombs, 1940–45: An Oral History* (Manchester: Manchester University Press, 2016), chapter 8.
19 A. Knapp, *Les Français sous les bombes allies* (Paris: Tallandier, 2014), p. 290.
20 L. L. Downs, *Childhood in the Promised Land: Working Class Movements and the* Colonies de Vacances *in France, 1880–1960* (Durham, NC and London: Duke University Press, 2002), pp. 138–9, 187, 353 (n119).
21 See Dodd, *French Children under the Allied Bombs*, chapters 5–7.
22 ADC, 288W 43.1: Intercepted telephone call between Chénérailles (Creuse) and Gouzougnat (Creuse), 13 April 1943.
23 ADC, 288W 43.1: Intercepted letter between Lachault (Creuse) and Treignat (Allier), 15 April 1943.
24 ADC, 288W 43.1: Intercepted phone call between Magnat-l'Étrange (Creuse) to Reignac (Indre-et-Loire), 20 April 1943.
25 ADC, 987W 110: Pecque (Secretary of the Service d'Accueil for the children from the Seine) to Secretary-General of Prefecture of the Creuse, 1 July 1943.
26 ADC, 987W 110: Extract from report by Killian (cantonal inspector), 10 March 1944.
27 ADC, 987W 110: Primary School Inspector (Guéret) to Inspector General of Primary Education in the Seine, 5 July 1943.
28 R. Payre, 'Henri Sellier et la réforme municipale en avril 1942', *Genèses 41* (2000), 143–63.
29 H. C. Stuart, 'Review of the evidence as to the nutritional state of children in France', *American Journal of Public Health*, 35.4 (1945), 299–307, p. 304. On child nutrition

and charitable feeding, see the chapters in this volume by Matthieu Devigne, Shannon Fogg and Jean-Pierre Le Crom.

30 ADC, 987W 110: Report of the Maison d'Accueil Chrétienne pour enfants (MACE), 8 December 1943. For more on this institution, which is more well known for hiding Jewish children, see C. Moreigne, 'Des Alpes-Maritimes à la Creuse: la Maison d'Enfants Franco-Tchéquoslovaque du Château du Theil (1943–44)', *Mémoires de la Société des sciences naturelles, archéologiques et historiques de la Creuse*, 56 (2010/11), 293–311.

31 ADC, 288W 43.1: Intercepted telephone call between locations Dun-le-Failletot (Creuse) and Guéret (Creuse), 18 May 1943; intercepted telephone call between locations Montluçon (Allier) to Chambon (Creuse), 3 June 1943.

32 ADC, 288W 43.1: Intercepted telephone call between locations Montluçon (Allier) to Chambon (Creuse), 3 June 1943.

33 AMBB, 6H 19: Bertrand (Primary School Inspector for the Prefecture of the Seine) to Mayor of Boulogne-Billancourt, 1 May 1943.

34 J. Welshman, 'Evacuation and social policy during the Second World War: myth and reality', *Twentieth Century British History*, 9.1 (1998), 28–53, p. 33.

35 Downs, 'Au revoir les enfants', p. 132.

36 Stewart and Welshman point out that Scottish understandings of evacuees' poverty hinged upon structural rather than behavioural interpretations; historians must be wary of generalizations about 'British' history. See John Stewart and John Welshman, 'The evacuation of children in wartime Scotland: culture, behaviour and poverty', *Journal of Scottish Historical Studies*, 26.1+2, 100–20.

37 ADC, 288W 43.1, Intercepted telephone call between Montluçon (Allier) to Chambon (Creuse), 3 June 1943.

38 ADC, 288W/43 1: Intercepted telephone call between Chénérailles (Creuse) and Gouzougnat (Creuse), 13 April 1943.

39 ADC, 987W 110: Report of the MACE, 8 December 1943.

40 ADC, 288W 43.1: Intercepted telephone call between locations Bonnat (Creuse) to Cheniers (Creuse), 24 April 1943.

41 AMBB, 6H 19: report on Dr Bezançon's visit to the Creuse, 17 August 1943.

42 AMBB, 6H 19: Mayor of Boulogne-Billancourt to Huré (cantonal inspector), 14 August 1943; Huré to Mayor of Boulogne-Billancourt, 4 August 1943.

43 Downs, 'Milieu social or milieu familial?', p. 60.

44 AMBB, 6H 19: Report on Dr Bezançon's visit, 17 August 1943.

45 ADC, 987W 110: Report of the MACE, 8 Dec. 1943; ADC, 288W 43.2: *Les Bras-ouverts*, April-May 1944.

46 AMBB, 6H 19: Reports on children in the Doubs, September 1943.

47 AMBB, 6H 19: Bourderau (cantonal inspector), report on children in the Lot, 20 December 1943–20 January 1944.

48 ADC, 288W 43.1: Pecque (Service d'Accueil), report on evacuated children, 22 September 1944.

49 AMBB, 6H 19: *Les Bras-Ouverts*, no. 2 ('Noël'), 1943.

50 AMBB, 6H 19: Denise Gardet to Prefect of the Creuse, 10 December 1943.

51 AMBB, 6H 19: Reports on children in the Doubs, September 1943.

52 ADC, 288W 43.1: Pecque (Service d'Accueil), report on evacuated children, 22 September 1944.

53 AMBB, 6H 19: Bourderau, report on children in the Lot, 16 November 1943.

54 AMBB, 6H 19: *Les Bras-Ouverts*, no. 2 ('Noël'), 1943.

55 See, e.g. F. Bodman, 'War conditions and the mental health of the child', *British Medical Journal*, 4 Oct. 1941, 486–8; W. M. Burbury, 'Evacuation and air raids: effects on children', *British Medical Journal*, 8 Nov. 1941, 660–2; E. Glover, 'Notes on the psychological effects of war conditions on the civilian population', part iii, 'The "Blitz" – 1940–41', *International Journal of Psychoanalysis*, 23 (1942), 17–37.

56 ADC, 288W 43.1: Pecque (Service d'Accueil), report on evacuated children, 23 March 1944.

57 ADC, 9BIB 129.74: *Le Courrier du Centre*, 'Les petits parisiens dans la Creuse', 8 May 1943.

58 M. H. Mercier and J. L. Despert, 'Psychological effects of the war on French children', *Psychosomatic Medicine*, 5.3 (1943), 266–72, p. 269.

59 ADC, 288W 43.1: Pecque (Service d'Accueil), report on evacuated children, 23 March 1944.

60 Women's Group on Public Welfare, *Our Towns: a Close-up* (Oxford: Oxford University Press, 1943), p. 81; I. L. Janis, *Air War and Emotional Stress. Psychological Studies of Bombing and Civilian Defense* (New York: McGraw Hill, 1951), p. 92, citing R. Titmuss, *Problems of Social Policy* (London, 1950).

61 ADC, 288W 43.1: Pecque (Service d'Accueil), report on evacuated children, 22 September 1944.

62 ADC, 987W 110: Notes on the evacuation of 'incontinent' children to Lourdes, 26–28 January 1943.

63 ADC, 288W 43.1: Service d'Accueil to Head of Refugee Services in the Creuse, undated (autumn 1944).

64 AMBB, 6H 19: Reports on children in the Doubs, September 1943.

65 AMBB, 6H 19: Reports on children in the Doubs, September 1943.

66 Downs, 'Au revoir les enfants', p. 140.

67 ADC, 288W 43.1: Report of Huré (cantonal inspector), 16 September 1944.

68 ADC, 288W 43.1: Denunciation of Monsieur M., anonymous and undated; letter from Monsieur M. to the Prefect, 11 November 1944; police report and witness statements, 13 November 1944.

69 ADC, 288W 43.1: Letter from girl's mother to Prefect of the Seine, 28 June 1945, forwarded to Prefect of the Creuse, 19 July 1945.

70 ADC, 987W 110: Report from the Service d'Accueil (Grand-Bourg), 21 February 1945.

71 Interview by L. Dodd with Yvette Chapalain, Brest, 23 April 2009 (see also Dodd, *French Children under the Allied Bombs*). As this book goes to press, I am working on a series of interviews I conducted in summer 2017 with people evacuated from the Paris suburbs to the Creuse during the war as children, and with people in whose families they were billeted. The interviews suggest both positive adaptation and cases of the opposite, including anxieties generated at the time and thereafter over family separation and reconfiguration after the war.

72 A.-M. Thiesse, 'Les deux identités de la France', *Modern and Contemporary France*, 9.1 (2001), 9–18, p. 13.

73 ADC, 288W 43.1: Pecque (Service d'Accueil), report on evacuated children, 4 November 1944.

74 O. Wieviorka, *La Mémoire désunie. Le souvenir politique des années sombres, de la Libération à nos jours* (Paris: Seuil, 2013), p. 16.

75 C. Nettelbeck, 'A forgotten zone of memory? French primary school children and the history of the Occupation', *French History and Civilization*, 14 (2011), p. 159. See, in particular, the chapters by Camille Mahé and Matthieu Devigne in this volume for discussions of children and childhood in wartime France.

Part Two

Confrontation and Challenge in Wartime France

8

Colonial Prisoners of War and French Civilians

Sarah Frank

This book thus far has examined a variety of experiences and people who lived through the German occupation of France and the Vichy regime: mostly French, mostly civilians and mostly white. In this chapter I turn to another group present in France during this period: prisoners of war from the French colonies. Both world wars brought soldiers from across the French territories in Africa, Madagascar, Indochina and the Antilles to fight alongside white French soldiers. At the fall of France, many of these colonial soldiers were among the 1.8 million prisoners taken by the German Reich. The subsequent occupation of France gave the Germans the opportunity to separate their prisoners racially, taking white prisoners to Germany and leaving the colonial prisoners of war (CPOWs) in France.[1]

The question of everyday life in wartime France must, in so many cases, be an exploration of abnormal circumstances. This was especially true for the CPOWs. Over the summer and autumn of 1940, the Germans built and renovated camps throughout the Occupied Zone of France and moved most of the white prisoners to Germany.[2] Among the 130,000 men who remained in these camps, called *Frontstalags,* were 85,000 CPOWs and 45,000 white metropolitan soldiers, some of whom fought in overseas regiments, and some without ties to the colonies.[3] Captivity in Occupied France was legally and practically problematic, but it did offer certain advantages. The international conventions governing prisoners of war, notably the 1907 Hague Convention respecting the Laws and Customs of War on Land and the 1929 Geneva Convention for the Protection of Prisoners, had not foreseen a situation where prisoners would be interned in their own country instead of that of the detaining power. While clearly the CPOWs were not in their own countries, France maintained legal jurisdiction over their movements and negotiated on their behalf. Both Germans and French saw that this legal ambiguity gave them scope to advance their own agendas. Germany wanted to punish the French for using colonial soldiers on European soil, and to maintain the supposed 'racial purity' of the Reich.[4] The traditional paternalism of the French army combined with Vichy's fears that German propaganda might sway CPOWs' loyalties created strong incentives to assert control over a population whose experiences in France could influence opinions in the colonies upon their return. Thus the French hoped that having the CPOWs in France would give them more influence over their colonial subjects, who, once repatriated, could shape the discourse around the defeat in favour of France.

Previous scholarship has painted the CPOWs' experiences of captivity as having been worse than other European prisoners', suggesting that the Vichy regime's racism led to them being neglected and abandoned to German prejudices.[5] The reality is much more nuanced. Rather, the peculiar flavour of French racism which, in the colonial context translated into paternalism, was exactly what obliged Vichy officials to 'protect' their colonial soldiers during captivity.

The CPOWs' everyday wartime experiences were determined by the way in which they were seen as 'other' – as non-white, colonial subjects – by the Germans and by Vichy. This chapter follows their progress from 1940, beginning with the racially-motivated dangers they faced during capture on the battlefield. It discusses their earlier and rather disorganized period of imprisonment in France, during which, nonetheless, relations developed with local people; it then moves on to the later period of their captivity where aid was offered under the aegis of the Comité central d'assistance aux prisonniers de guerre (Central Committee for the Assistance of Prisoners of War – CCAPG). Various charities worked under the umbrella of the CCAPG, including the French Red Cross which recruited French civilians to contribute deliveries of food and parcels to the CPOWs. Such official, top-down aid was designed to reinforce ties between CPOWs and the French, and thus to France. At the same time, the regime tried to cultivate personal attachments between French civilians and these colonial subjects; certain gendered relations of solidarity developed with local women, as did practical acts of solidarity with other civilians. These individual connections at times escaped the control of the authorities, leading to everyday, bottom-up interactions between the French population and the CPOWs, bolstered by feelings of humanitarianism and solidarity in the face of the shared burden of Occupation. These less formal interactions sometimes turned into relationships outside official boundaries, and must be seen as contributing to the higher proportion of CPOWs escaping from camps in France than French POWs from German *Stalags*.

In this chapter, I will suggest the way in which the abnormal circumstances of the CPOWs' daily lives created an atypical interaction with the French population, and that this interaction is a crucial part of their imprisonment as it gave opportunities for escape and survival. Drawing in particular on CPOWs' own accounts, I will show that the CPOWs were not neglected, either by Vichy or by local populations, and that the growth of a bottom-up solidarity which developed from Vichy's top-down efforts to secure colonial loyalties facilitated their survival and escape.[6] Yet while many of these relationships challenged social norms, they were by no means removed from racism or racist ideals. On the contrary, paternalism and the desire to protect the soldiers from German propaganda underscored many interactions. The abnormality of this wartime interaction, however, is highlighted by the disillusionment felt by many CPOWs on their repatriation after the war when French colonial dominance was vigorously reasserted.

Capture and defeat

The weeks of fighting in May and June 1940 were marked by chaos and confusion. Eight million displaced civilians flooded the roads in front of the advancing German armies. While colonial and French soldiers struggled to hold positions along the Maginot line, in the Aisne, the Argonne forest and the Somme, the German Blitzkrieg overwhelmed the French defences and enabled the Wehrmacht to reach Paris in only six weeks.[7]

During the short-lived battle for France, stereotypes and racism put the colonial soldiers at greater risk than white soldiers. Both the French and the Germans were influenced by stereotypes of colonial soldiers, sometimes with deadly consequences. In France colonial soldiers were portrayed as warriors who did not fear death.[8] The Germans, from their earliest experience fighting against French colonial soldiers in the Franco-Prussian war, considered their use in Europe as simply unacceptable. The Germans' own experience of colonial warfare, described as 'enemy barbarism' – especially in relation to the Herero in South-West Africa in 1904–7 – had reinforced this hostility, which was reapplied to Europe.[9] The German colonel Nehring cautioned his troops that, in the past, 'French colonial soldiers mutilated German soldiers in a beastly manner. Any goodwill towards these native soldiers would be an error'.[10] For some Germans, seeing a colonial soldier use a *coupe-coupe* or machete, which was legal under the rules of war, confirmed their assumed status as 'barbarians' and justified treating them with extreme violence.[11] North African infantryman Manuel Aldeguer witnessed a group of German soldiers force 200 West African soldiers into a field and begin shooting at them.[12] While all surrendering soldiers were at risk, these acts of violence fell disproportionally on black soldiers.[13] The most dangerous time was surrender and capture where institutional racism, rumours of illegal warfare, and ferocious hand-to-hand combat influenced German behaviour.[14]

Having already killed a number of black soldiers, the German military authorities tried to force Jean Moulin, prefect of the Eure-et-Loir, to sign a false declaration accusing Senegalese troops of atrocities. This would then serve to justify killing them after their surrender. Moulin attempted suicide rather than lie about the CPOWs.[15] His attempt was unsuccessful and, as is well known, he later became a key leader of the French resistance. This incident reveals something about both the French and German reactions to colonial troops. The styling of colonial soldiers as 'savages' meant that some German soldiers felt justified in killing them. Yet that was not sufficient legally to defend their murder – hence the need for Moulin's false declaration to legitimize the action. This inadvertently demonstrated a desire to respect international law, at least in appearance. Total abandonment of the 1929 Geneva Convention for the Protection of Prisoners would have allowed them to shoot colonial soldiers or even French soldiers without justification. Instead, after these isolated incidents in May and June 1940, the Germans changed their behaviour towards colonial prisoners. That the CPOWs were accorded Geneva Convention protection was crucial to their survival. Indeed, the contrast in treatment between colonial prisoners and Soviet ones bears noting. Only 5 per cent of CPOWs died in captivity compared with 60 per cent of Soviet prisoners, who were not given Geneva Convention protection.[16] French military officers and soldiers had long been encouraged to infantilize 'their' colonial soldiers and the seemingly dramatic shift in German attitudes towards the colonial prisoners worried soldiers and officials alike. Some German soldiers joked with the CPOWs and took photographs of them wearing silly hats.[17] Drawing on its long-standing paternalism, French concern manifested itself in a desire to protect the CPOWs both from German influence and their own supposed naivety.

The reaction of the French government and of local civilians suggests that France would defend both its colonial soldiers and their use in Europe as legitimate. Some of the first interactions between French civilians and CPOWs occurred during 1940, when ordinary people witnessed these massacres along the front. Colonial soldiers were highly visible in the racially homogeneous French countryside. Locals were aware of their contributions to the war effort, and of their murders. They carefully recorded the location of CPOW graves and passed this information on to the colonial authorities, which informed families. The sheer number of reports from civilians and soldiers shows that the French did not consider violence against them as acceptable, even within the context of war. The vast majority of the CPOWs survived capture and captivity. However, they were obviously affected by witnessing or hearing about their friends' and countrymen's deaths.[18] The CPOWs were forced into a captivity that felt unstable and violent. Historians are rightly critical of this beginning stage of captivity where physical conditions were terrible.

Imprisonment and interaction

The defeat rendered French confidence in institutions and traditions fragile. The fear that this might spread to colonial populations, who might then question France's right to rule, prompted efforts to mitigate the consequences of the defeat in the colonies, and later, to avoid discussions of collaboration. General Weygand explained after a visit to the African colonies that:

> on this continent, Germany and Italy remain the enemy. Any concessions that may be made to one or other of these powers of our naval and air bases in any of our African territories will ruin [the natives'] trust in their leaders and provoke reactions that may divide the French Empire.[19]

Indeed, the fear of German propaganda influencing the colonial populations was widespread among the colonial administrations, which actively fought against it.[20] Charles de Gaulle's success in rallying French Equatorial Africa to his cause meant that the colonial subjects were presented with two 'Frances' both claiming legitimacy. For the first time, the French found themselves in the awkward position of asking colonial subjects for the right to rule.[21] One important way of maintaining the CPOWs' loyalty was through improving their conditions of captivity, distributing packages and hot food, and gentle reminders of imperial solidarity.[22] Helping the CPOWs through their captivity now became more than a question of both the French civilizing mission and Christian duty; it was a guarantee of continued French influence in the colonies.

It also became a major negotiating point in French collaboration with the Germans. While rejecting the ideals and politics of the Third Republic, Vichy reiterated its imperial rhetoric. As Philippe Pétain's new Vichy regime grappled with the consequences of the defeat, two powerful symbols emerged as rallying points: that of the prisoners of war, who unlike the dead could be brought home, and that of the Empire, which remained both free and French. This rhetoric encouraged ideas of imperial duty, an abstract image. However, for those living near a *Frontstalag* where the CPOWs were imprisoned, that duty could become a more concrete reality.

Contact between civilians and CPOWs was regulated to varying degrees depending on the period. During the summer of 1940, prisoners were sent almost haphazardly onto French farms to help bring in the harvest. This allowed farmers to choose how many prisoners to employ and at what tasks. For example, French farmer Charles Metton collected four Algerian workers every morning from the camp and set them to work on his farm, helping to drain the fields. He returned them to the camp each evening.[23]

The CPOWs were engaged in essential economic sectors like agriculture and forestry to make up for the missing French prisoners, 36 per cent of whom were farmers.[24] They were seen as an inexpensive labour force to exploit.[25] Additionally, they did unskilled labour like repairing roads, clearing out ditches, cutting down isolated trees, breaking stones, excavating cesspools, cleaning bridges and quarries, digging fields and repairing waterways.[26] This brought them out of the confines of the *Frontstalag*, gave them a chance to earn wages, and afforded them the opportunity to interact with French civilians. Most often contacts were through work or over meals. In Saint-Jean-sur-Erve (Mayenne), CPOWs and locals ate together sharing soup, meat, potatoes or beans, jam or cheese, bread and coffee, red wine or cider.[27] In Commercy (Meuse), CPOWs appreciated that despite the difficulties, locals slipped them extra food and did what they could to improve conditions.[28] A few women in the suburbs of Épinal (Vosges) would run errands for the CPOWs, buying them potatoes, tobacco, bread or supplying hot soup to those working nearby.[29] This solidarity extended to improving the CPOWs' moral standing. In the Ille-et-Vilaine, Madame Le Gourain fed the CPOWs, held classes, prepared baptisms, provided light medical care and hosted parties for festival days.[30] In some instances it even continued after death. At Chaumont (Haute-Marne), the doctor placed a notice in the local paper following the death of a CPOW. About thirty people attended his funeral.[31] In many cases, it appears that French men and women responded well to the needs of the CPOWs, creating personal attachments to these men, who were frequently referred to as 'our natives'.[32]

As the Occupation advanced, administrative and physical structures were put in place to facilitate negotiations over the prisoners and to improve the conditions of their captivity.[33] This effectively reduced the freedoms of that first summer and placed increasing restrictions on both the French and the CPOWs. As the Germans imposed greater financial responsibility for the CPOWs on the French, smaller towns found their budgets increasingly stretched. This resulted in some racist pushback from local leaders like the mayor of Selle-Craonnaise (Mayenne) who explained that he could find jobs for white prisoners, even Bretons, quite easily, but no one would want to hire Arabs, Indochinese or 'others'.[34] Surprisingly such blatant racism was rather limited and usually rejected by the local population. CPOWs of all ethnicities worked successfully with the French throughout the Occupation. As the war continued, this solidarity never entirely vanished; rather, it took forms that sometimes challenged the National Revolution's conservative values. As French citizens responded to Vichy's calls to assist the CPOWs during their captivity, the lines between colonized and colonizer became increasingly blurred. Over time the CPOWs became more and more familiar to French civilians. Interactions moved from simply providing food to smuggling in parcels and letters to avoid the camp censor.[35] This bottom-up assistance was unregulated, fell outside official propaganda guidelines, and sometimes included illegal activities.[36]

Patriotic maternalism, colonial paternalism

Through the connections they forged with the CPOWs, French women personified the fluidity between the top-down Vichy sanctioned aid and the bottom-up organic and sometimes spontaneous support from the population. The parallels between Vichy's gendered and its imperial propaganda were striking, in terms of paternalism, protection and prescription. In its rhetoric at least, Vichy valued women, as mothers first and foremost.[37] As such, they could also take on a maternal role for the CPOWs. Even the language of parenthood, family, motherhood was co-opted by the National Revolution and sometimes echoed by the CPOWs themselves. In August 1941, one West African prisoner wrote to Pétain: 'Without France's benevolent attention, we do not know what severe treatments would be inflicted on us natives. But our good mother, watching over her children, knew how to soften yesterday's enemies and managed to care for us through the mesh of the barbed wire.'[38] Here France is personified as the motherland – the 'mère-patrie' – watching over her charges alongside Pétain, who presented himself as the father of the French nation. This left the CPOWs as the children of Empire and all French citizens had a responsibility towards them.

This familial vocabulary even influenced the CCAPG's mission statements. Individual parcels for prisoners were an archetypal aspect of the prisoner experience and of Vichy's top-down aid. The CCAPG argued that the sender of the package effectively 'brings the native the proof of solicitude, not only of the nation but of a particular element in this community [...] [and] substitutes itself for the prisoner's far-off family'.[39] Parcels not only provided extra food or woollen socks. They were a link to the outside world and to home, provided by the French government. French officials understood their importance. Aid needed to appear individualized to be an effective replacement for the family, even if this increased cost and time.[40] Successful packages would create and reinforce ties to, and thus dependence on, France.

The camps themselves were male-only worlds, and yet the nature of the occupation created opportunities for exchanges with French women that would not have occurred under normal circumstances in France or in the colonies. With so many French men of working age held prisoner in Germany, many French women stepped in to fill the void, especially on family farms. Additionally, women held important roles within charitable organizations, coordinating efforts in North Africa or with the French Red Cross driving trucks, transporting food deliveries, and even inspecting camps.[41]

Maternal role models, in the form of *marraines* (godmothers) became the acceptable way for CPOWs and the French to interact. Many young women near Epinal (Vosges), a town with a large *Frontstalag* and a local population particularly concerned for its prisoners' well-being, adopted a CPOW or two. Pierre Jean Prost, a French prisoner, recalled how the camp's medical staff coordinated meetings between the CPOWs and their godmothers:

> we sent the [godsons] for medical visits in Haxo on prearranged days and along the road to the hospital [the godmothers] had all the time they needed to meet a Samba Diouf or a Santa Troaré transformed into Jean Jacques or Jean Louis (those were the fashionable first names) and very impressed with their recent promotion to an apostle and proud to have a godmother who sends them, from time to time, a parcel or a letter.[42]

Receiving letters, especially when news from home was scarce, greatly improved CPOW moral and created a sense of attachment to these French women – attachment that could become problematic in the Vichy officials' eyes, however, if too close.[43]

Even so, Vichy sponsored the godmothers, providing them with the same *carte de colis* as poor French families were given to offset the financial cost of sending parcels to their own prisoners in Germany.[44] It was an attempt to put names and faces to the aid the prisoners received. The godmothers could do exactly what official anonymous deliveries could not: create ties between the CPOWs and the French. However, the friendships that emerged, by their very nature, were not dictated by paternalism or propaganda goals, and thus moved these relationships out of the realm that Vichy controlled. Thus what began as official became more organic through the growth of genuine emotional and friendly attachments. Léopold Senghor, CPOW and later first president of Senegal recalled that 'The Frenchwomen, through their selfless generosity and courage were the best propagandists for France'.[45] Overall, Vichy decided that the benefits, good propaganda for France and improved morale, outweighed the potential costs.

Nevertheless, Vichy's return to 'traditional' French values condemned sexual relations for both women and colonial soldiers. Some camp guards shared these values and even disapproved of friendships between prisoners and local women. Two German guards attacked a 23-year-old prisoner, Tayeb, when they surprised him talking to a young French milkmaid who made daily deliveries to the camp and with whom he was suspected of having a relationship. The post-mortem examination contradicted the guards' claim that he was killed while escaping.[46] What caused this overreaction by Tayeb's guards? Was it an expression of white solidarity, sexual jealously that a French woman preferred a North African prisoner, an act of terror to serve as an example for other CPOWs, or simply an example of violent treatment of a colonial prisoner? It should also be noted that prisoners in Germany were also forbidden from having relations with local women, supposedly to protect the purity of German women. While French authorities called for an investigation into Tayeb's death, this certainly did not imply consent or encouragement for relations between French women and the CPOWs. Both French and Germans preferred interactions that did not damage European prestige. Indeed, the postal censor regularly removed photos and edited claims from Madagascan prisoners that they had married French women who were reportedly 'easier' than those in the colonies.[47]

Solidarity and escape

Friendships between local women and CPOWs may have begun to obscure invisible hierarchies, but helping CPOWs to escape took French commitment to the prisoners in a different direction. If caught, these civilians risked arrest or even deportation.[48] For many French people it was not worth the risk: some turned escaped prisoners directly over to the German authorities.[49] Others, like the locals in the Gironde, were generally indifferent to the fate of the CPOWs, which made escape far more difficult there.[50] Employers were held responsible if 'their' CPOWs escaped during work hours and could be made to report directly to the German authorities.[51] This forced local employers into the legal remit of the *Frontstalag* and effectively made them representatives of the detaining power: an ambiguous position for a patriotic Frenchman to inhabit, and a good example of the expression of German power in the economic sphere. Usually, German guards accompanied the CPOWs when they worked in local communities. This was ostensibly to remove any French responsibility for the prisoners should they attempt an escape.[52] Local administrators such as prefects or mayors were required to stop escaped prisoners and provide any information the *Frontstalag* commanders might require.[53]

It was often difficult to know whether local figures were complicit in the escapes. In one example in the Yonne department, the mayor was called to account for the escape of three Tunisian prisoners who had been working in his community. Since the prisoners escaped on a Sunday, when they were under the German guard's responsibility, the mayor and the men's employer had plausible deniability. Considering the prisoners left just after receiving their salaries, the choice of day might not have been a coincidence.[54] When CPOWs decided to escape from captivity, they depended on French civilians not just for assistance but for their very survival. Civilians could help lead CPOWs away from the camps, or alternatively, could turn them in to the German authorities. Sometimes CPOWs managed to link up with local resistance networks which had well-planned systems for managing escape routes. Prisoners in the Haute-Saône were lucky that the leader of the local resistance was also the locksmith for the camp.[55] There were several group escapes and many individual ones. After each breach, he was called in to change the locks. Once the CPOWs escaped the camp, they were given false papers, food, hidden in the nearest town and later drivers from the nearby Citroën factory moved them away from the *Frontstalag*.[56]

Civilian assistance was so essential that some CPOWs, such as Michel Gnimagnon, organized their entire escape around the help of one trustworthy individual. Gnimagnon met Madame Bruand on her regular soup delivery to prisoners near Golbey at Épinal. When Gnimagnon approached Bruand with his desire to escape, she had already helped many white prisoners and was willing to assist him as well. However, as Bruand was the only French civilian to come into personal contact with the CPOWs, she would be an obvious suspect. Gnimagnon needed to organize his escape from somewhere else. Not only did Bruand facilitate Gnimagnon's departure, she sent him encouraging notes to keep his morale up while waiting for the opportune moment.[57] Over the next six weeks Gnimagnon studied the options. Eventually, he managed to escape by hiding during work, scaling a wall after dark, and navigating through the barbed wire and snow, after which his contact led him to Bruand's house where he spent the night. The next day, armed with food and the supplies she provided, a third person with possible ties to the intelligence services escorted Gnimagnon by bicycle to the train station, where he was hidden on a mail train headed for Marseille.

Physical appearances of course made escape more difficult for CPOWs. However, creativity and daring helped overcome their inability to blend in with the white civilian population, as did an understanding of how racial stereotyping operated. Albin Bancilon was hidden in plain sight on a French farm whose owners pretended he was their servant.[58] Mohamed Ben Ali took a risky but simple approach: dressed in civilian clothes and carrying a bucket, he pretended to be a North African civilian worker.[59]

For the CPOWs, the French countryside was unfamiliar territory riddled with German patrols. Locals, even those not engaged in the resistance, knew the back roads and how to circulate in relative safety. CPOWs found help, food, clothes and directions throughout the Occupied Zone. One former POW from the Great War fed escaped CPOWs, advised them how to avoid the Germans and supplied directions to the demarcation line.[60] Here, it seems, ordinary people were not thinking about the lofty ideals of imperial *grandeur*, but rather how to help other men escape from the common enemy.

The demarcation line was the most challenging part of the escape. While the French had initially understood it as an administrative marker, it rapidly became a closed border. Everyone needed a pass to move from the northern zone to the southern zone. Without the required paperwork, the CPOWs took alternative routes. For many this meant reliance upon an underground organization, such as the one at Dole (Jura) which was run by two brothers. Together they helped over 400 prisoners cross the line.[61] CPOW Hassen-Ladjimi described his experience at another such border crossing:

> I crossed at a farm that had expressly installed a millstone along the border. While two women were lookouts, a child brought the prisoner thirty metres along the road where the track was made in such a way that it was always camouflaged and all the difficult parts were fitted with a ladder or holes in the fences. A dozen prisoners took this route every day. The day before, two Senegalese, armed and in uniform, crossed.[62]

The structures and dynamics of escape changed completely after the Allied landings in North Africa and subsequent German invasion of the southern zone in November 1942. Before that time, prisoners who had escaped to the 'Free' Zone were not returned to their camps. However, with all of France now under German occupation, escaped prisoners could be forcibly sent back to captivity. Even those who managed to remain free could not return home to the colonies since Vichy no longer controlled them.

Overall, CPOWs escaped at a higher rate than French prisoners in Germany. Approximately 6.7 per cent of CPOWs[63] escaped while fewer than 5 per cent of French prisoners did.[64] Three reasons could explain the difference. First, while some French prisoners received help from some German civilians, CPOWs in France benefitted comparatively far more from the sympathy of the local population. Second, from a practical point of view, CPOWs had a shorter distance to travel to escape captivity than French prisoners in Germany. Finally, CPOWs had French francs earned at work which could help purchase food or clothes. French prisoners in Germany were paid in *lagergeld* which could not be spent outside the camps.

After a few high-profile escapes from Germany, Georges Scapini, head of all POW affairs, publicly requested that all prisoners stop escaping.[65] In eastern France, the *Petit Vésulien* had warned in October 1940 that unless the 'selfish' escapes stopped, all workgroups of French and colonial prisoners would be confined to their camps indefinitely.[66] Yet of course, this did not stop escapes from happening, and privately Vichy condoned them. There was a delicate balance between the legal concerns and the potential benefits of CPOWs escaping. Colonial officials recognized that 'our best propagandists on this subject are the escaped soldiers who all emphasize the kindness shown them by the metropolitan French, and blame [Germany] for the beatings and brutality they suffered during captivity'.[67] Much of Vichy's information about captivity came from the escaped prisoners. In the end, Vichy preferred to denounce the escapes while reaping the benefits.

Escape for CPOWs did not translate to an immediate return home, but rather to Vichy-run camps in the southern zone until they could be repatriated. Instead of experiencing an increase of imperial solidarity, which positive everyday interactions with local French people may have led them to expect, CPOWs found themselves back inside the familiar, strict and hierarchical regimes they had known before the war. This continued during and after their voyages home. French officials considered the return from captivity to be a crucial time in terms of the mental stability and loyalty of the men who would 'discover, with love, the new face of France'.[68] However, for the CPOWs, the new face of France was actually the old, conservative, colonial one. By providing shelter and guidance, a paternalist Vichy hoped to reorient the CPOWs to their proper role in French society, a role that was subservient to that of returning white prisoners. As Admiral Darlan argued in 1941: 'It is essential that these men are informed [...] of the Marshal's work, his politics, and his government's actions and that they do not feel they have arrived in a country where they will find indiscipline and slackness.'[69] Darlan wanted the CPOWs to understand that their sacrifice had been recognized but that it had already been rewarded through French efforts on their behalf while in captivity. In turn, they were expected to respond with loyalty and, more importantly, discipline.

Conclusion

By paying attention to the top-down as well as the bottom-up interactions of the CPOWs in Occupied France, many nuances about the nature of their captivity, their relations with French civilians and about gender and race are revealed. In some ways, the Occupation served to flatten many previously hierarchical relationships through interactions which would not have taken place under normal circumstances. Colonial soldiers and French women would not have normally exchanged private correspondence or met along the road to chat while walking to a doctor's appointment. While many of these relationships were certainly sincere, they did not mean racial boundaries were erased. If anything, the French authorities thought that these connections would reinforce traditional French values by tethering the CPOWs to the French and their protection while under German domination. While the paternalism never changed, the Occupation provided a context in which solidarity appeared to be more important than racial constructs. After the war, CPOWs believed that their sacrifice deserved recognition and fair compensation. However, the French felt that they had already played their part by improving their conditions during captivity. German propaganda was ultimately blamed for the CPOWs' frustration. The general feeling of unease and lack of recognition among returning POWs – both French and colonial – went unexamined. The French reaction – from the Vichy regime and later from the Provisional Government – was that reclamations must be quashed and the traditional discipline of the colonial troops reinstated. After a long and difficult captivity, CPOWs were disappointed to see the solidarity they experienced while prisoners evaporate as French priorities once again took precedence.

Notes

1 For this chapter, I use 'colonial prisoners of war' to refer to all men, both citizens and subjects, from the French territories outside of metropolitan France.

2 Over fifty camps existed on 24 September 1940 and housed both colonial and white prisoners before white prisoners were transferred to Germany (M. Thomas, 'Les Prisonniers coloniaux' in J.-L. Leleu, F. Passera and J. Quellien (eds), *La France pendant la seconde guerre mondiale, atlas historique* (Paris: Fayard and Ministère de la Défense, 2010), p. 114. By the next summer twenty main *Frontstalags* remained: Archives Nationales de France (AN), F/9 2959: *Frontstalags* in France, 1 March 1941.

3 AN, F/9 2351: Approximations concerning prisoners from Algeria, the colonies, protectorates and countries under mandate for General Andlauer, 5 May 1941; AN, 72 AJ/291: Lieutenant Jeanmot, *Les Prisonniers de guerre dans la deuxième guerre mondiale, plan d'études* (Vincennes: Service Historique de la Défense (SHD), 20 January 1956).

4 N. Lawler, *Soldiers of Misfortune: Ivorien Tirailleurs of World War II* (Ohio: Ohio University Press, 1992), p. 104.

5 See, for example, Lawler, *Soldiers of Misfortune*; M. Echenberg, *Colonial Conscripts: the Tirailleur Sénégalais in French West Africa, 1857–1960* (London: James Currey, 1991); A. Mabon, *Prisonniers de guerre 'Indigènes': visages oubliés de la France occupée* (Paris: La Découverte, 2010); M. Thomas, 'The Vichy government and French colonial POWs, 1940–1944', *French Historical Studies,* 25.4 (2002), 657–92.

6 Very few first-person narratives exist for the CPOWs' experience. However, in 1940 Vichy created the *Commission sur les replis suspects* to investigate and eventually bring to justice French officers who had retreated or surrendered against their orders. Testimonies from escaped prisoners were sent to this commission whose work was continued by the Provisional Government until after the Liberation. Vichy used this structure to question escaped CPOWs about German propaganda they might have encountered. It is important to remember that the CPOWs were reporting to French military authorities which clearly influenced what they chose to report and how. An effort has been made to cross-reference each claim with other sources and material.

7 Echenberg, *Colonial Conscripts,* p. 92.

8 SHD, 27N 70: Colonel Gauche, daily summary of military postal censorship, 7 June 1940.

9 H. Jones, *Violence Against Prisoners of War in the First World War* (Cambridge: Cambridge University Press, 2011), p. 74.

10 E. Deroo and A. Champeaux, *La Force noire: gloire et infortunes d'une légende coloniale* (Paris: Tallandier, 2006), p. 174.

11 SHD, 34N 1081: Sous-Lieutenant Gilbert, combat report for the 7th company of the 53 Régiments d'Infanterie Coloniale Mixte [RICMS], 5–7 June 1940.

12 SHD, 14P 16: Zouave Manuel Aldeguer, captivity report, 4 November 1940.

13 S. P. Mackenzie, *The Colditz Myth: British and Commonwealth Prisoners of War in Nazi Germany* (Oxford: Oxford University Press, 2004), p. 37.

14 Mackenzie, *Colditz*, p. 36; R. Scheck, *Hitler's African Victims: the German Army Massacres of Black French Soldiers in 1940* (Cambridge: Cambridge University Press, 2006), p. 24; Scheck estimates that during the battle for France, German soldiers killed approximately 3,000 black soldiers illegally (p. 58).

15 Deroo and Champeaux, *Force Noire*, p. 168.

16 C. Streit, 'Prisonniers de guerre allies aux mains des Allemands', in J.-C. Catherine (ed.), *La Captivité des prisonniers de guerre: histoire, art et mémoire 1939–1945: Pour une approche européenne* (Rennes: Presses universitaires de Rennes, 2008), pp. 31–2; R. Scheck, 'French colonial soldiers in German prisoner of war camps, 1940–1945', *French History*, 24.3 (2010), 420–46, p. 436.

17 AN, 72 AJ/1965: Jean Cavaillès, 'La Guerre', in G. Ferrières, *Jean Cavaillés, philosophe et combattant* (Paris: Presses Universitaires de France, 1950).

18 Archives Nationales du Sénégal (ANS), 2D 23/28: intelligence forwarded to the Direction des affaires politiques et administratives and Surêté générale, 22 August 1941.

19 SHD, 1P 89: Weygand to Pétain, 10 November 1940.

20 AN, AJ/ 41/ 1788: Doyen to Vogl, 22 March 1941.

21 R. Ginio, *French Colonialism Unmasked: the Vichy Years in French West Africa* (Lincoln, NE: University of Nebraska Press, 2006), p. xiv.

22 SHD, 1P 200: report, escaped prisoner from Frontstalag 184 for the Delegation for Armistice Services (*Délégation des services de l'Armistice* [DSA]), 1 July 1941.

23 J.-J. François, *La Guerre de 1939–1940 en Eure-et-Loir: le courrier des lecteurs* (Luisant: La Parcheminière), pp. 304–5.

24 R. O. Paxton, *Vichy France, Old Guard and New Order 1940–1944* (New York: Columbia University Press, 1972, 2001), p. 209.

25 Scheck, 'French colonial soldiers', p. 425.

26 Archives départementales de la Vienne (ADV), 1566W 2: use of prisoners in the following camps: Latille, Vouzailles, Vouille, Neuville, Mirebeau, Scorbe-Clairevaux, [n.d.]; see also Archives départementales de la Marne (ADM), 7W S5989: Engineer-in-chief to local engineers, 13 November 1941.

27 Archives départementales de la Mayenne (ADMay), 227W 6: Mayor of Saint-Jean-sur-Erve to Prefect of Mayenne, 26 March 1941.

28 SHD, 14P 17: Chef Haim, report, 23 October 1940.

29 SHD, 14P 46: Gnimagnon, captivity report, 7 February 1941.

30 Mabon, *'Indigènes'*, p. 87.

31 AN, F/9 2351: Mission Brault in the Eastern Region, 27 October to 9 November 1941.

32 For other examples see, SHD, 7NN 2022: Huntziger to Admiral of the Fleet (Darlan), 23 May 1941; ADMay, 227W 6: Mayor of Chatelain to Prefect of Mayenne, [n.d.]; Mabon, *'Indigènes'*, p. 87.

33 AN, AJ/ 41/ 1835: state of negotiations, sub-committee for POWs, 8 October 1940; AN, F/9 2007: Doyen to Scapini, 21 January 1941; Annexe IV questions du cadre de la Convention de Genève traitées par le SDPG, [n.d.]; Annexe V questions hors du cadre de la Convention de Genève traitées par le SDPG, [n.d.]; Archives départementales de la Yonne (ADY) 1W 655: Mathès to Prefect of the Yonne, 14 March 1941.

34 ADMay, 227W 6: Mayor of Selle-Craonnaise to Bussière, 22 March 1941.

35 AN, 72/ AJ/ 291: Roger Dabin to the Secrétaire général de la Communication d'histoire de la captivité, 14 August 1958.

36 Archives départementales du Loiret (ADL): 11R 14, Secretary of State for National Education and Youth to the prefects, rectors and academy inspectors, 2 April 1941.

37 M. Pollard, *Reign of Virtue, Mobilizing Gender in Vichy France* (Chicago and London: University of Chicago Press, 1998), p. 42.

38 AN, F/9 2351: Bonko Hambrié to Pétain, no date but response dated 11 August 1941.

39 AN, F/9 2959: CCAPG, minutes, 13 January 1942.

40 SHD, 9R 38: Honnorat, report of the enquiry into the supplying of clothing and rations to prisoners by individual package, 22 May 1942.

41 SHD, 1P 33: French Red Cross of Algiers, meeting, 28 June 1941; AN, F/9 2351: Bonnaud to Commandant Jalluzot, 15 December 1941; AN, F/9 2351: International Committee of the Red Cross (ICRC), visit to Montargis, 18 June 1941; Madame Duhau, 'Quelques suggestions au sujet des camps de prisonniers indigènes présentées', 26 May 1941.

42 SHD, 14P 46: Pierre Jean Prost, escape report [n.d.].

43 Mabon, *'Indigènes'*, pp. 94–5.

44 AN, F/9 2351: Andlauer to the sous-délégués d'outre-mer aux associations marraines, 27 April 1942.

45 SHD, 2P 70: Léopold Senghor, captivity report, 7 July 1942. This prisoner was identified as Senghor by Raffael Scheck. See R. Scheck, 'Léopold Sédar Senghor prisonnier de guerre allemand: Une nouvelle approche fondée sur un texte inédit', *French Politics, Culture & Society*, 32. 2, pp 76–98.

46 AN, F/9 2351: Letter from Besson to Scapini, 18 September 1942.

47 Archives Nationales d'Outre-Mer (ANOM), FM 1 AFFPOL/929/Bis: Service des Contrôles Techniques des Colonies, Secretary of State for Colonies, 5 November 1941.

48 Archives départementales de la Haute-Saône (ADHS), 9J 10: Journal de marche du 'Mouvement Lorraine' de la Haute-Saône, 28 September 1940.

49 SHD, 14P 46: Michel Gnimagnon, report on captivity, 7 February 1941.
50 SHD, 2P 70: Senghor, captivity report, 7 July 1942.
51 ADHS, 27W 63: Lieutenant-Colonel Laub, poster: 'Consignes pour les prisonniers aidant aux travaux des champs' [n.d.].
52 ADY, 1W 655: French forestry department inspector to Prefect of the Yonne, 24 May 1941.
53 Archives départementales de la Gironde (ADG), 45W 82: Tribunal de la Feldkommandantur 529 to Prefect of Gironde, 14 December 1940.
54 ADY, 1W 652: Procès-Verbal, 6 October 1941.
55 ADHS, 9J 10: Journal de marche du 'Mouvement Lorraine' de la Haute-Saône, 28 September 1940.
56 ADHS, 9J 10: Pierre Choffel, isolated resistance: escapes from Stalag 141, 22 June 1956.
57 SHD, 14P 46: Michel Gnimagnon, report on captivity, 7 February 1941.
58 SHD, 14P 16: Nussard, recommend Albin Bancilon for commendation, 1 August 1940.
59 SHD, 14P 17: Mohamed Ben Ali, escape report, translated by Ould Yahoui, 7 November 1940.
60 SHD, 14P 17: Sergeant Mohamed Ben Mohamed Ben El Habib, escape report, 29 August 1941.
61 SHD, 14P 46: De Peralo, captivity and escape report [n.d.].
62 SHD, 14P 16: Hassen-Ladjimi, escape report, 28 September 1940.
63 Calculations based on the ICRC 'capture cards' at the Bureau des Archives des Victimes des Conflicts Contemporains (BAVCC), Caen.
64 Y. Durand, *La Vie quotidienne des prisonniers de guerre dans les Stalags, les Oflags, et les Kommandos 1939–1945* (Paris: Hachette, 1987), p. 107.
65 H. Bories-Sawala, 'Les prisonniers dans l'industrie de guerre allemande: une composante parmi la main-d'œuvre forcée, composite et hiérarchisée', in J.-C. Catherine (ed.), *La Captivité des prisonniers de guerre. Histoire, art et mémoire 1939–1945: Pour une approche européenne* (Rennes: Presses universitaires de Rennes, 2008) pp. 95–104, p. 97.
66 *Le Petit Vésulien*, 22 October 1940.
67 SHD, 3H 159: political and economic information bulletin, 9–15 March 1941.
68 SHD, 2P 82: Barret, note, 25 July 1941.
69 SHD, 2P 82: Darlan to Secretaries of State for War and Information, Scapini, président de la commission du retour des prisonniers, 25 June 1941.

9

Wehrmacht Brothels, Prostitution and Venereal Desire

Byron Schirbock

In the spring of 1940, a German propaganda pamphlet accused France of being the nerve centre for the international trafficking in women for sexual exploitation. It was depicted as a country where sexually transmitted diseases (hereafter STDs) flourished due to unregulated prostitution, and where women were being billeted in bordellos and exploited: 'On French soil prostitution is blooming in every form. Alongside secret and public street prostitution the country is flooded with an endless number of brothels, where the unlimited craving for pleasure takes place.' The diatribe ended not with a plea against prostitution in general but one in favour of stricter state control in order to prevent human trafficking, the women's exploitation and to maintain public health.[1]

Only a few months later, France was vanquished and occupied by German forces and it did not take them long to implement what they envisioned: hand in hand with the collaborating Vichy regime, with its distinctly conservative morality, prostitution was regulated under German supervision. Soon, and despite their own pretention to be setting things in order, the Germans themselves became part of what they had scourged – the systematic exploitation of female bodies, and of course the women they belonged to – which was itself a manifestation of foreign rule imposed on Occupied France.

This chapter seeks to highlight the system of the Wehrmacht brothels as part of the quotidian life of the occupiers in wartime France. In contrast to the everyday struggle of the French population, German soldiers in the occupied territory underwent a substantially different and in many cases rather positive experience. Across the chapter, I consider the social reality of the confrontation of a civil population with a higher percentage of women and the male occupiers and offer a different perspective on daily face-to-face interactions between

French women and German men, but also between Vichy and Wehrmacht authorities on an administrative level.

Nicholas Stargardt has recently claimed that sexual encounters in Western Europe remained unregulated by the occupation authorities.[2] At first sight this might be true, although the reality was more complex. Social contact and even intercourse with French women were not actually forbidden, but were not encouraged either. While individual encounters on a private level remained untouched as long as the participants kept them out of sight, prostitution was indeed on the authorities' minds as a potential spreader of STDs. Whereas sexuality in the Third Reich in general and prostitution in Nazi Germany in particular have caught scholarly interest, brothels for Wehrmacht troops in occupied territories have been less well explored to date. The first work on the subject was published by Franz Seidler in 1977, and provided a basis for understanding the topic of STDs and prostitution as a problem for the German Army.[3] His approach being rather descriptive, at times uncritical with the material and neglecting gender issues, Seidler did, however, depict bordellos for German troops as an effective means against the threat of venereal diseases. A ground-breaking case study by Insa Meinen appeared in 2002, which revealed the complexity of the Wehrmacht's politics of controlling prostitution in Occupied France alongside its cooperation with the French authorities.[4] By criticizing Seidler's perspective, Meinen emphasized the power over women and their bodies and read the politics of prostitution in Occupied France less as an answer to the threat of STDs but instead as an attempt to gain control over gender relations in Occupied France as well as control over the female French population. Although her interpretations did not go undisputed,[5] Meinen set the frame for the future research. Scholarship on Vichy's policies towards prostitution issues revealed that the agenda of the *Révolution nationale* was mostly driven by concerns over moral hygiene rather than public health.[6] However, although the Germans' and Vichy's aims were different, they nevertheless agreed on the means of reaching the latter, resulting in a system scholars have called 'proxénétisme d'état' ('state pimping').[7]

In this chapter, I focus attention on the southwest military district of France, although my conclusions are not confined to that region. The German administration divided France into four districts (Paris and its suburbs, northwest France, northeast district, southwest district). Between 10 September 1940 and 15 January 1942 a fifth district existed, which included the coastal departments from the Spanish border up to the Charente region. It was incorporated into the southwest district in spring 1942, which by then included

Brittany, the Loire Valley, the Charente and Aquitaine – seventeen departments in total. After the occupation of the former 'Free' Zone in November 1942, a distinct district of the commander in chief in southern France was created. This regional focus comes in part from the fact that a small corpus of personal records of the high ranking German medical officer responsible for the military district southwest France is available.[8] This corpus is complemented by sources from various archives across France which provide insight into the everyday functioning of the Wehrmacht brothels.

By analysing the mechanisms for regulating sexual activity between the male occupier and the female occupied, I will demonstrate the ways in which control was exercised in soldiers' and prostitutes' everyday lives. This control manifested unequal power relations between Germans and French, as well as between men and women; it acted upon the spaces of leisure and work; and it shaped the ways in which both German military personnel and French sex workers related to people other than each other. Controlling both the supply and demand ends of the chain in this transaction, which should be seen as more than a simple business exchange, was a task shared – again unequally – by the French and German authorities. It is clear that the exercise of the occupier's control in respect to prostitution was not only due to anxieties over the spread of STDs, but also a result of fears of the moral corruption of German men by French women, often stereotyped by Germans as vain and loose-moralled – but desirable nonetheless, as the evidence shows. I will show that control was not only exercised through regulation, sanitary obligation and moral pressure, but also through the regulation of space and mobility. This chapter will conclude that brothels functioned as manifestations of German foreign rule as social practice; it is by considering these everyday interactions between German men and French women that this becomes clear.

Balancing the 'urges' of venereal desire and the threat of venereal disease

In the course of the Second World War, the German Army tried to manage sexual encounters between its soldiers and foreign civilians in occupied territories as STDs, especially syphilis and gonorrhoea, were seen as a major potential threat to the troops' health.[9] As a lesson from the control practised in occupied Belgium and Northern France during the Great War,[10] where, despite supervision and cooperation with local authorities, large numbers of sexually-transmitted infections still occurred, the Wehrmacht High Command sought to intensify its mechanisms and practices of surveillance.[11] One basic means to influence social encounters was to appeal to the soldiers' sense of honour. In various pamphlets and leaflets they were instructed 'to pull themselves together' in foreign occupied countries.[12] Unrestrained behaviour was regarded as a danger to family life and to the honour of being German (*Deutsch sein heißt treu sein!*).[13] Superiors should serve as role models: 'Sexual energy is the engine of joy and vigour', stated an article encouraging commanding officers to make sexual intercourse a discussion topic among their men.[14] Saving up for family life at home was articulated as the ideal to follow,[15] as well as the maintenance of 'moral reliability' (*sittliche Zuverlässigkeit*) in their behaviour towards foreign women.[16]

Although sexual encounters in the East were more consistently categorized as racial ones,[17] this did not mean that the German authorities were not similarly concerned about sexual encounters in the West. In France, soldiers were told to keep their distance from the local population by depicting especially French women through a lens of stereotypes.[18] Although such appeals may have had some effect here and there, their impact remained limited. For example, when asked by his wife in a letter about the French women in Paris, a German soldier awkwardly responded: 'mainly, because they are French women, they should have lost every attraction in the eyes of a German soldier.' He continued: 'emphasis is placed on should . . . .' The author had previously claimed to dislike the style of Parisian women, whom he found too 'swanky'.[19] Since prostitution was the main location of soldiers' sexual encounters with French women, the German authorities sought to control this sector by forcing local administrations to cooperate. According to Luc Capdevila and others, Vichy's main concern was public morality; thus it aimed at reducing the visibility of prostitution rather than eradicating it.[20] The occupiers, on the other hand, had no interest in establishing a moral order in France; instead their interest was the eradication of STDs.[21] Thus restrictions and surveillance provided the common ground for the monitoring of bordellos which suited the two authorities.

German supervision was regarded as the most effective means of both controlling the spread of STDs and reducing sexual violence. Although the system of coerced registration of sex workers was not totally new, the German authorities acted with cruel efficiency and under Vichy's endorsement.[22] Usually, existing brothels (*maisons de tolérance*) were put under control and opened exclusively for a German clientele, who were forbidden from entering French brothels. Where new facilities were required, buildings, often hotels, were turned into brothels. For officers and higher ranks, existing luxury bordellos – preferably in less visible sites, distant from the troop brothels – were seized.[23] The request to open a new brothel had to be made by the local Wehrmacht commander, who submitted it to the district chief for his final say.[24] When in 1943 a Waffen-SS unit illicitly opened a bordello it was closed down by local German authorities right away.[25] To ensure every soldier with 'urgent needs'[26] found his way to the houses, leaflets with maps and the houses' opening hours were circulated, thus normalizing the use of brothels as part of soldiers' daily lives in France.[27] The entrance fee was set at 3 Reichsmarks, a rather low price compared to rates on the street.

Although such establishments were referred to internally as Wehrmacht brothels (*Wehrmachtbordell*), the German authorities depicted them as French brothels under German surveillance, and in consequence bound by French law.[28] Medical check-ups at least twice a week were mandatory for the women working in the bordellos. The German authorities co-opted French public health officers or registered doctors to conduct these examinations.[29] Those sex workers who were not registered by the authorities were labelled 'illegal prostitutes'. The French police were put in charge of the surveillance of these non-registered women[30], and to support their task, 'experienced' policemen from Germany were transferred to France.[31]

Compared to methods of regulation during the Great War, the German Army in the Second World War exercised coercion vigorously as a means of control by targeting not its soldiers but French prostitutes. They had to follow a set of rules that significantly changed the way they practised their work. The French authorities, the police and public health officers, endorsing this shift of policy, worked hand in hand with the occupier who managed to install a system reaching far into the lives of German soldiers and French women, and at the same time keeping both groups under surveillance as well as controlling their relations towards each other.

Managing Wehrmacht brothels in the French southwest

From the Spanish border up to the northeast of Brittany, the density of German troops was high. In particular, at the submarine bases in Bordeaux, La Pallice (the deep-sea port of La Rochelle), Saint-Nazaire (including La Baule), Lorient and Brest around 10,000 Germans were garrisoned.[32] During the Occupation the Wehrmacht maintained 156 brothels in the region, most of them in city areas along the coast.[33] The majority were existing bordellos taken over right after the invasion in June 1940. Their number grew over time, and many existed up until the Liberation; yet due to variations in the number of troops stationed in France, some were closed down as they were under-used. In October 1941 78 brothels for troops and 7 for higher ranks were open;[34] one year later they numbered 132 for troops and 11 for officers.[35] Between 1942 and 1943 about 120 brothels were constantly open in the district. The average number of women working in each house was eight, but some bigger brothels such as those in Nantes had some twenty prostitutes, while those in the more rural hinterlands might only have had two. After Paris and Lille, Bordeaux was a hot spot for German troops due to its geographical position. Eleven brothels were open in the city centre, employing 115 women, for use by German soldiers, German civilian personnel and construction workers of the *Organisation Todt*. A brothel reserved for officers also existed. In contrast to the more lowly ranks, officers did not have to undergo the medical sanitation process, but were expected to take care of such a procedure themselves.[36]

The Wehrmacht district medical officers kept meticulous statistical records. During the last quarter of 1941, Wehrmacht brothels in France counted 382,167 visitors of whom 264,171 had intercourse (about 70 per cent). Every day in southwest France 3,133 German soldiers went to have sex in the establishments provided for them.[37] Interestingly, these statistics also show about 30 per cent of the visitors were onlookers who came to have fun drinking and dancing, but did not buy sex. This goes against the idea that these *maisons de tolérance* served the sole purpose of catering to soldiers' 'urgent needs', and reveals them as spaces where other forms of leisure and relaxation also took place.[38] As figures show after just six months of occupation in France, going to a brothel had become a normalized form of escaping 'the everyday duty', like going to a bookshop or spending time at the Soldiers' Home.[39] Even if the authorities understood sex between registered prostitutes and German soldiers in controlled areas as a 'business-like-economic transaction' (*sachlich-wirtschaftlicher Akt*),[40] soldiers might have seen it as 'recompense for their war efforts'.[41] Especially in Bordeaux, the number of visitors during 1942 who did not have sex is surprising: 38 per cent.[42] They left the house with their card – on which they were obliged to record the name of the prostitute with whom they had had intercourse – empty. Yet these men still went to get sanitized afterwards, in order to retrieve their pay book. This phenomenon was not restricted to ordinary soldiers; young officers also went in groups to drink and dance in brothels without having intercourse.[43] By undermining the idea of handling their sexual urges these onlookers still profited from the exploitation of women by enjoying their company on a business-like basis.

It is difficult to know whether systematic and continuous recruitment of women for the *maisons de tolérance* outside towns and cities took place, but there is evidence of a recruitment office in Paris,[44] and a system whereby prostitutes were rotated around the bordellos in the capital.[45] To ensure that German rules were enforced, the Madams ran their businesses under the constant threat of sanctions in case of infraction.[46] Yet the ambition of achieving total control over sexual encounters was limited by ongoing challenges. The only effective means to fight 'illegal prostitution' which was developed during the occupation was to use round-ups of prostitutes and raids on brothels.[47] Since these were personnel-intense, the German field gendarmerie required assistance from French police forces. Outside towns and cities, cars and fuel were short due to rationing. In fact, as with so many administrative requirements on both German and French sides, the efforts to ensure medical controls and effect raids in certain areas had to be dropped because of scarce resources, such as suitable transportation and fuel. Thus, the hindrances caused by everyday privations made their mark in the policing and control of desire and sexual interaction, as elsewhere.[48]

The Germans were also kept busy with other problems. First, an argument about sanitary control developed between medical officers of the occupation administration and combat troops. Having introduced obligatory sanitary control procedures, medical officers faced an onslaught of demand, with soldiers queuing very visibly outside their offices. Furthermore, in order to speed through the large numbers who required the procedure, it became lax and unprofessional. Inspections uncovered hygienic defects and a lack of basic sanitary material like towels or condoms. Since the efficiency of these sanitary controls could not be guaranteed, the chief medical officer of First Army Corps voiced concerns about the whole routine, arguing that soldiers were frightened of the imposition of queuing out the front, fearing the sanitation procedure and were thus more likely to visit illegal prostitutes instead.[49] As a consequence he demanded to shut down the obligatory but rather pointless sanitation, but his efforts did not meet with success.[50]

Second, there was a growing number of foreign auxiliary forces from Eastern Europe stationed in France. As more German soldiers were drafted to the Eastern front, security tasks in occupied territories were carried out by volunteers of various nations such as Russians, Ukrainians, Georgians, Cossacks and even Indians. Whereas in Bordeaux, Italian sailors were also granted access to Wehrmacht bordellos, other foreign volunteers were not. Their demands for access caused doubts among regular German troops. Racial as well as logistic arguments were raised both by German soldiers and by the prostitutes themselves, and since no general answer was found, individual solutions were applied.[51] Some brothels established separate opening hours for Eastern troops. In regions where those soldiers were more numerous, separate houses were opened. Sometimes it was difficult to find enough women willing to work in a brothel for men of Eastern descent. Especially Russians and Indians were at times rejected as clients by the women themselves.[52] However, in any case a separation of German and other foreign clients took place.

Despite the claims made by soldiers to their wives back home that they found French women showy and unattractive,[53] many engaged in sexual encounters while stationed there.[54] The experiences they had there reinforced their commonly-held stereotypes about French women and shaped individual memories. It appeared that the prophecy had fulfilled itself: here were the supposedly 'debauched' French women that they had heard about, served up in brothels for their pleasure and use.[55]

To satisfy the enormous demand, an immense number of brothels were rapidly set up including an elaborate system of circulation not only to allow hundreds of thousands of soldiers to have sex but to even give them the benefit of an alternating choice of women. Discussions among German authorities circled around how far paternalism could go and what to demand from the soldiers. The women's interest never played a substantial role in these discussions. Once they had opted to work according to the rules, they had to obey them. For the soldiers this system granted easier access to women. The German authorities tried at least twice by monitoring a market they feared and by keeping their soldiers away from STDs and satisfied at the same time. Manifesting German rule in France by administrating the modes of sexual encounters, the bordellos also became – unintentionally – spaces of relaxation and leisure for soldiers, which nonetheless still demonstrated German male dominance.

Sex work: control, danger and retaliation

Private accounts of sex workers during the occupation are rare.[56] Reasons for engaging in prostitution were manifold, but between 1940 and 1944 two main causes played a role: first, an increase in demand for paid-for sex. Many prostitutes continued working as such after the defeat, and, registered or not, women kept serving a demand that grew with the presence of hundreds of thousands of

German soldiers in France. And second, there was a shift in the job market created by the absence of men as breadwinners or as workers.[57] Forced by circumstance, some women stepped into the shoes of absent men. Others took on new jobs provided by the occupier, becoming cleaners, cooks or kitchen hands. Others still were drafted to work in Germany.[58] Some decided to sell sex to soldiers for various reasons. In contrast to the situation in German-occupied Eastern Europe, women were not directly forced to prostitute themselves in Wehrmacht bordellos; yet the line between forced and voluntary work was sometimes thin and often blurred.[59] Only registered sex workers were tolerated either as 'free' prostitutes (those working independently) or in bordellos under surveillance. Once women decided to work in a brothel, their mobility was strictly limited to lower the visibility of prostitution in general. A complete transformation of the spaces of daily life, their place of work now became a 'home' of sorts, and leaving it was only permitted under supervision. Public spaces such as cinemas were forbidden to them.[60] Still, working in a Wehrmacht brothel was perhaps safer than working on the streets, as the bordellos at least provided a roof and ensured a regular income.

While mobility and transportation were very restricted during the years of the Occupation, independent 'free' prostitutes and prostitutes who were unregistered were able to move to respond to increased demand for sex as the density of troops fluctuated. This also increased the risk of infection from STDs, particularly when unregistered sex workers were present in large numbers and the sanitary controls could not be applied. At all times, though, the women were at the Germans' mercy. Regarded as vain, lazy and 'easy', French women and prostitutes in particular were created as a social other.[61] Medical officer Schmidt referred to the sex workers mostly as 'girls' instead of women, even though French law forbade the procurement of women under twenty years old. He essentialized them as being naturally promiscuous and sexually dominant.[62] By generally accusing them of spreading STDs, German medical personnel created a threat scenario which legitimized the placement of sex workers under constant surveillance, and thus 'rendering [them] harmless'.[63] This led to a simple dichotomy: French prostitutes needed to be monitored and German soldiers – as potential victims – safeguarded and forewarned. And yet the evidence demonstrates that the soldiers themselves acted promiscuously not only by frequenting brothels but also using unregistered prostitutes and refusing to use condoms. Thus they evidently played a role in spreading STDs, but were only ever considered as deserving of protection.[64] Whereas the only obligation for soldiers was to get sanitized after intercourse, it was the sex workers who were obliged to use condoms. Twice weekly medical examinations took place. In case of infection with STDs, hospitalization of up to two-and-a-half months was ordered; this evidently posed a problem to women earning their livelihood through prostitution, but also those with family responsibilities.[65] Any infringement was punished, and could lead to arrest and placement in a detention camp.[66]

Aside from that, the women had to face their clients. Only light alcohol was served within the brothels, and the sanitation offices' staff were required to deny drunken soldiers access to the bordello.[67] Yet bribery was not uncommon, and some men turned up at brothels already drunk;[68] indeed in one case in Saint-Malo, drunken soldiers threatened the prostitutes and then resisted arrest, pulling a gun on the military police.[69] Women outside the bordellos were in even greater danger. They feared police raids and imprisonment as well as sexual and other forms of physical violence. On 15 July 1943 in Bordeaux, for example, a German sailor so seriously injured a registered prostitute in the street that she died the next day. While this was but one attack among many during the Occupation, sexual violence did not reach the same level in France as in the Eastern occupied territories; it nonetheless increased significantly as battle troops were relocated from the Eastern front during the period from 1943 to 1944.[70]

Furthermore women who engaged in sexual encounters with Germans or who were accused of having done so, were stigmatized in many ways. It was not only after the Liberation that they were seen as traitors who sold both just their bodies but also their nation to the enemy. The women were subjected to public humiliation.[71] As is well known, as the liberation of French territory progressed across the summer of 1944, women were denounced and rounded up, their heads shaved in public spectacles; some were branded and tattooed, and then paraded through the streets, harangued by the mobs of onlookers. While it has been said that, in particular, *résistants de la dernière heure* (i.e. those who joined the resistance very late in the day) used this practice to restore their male domination over female bodies, it is clear that women remained objectified by these acts.[72] Such punishments seemed to fulfil a double goal, condemning both their 'treason' and their deviation from acceptable female social roles.[73] Although some have considered the Occupation and its sexual encounters to have had a rather positive impact by reshuffling gender hierarchies,[74] the legacies for French women were as asymmetric as the Occupation itself. Although not every woman experienced this kind of public humiliation, some had to face pregnancy and the lasting stigma of a child born to a German father.[75] Some women were shot for their past sexual activity during the period of the *épuration*.[76]

French sex workers under the Occupation, no matter if registered and in a brothel or unregistered and working on the streets, experienced everyday life as a quotidian threat. Not only in the eyes of the authorities, but also of German medical personal, they were firstly considered as immoral, and secondly as a threat. In consequence they were totally exposed to the coercive manipulation of the public authorities, the German administration, of French and German doctors and, most notably, of the German soldiers. Furthermore, their social status as prostitutes led to further stigmatization among their compatriots, and thus working in a brothel could lead to total social isolation.

Conclusion

The Wehrmacht brothel system and the regulation of prostitution in general was an essential part of German foreign rule and of soldiers' everyday life in Occupied France during the Second World War. Established as a result of health and security concerns, the Wehrmacht bordello system may have achieved the aim of lowering the number of infections of STDs among soldiers. Although unregistered prostitutes remained present in numbers, and infections persisted, the German Army succeeded in channelling a large number of sexual contacts into monitored brothels, and exercised a scripted procedure of intercourse and sanitization. However full control over sexual encounters between German soldiers and French women was an aspiration rather than a goal which was actually reached. In addition to private affairs, which remain uncounted and uncountable, many soldiers preferred to go to unregistered prostitutes to avoid this clinical system. On the other hand, the normalization of buying sex which this official system provided may well have lowered the threshold of inhibition, leading sexual newcomers to have their first experiences. Despite the claim that this was simply an exchange of a service for money between soldiers and sex workers, the bordellos also became places of leisure alongside the *Soldatenheime*, cinemas, theatres and bookshops.[77] Since 20 to 30 per cent of visitors – and sometimes more – claimed not to have had intercourse while at a brothel, it seems that the Wehrmacht unwittingly created a distinct 'contact zone' for social interaction, between soldiers and French women as well as among soldiers.[78] Yet that social interaction between men and women was profoundly unequal.

The presence of German troops in France was linked to the presence of a controlled system of sex work. In nearly every bigger town of a *département* (or at least its *chef-lieu*) a Wehrmacht brothel was set up. While the German and the

French authorities sought to reduce their visibility, these *maisons de tolérance* were both present and acknowledged in towns (even disguised as bars or hotels), as were the soldiers frequenting them. Furthermore, brawls between drunken soldiers on the streets in front of the sanitary offices and brothels, and police round-ups of prostitutes took place day and night: these sexual encounters were hardly a secret. Such restricted areas or red-light districts were themselves expressions of the Occupation: the appropriation and transformation of space with a newly defined geography, and distinct rules of mobility and access, underlining still further the Occupiers' claim to power.[79]

Wehrmacht medicals, German military police and French vice squads eagerly cooperated by monitoring sexual interaction, exerting control over thousands of women, threatening them with sanctions, limiting their mobility, at times diminishing their income, and affecting their options, choices and decision-making. Inequality was thus twice stipulated: first, between the occupier and the occupied and second, between men and women. For German soldiers, such sexual experiences in France became part of a rather positive memory of their wartime French lives, which many, at least partially, experienced as a light-hearted period in otherwise complicated times. The women and their bodies on the contrary had been transformed into a yet another French resource placed at the Germans' disposal.[80] So for women, the memory must remain at – the very least – more ambivalent. Soldiers and officers made French women into objects of their venereal desire. Sexual encounters with Germans were an everyday occurrence for a large number of French women and on the 'horizon of possibility' for many more whose resources were limited by the conditions war and occupation imposed on France. For German soldiers, sex with prostitutes was an integral and normalized part of their daily lives in Occupied France. Thus the Wehrmacht brothels suggest some of the multiple levels at which Occupation – and its acts of dominance and subjugation – was carried out in everyday life, whether through the rules and regulations imposed upon sex work, or through the control exerted over the bodies of a vanquished population.

Notes

1 F. Seekel, *Frankreich. Zentrale des internationalen Mädchenhandels* (Berlin: Junker und Dünnhaupt Verlag, 1940).

2 N. Stargardt, *The German War: A Nation under Arms 1939–1945* (London: The Bodley Head, 2015), 129.

3 F. W. Seidler, *Prostitution, Homosexualität, Selbstverstümmelung. Probleme der deutschen Sanitätsführung 1939–1945* (Neckargemünd: Vowinckel, 1977).

4 I. Meinen, *Wehrmacht und Prostitution während des Zweiten Weltkriegs im besetzten Frankreich* (Bremen: Edition Temmen, 2002); French version, *Wehrmacht et prostitution sous l'Occupation (1940–1945)* (Paris: Payot, 2006). For a condensed summary see also Meinen, 'La réglementation de la prostitution et des relations sexuelles par les occupants', *Travail, Genre et Sociétés*, 10.2 (2003), 69–82.

5 M. Plassmann, 'Wehrmachtsbordelle. Anmerkungen zu einem Quellenfund im Universitätsarchiv Düsseldorf', *Militärgeschichtliche Zeitschrift* 62.1 (2003), 157–73.

6 M. Boninchi, *Vichy et l'ordre moral* (Paris: Presses universitaires de France, 2005); C. Olivier, 'Bucoliques et emmurées. Les prostituées et le régime de Vichy', *Travail, Genre et Sociétés*, 2003, 55–68.

7 L. Capdevila, F. Rouquet, F. Virgili, D. Voldman, *Hommes et femmes dans la France en guerre, 1914–1945* (Paris: Payot, 2003), p. 147; Meinen, 'La réglementation', p. 74.

8 Held at the University Archives of the Heinrich-Heine-University in Düsseldorf (UAD) in Germany. I am grateful to Dr Julius Leonhard for granting me access. See H. Umbreit, *Der Militärbefehlshaber in Frankreich 1940–1944* (Boppard am Rhein: Boldt, 1968), p. 40.

9 For anxieties prior to 1914, see S. Kuss, *Deutsches Militär auf kolonialen Kriegsschauplätzen. Eskalation von Gewalt zu Beginn des 20. Jahrhunderts* (Berlin: Christoph Links Verlag, 2010); D. J. Walther, *Sex and Control. Venereal Disease, Colonial Physicians, and Indigenous Agency in German Colonialism, 1884–1914* (New York: Berghahn, 2015). On the fear of STDs resulting from the First World War see M. König, 'Syphilisangst in Frankreich und Deutschland. Hintergrund, Beschwörung und Nutzung einer Gefahr 1880–1940', in M. König (ed.), *Infiziertes Europa. Seuchen im langen 20. Jahrhundert* (Munich: De Gruyter, 2014), 50–75.

10 For sexual encounters during the First World War see J. Connolly, 'Encountering Germans: the experience of Occupation in the Nord, 1914–1918' (unpublished PhD dissertation, King's College London, 2012); E. Debruyne, 'Les "femmes à Boches" en Belgique et en France occupée, 1914–1918', *Revue du Nord*, 96.404–5 (2014), 157–85; M. Röger and E. Debruyne, 'From control to terror: German prostitution policies in eastern and western European territories during both World Wars', *Gender & History* 28.3 (2016), 687–708.

11 On the mechanisms of prevention during the First World War see L.Sauerteig, *Krankheit, Sexualität, Gesellschaft. Geschlechtskrankheiten und Gesundheitspolitik in Deutschland im 19. und frühen 20. Jahrhundert* (Stuttgart: Steiner, 1999), p. 441.

12 Hauptstaatsarchiv Stuttgart (HS), J 150/412–8 leaflet collection: Bruno Brehm, *Deutsche Haltung vor Fremden. Ein Kameradenwort an unsere Soldaten* (Berlin: 1940–41), p. 1.

13 HS, J 150/320–4: leaflet collection: M. Staemmler, *Deutsche Rassenpflege* (Berlin: 1941), p. 49.

14 UAD, 8/4, no. 19: 'Wie spricht man mit einen Unteroffizieren und Mannschaften über das Thema Mann und Frau', *Mitteilungen für das Offizierskorps*, February 1944.

15 Major Ellerbeck, 'Der deutsche Unteroffizier und das Thema "Frauen und Mädchen"', *Die Zivilversorgung*, 15 October 1942, p. 281.

16 UAD, 8/4, no. 19: *Mitteilungen für die Truppe*, no. 244, January 1943.

17 R. Mühlhäuser, 'Between "racial awareness" and fantasies of potency. Nazi sexual politics in the occupied territories of the Soviet Union, 1942–1945', in D. Herzog (ed.), *Brutality and Desire. War and Sexuality in Europe's Twentieth Century* (Basingstoke, New York: Palgrave Macmillan, 2009), 197–220; R. Mühlhäuser, *Eroberungen. Sexuelle Gewalttaten und intime Beziehungen deutscher Soldaten in der Sowjetunion 1941–1945* (Hamburg: Hamburger Edition, 2010).

18 Archives Nationales (AN), AJ 40 45: *Merkblatt für den Aufenthalt in Paris.*

19 Württembergische Landesbibliothek Stuttgart (WLB), Sterz collection, letter from Siegfried B. to his wife, 12 September 1943.

20 Capdevila et al. *Hommes et femmes*, p. 147.

21 E. M. Place, 'Wehrmacht soldiers in Paris 1940–1944' (unpublished PhD dissertation, University of Birmingham, 2007), p. 52.

22 On the regulation of prostitution in France and Germany, see M. König, *Der Staat als Zuhälter. Die Abschaffung der reglementierten Prostitution in Deutschland, Frankreich und Italien im 20. Jahrhundert* (Berlin: De Gruyter, 2016).

23 Place, 'Wehrmacht soldiers in Paris', p. 56.

24 UAD, 8/4, no. 12: *Wehrmacht-Bordelle*, undated, pp. 1–2.

25 UAD, 8/4, no. 49: report 29 April 1943.

26 UAD 8/4, no. 12: *Wehrmacht-Bordelle*, undated, p. 4.

27 UAD, 8/4, no. 18: leaflet with map indicating the German bordello quarter; Archives départementales Loire-Atlantique (ADLA), 52J 10: *Standortbefehl* no. 143/43.

28 AN, AJ 40 923: letter from chief medical officer of the Bordeaux district, October 1941.

29 E.g. Archives départementales de la Somme (ADS), 26W 575: attestation of the German *Kommandantur* in Amiens, stating that a Doctor Ponthieu conducted examinations, 15 June 1942. French women working in German garrisons, such as cooks and cleaners, were also mistrusted and subject to examinations. See, for example, Archives départementales Indre-et-Loire (ADIL), 4ZA: report on female kitchen staff in the *Soldatenheim II* in Tours, 9 November 1943.

30 See, e.g. police reports in Archives départementales Seine-et-Marne (ADSM), SC 26444 to 446.

31 Archives de la Préfecture de Police, DA 851: Internal documents of the *police de mœurs* of 1941–42 in Paris stated that a Captain Hauke form Berlin vice police was now active in Paris.

32 P. Lieb and R. O. Paxton, 'Maintenir l'ordre en France occupée. Combien de divisions?', *Vingtième Siècle. Revue d'histoire*, 112 (2011), 115–26.

33 Author's estimation based on figures and reports in UAD, 8/4, no. 14.

34 At the same time (November 1941) the German military district northwest France numbered 143 bordellos with 1,166 women working there, see Meinen, 'La réglementation', p. 75

35 UAD, 8/4, no. 13: report on 1941–42, 6/43, p. 6. In April 1942 Bordeaux was reincorporated into the district which explains the enormous growth in numbers.

36 UAD, 8/4, no. 12: *Hinweise zur Errichtung und zum Betrieb von Absteigehotels für Offiziere.*

37 UAD, 8/4, no. 19: report on the period from 1 September to 31 December 1941, undated.

38 UAD, 8/4, no. 13: report on 1941–42, 6/43, p. 6.

39 Place, 'Wehrmacht soldiers in Paris', p. 61; Meinen, 'La réglementation', p. 69.

40 Seidler, *Prostitution, Homosexualität, Selbstverstümmelung*, p. 180.

41 Meinen depicts brothels in France as the functionalization of space for the détente of troops battling in the East, Meinen, 'La réglementation', p. 70.

42 UAD, 8/4, no. 13: report on 1941–42, 6/43, p. 9.

43 UAD, 8/4, no. 13: report on 1943, undated, p. 11.

44 UAD, 8/4, no. 13: report on 1943, undated, p. 7.

45 UAD, 8/4, no. 13: report on 1941–42, 6/43, p. 5.

46 UAD, 8/4, no. 19: statistical results from September to December 1941; see also UAD, 8/4, no. 13: report on 1941–42, p. 2.

47 UAD, 8/4, no. 13: report on 1943, p. 13.

48 UAD, 8/4, no. 11: medical officer of Bordeaux's reports to district medical officer, 5 June 1942 and 5 February 1943.

49 Museum Foundation Post and Telecommunication, Berlin site, no. 3.2009.1998: letter from Erich D. to his wife and daughters, 6 October 1940. Aavailable online at http://www.museumsstiftung.de/briefsammlung/feldpost-zweiter-weltkrieg/brief.html?action=detail&what=letter&id=1438 (last checked 23 May 2017).

50 UAD, 8/4, no. 13: Correspondence between medical officer Schmidt and his counterparts, *Betrieb von Sanierstuben.*

51 UAD, 8/4, no. 13: *Bordellwesen bei den fremdländischen Truppenteilen*, 4 December 1943 and *Zur Bordellfrage der Osttruppen*, 15 March 1944.

52 UAD, 8/4, no. 13: *Bordellwesen bei den fremdländischen Truppenteilen*, p. 3 and *Zur Bordellfrage der Osttruppen*, p 1.

53 A. Luneau, J. Guérot, S. Martens, *Comme un allemand en France. Lettres inédites sous l'occupation 1940–1944* (Paris: Vendémaire 2016), p. 65.

54 The wives at home however did learn about the sexual exploits of their husbands, see S. Steinbacher, *Wie der Sex nach Deutschland kam. Der Kampf um Sittlichkeit und Anstand in der frühen Bundesrepublik* (München: Siedler, 2011), pp. 98–100.

55 S. Neitzel and H. Welzer, *Soldaten. Protokolle vom Kämpfen, Töten und Sterben* (Frankfurt/Main: Fischer 2011), pp. 225–6.

56 Marie Thérèse, *Histoire d'une prostituée* (Geneva, 1968); F. Jamet, *One Two Two* (Paris: Olivier Orban, 1975); Beate Schaefer, *Weiße Nelken für Elise. Die Liebe meiner Großeltern zwischen Wehrmachtsbordell und KZ* (Freiburg: Herder, 2013); C. Olivier, 'Un proxénète écrit à Suzy en 1941', *Clio. Femmes, Genre, Histoire* 17 (2003), 115–36.

57 Richard Vinen states that while war and ocupation destroyed many jobs, it also created new opportunities, see R. Vinen, *The Unfree French. Life under the Occupation* (London: Penguin, 2007), p. 116.

58 Vinen, *The Unfree French*, p. 116.

59 C. Paul, *Zwangsprostitution. Staatlich errichtete Bordelle im Nationalsozialismus*, (Berlin: Edition Hentrich 1994), 103–5. Meinen states, that women arrested and accused of spreading diseases were offered to work in brothel after convalescence instead of imprisonment in a camp (Meinen,'La réglementation', p. 74); H. Diamond, *Women and the Second World War in France, 1939–48. Choices and Constraints* (London: Longman, 1999), p. 36; K. H. Adler,'Reading national identity. gender and "prostitution" during the Occupation', *Modern & Contemporary France*, 7.1 (1999), 47–57, p. 55. Adler states that French women who volunteered to work in Germany were sometimes coerced to work in camp brothels for forced labourers.

60 UAD, 8/4, no. 12: guidelines for women working in Wehrmacht bordellos; UAD, 8/4, no. 12: remarks on instructions for prostitutes working in German Wehrmacht bordellos UAD, 8/4, no. 19, Betriebsanweisungen, 20 September 1942, p. 5.

61 See, for example, WLB, Sterz Collection: Letter of Willy B., 30 June 1940. On this kind of 'othering', see H. Footitt, 'The underside of "Occupation"', in H. Footitt and A. Knapp (eds), *Liberal Democracies at War. Conflict and Representation* (London: Bloomsbury, 2013), 157–78, p. 165.

62 Schmidt depicted them as 'sexually very demanding' in UAD, 8/4, no. 15: statistical journal on Wehrmacht bordellos 1943 (undated). UAD, 8/4, no. 13: report on Wehrmacht bordellos in southwest France from 1 September 1941 to 31 December 1942, p. 8.

63 A. Neumann, *'Arzttum ist immer Kämpfertum'. Die Heeressanitätsinspektion und das Amt 'Chef des Wehrmachtsanitätswesens' im Zweiten Weltkrieg (1939–1945)* (Düsseldorf: Droste, 2005), p. 250.

64 See UAD, 8/4, no. 13: report on Wehrmacht bordellos in southwest France from 1 September 1941 to 31 December 1942, p. 14.

65 In December 1940, 20 women in Berck (Pas-de-Calais) were hospitalised. They wrote collectively to the local German commander requesting their release over the Christmas period. Some had four children to feed (Archives départementales du Pas-de-Calais (ADPC), 27W 77).

66 UAD, 8/4, no. 11: letter of the local German commander in the city of Bordeaux to the regional prefect, dated 4 July 1942.

67 UAD, 8/4, no. 19: Betriebsanweisungen 20 September 1942, p. 4. Reports for the years 1941 to 1943 stated that this policy was quite successful, see UAD, 8/4, no. 13: reports 1941–42, p. 6 and 1943 p. 7; Neumann, '*Arzttum ist immer Kämpfertum*', p. 243.

68 Medical officers suspected the soldiers of bribing both prostitutes not to use condoms and corpsmen to facilitate the process of sanitation. However, tips were quite common as reports state. Some sailors left tips three times higher than the actual price for entering the brothel (UAD, inventory 8/4: no. 13, report of medical officer Schmidt, June 1943); Place mentions a case in Fougères (Ille-et-Vilaine) where the local German commander reprimanded a local Madam, compelling her to ensure that tips were not used as a bribe to avoid condoms ('Wehrmacht soldiers in Paris', pp. 47–8).

69 UAD, 8/4, no. 19: two reports of the local German commander's office of St Malo, 26 April 1944.

70 UAD, 8/4, no. 11: report local medical officer of Bordeaux, 5 July 1943. See also Mühlhäuser, *Nazi sexual politics* and Mühlhäuser, *Eroberungen*; and M.Röger, 'Le (non)quotidien pendant l'occupation allemande en Europe occidentale et orientale. La prostitution, les relations intimes et "les enfants de la guerre" en France, en Belgique et en Pologne', in W. Grabowski (ed.), *L'Europe occupée. Similitudes et différences* (Warsaw: IPN, 2014), 79–99, p. 88.

71 Marie Thérèse, *Histoire d'une prostituée*, p. 30.

72 F. Virgili, *La France virile. Des femmes tondues à la Libération* (Paris: Payot, 2000).

73 L. Capdevila, F. Rouquet, P. Schwartz, F. Virgili, D.Voldman, '"Quite Simply, Colonel . . .": gender and the Second World War', in H. Diamond and S. Kitson (eds), *Vichy, Resistance, Liberation. New Perspectives on Wartime France* (Oxford and New York: Berg, 2005), 51–8, p. 57.

74 Taking a rather uncritical approach, Patrick Buisson argued that sexual encounters between French women and German soldiers resulted in sexual liberation, P. Buisson, *1940–1945: années érotiques*, 2 vols (Paris: Albin Michel, 2008 and 2009).

75 On these children born of war, see J.-P. Picaper and L. Norz, *Enfants maudits. Ils sont 200,000, on les appelait les enfants de Boches* (Geneva: Éditions des Syrtes, 2004); F. Virgili, *Naître ennemi. Les enfants de couples franco-allemands nés pendant la seconde guerre mondiale* (Paris: Payot, 2009).

76 F. Leclerc and M. Weindling, 'La répression des femmes coupables d'avoir collaboré pendant l'Occupation', *Clio. Femmes, Genre, Histoire* 1 (1995).

77 Meinen 2002, 'La réglementation', p. 8.

78 M. L. Pratt, 'Arts of the contact zone', *Profession* (1991), 33–40.

79 Footitt, 'The underside of "Occupation"', p. 161.

80 Neitzel and Welzer, *Soldaten*, p. 229.

10

Madeleine Blaess: An Emotional History of a Long Liberation

Wendy Michallat

In July 1939, Madeleine Blaess graduated with a first-class honours degree in French from the University of Leeds. Passionate about her studies and wanting a career in academia, she was awarded a grant by the City of Leeds to study for a doctorate at the Sorbonne in Paris. Undeterred by Britain's declaration of war on Germany, she left for France in November 1939 and spent the next six months studying and sharing a life full of exciting interactions in the Paris boarding house *Les Marronniers,* with students, refugees from Eastern Europe, soldiers on leave, novelists, actors and actresses and sundry other short-stay lodgers. Madeleine's letters home told of her Sorbonne experiences and of the social whirl of *Les Marronniers* but the carefree tone of the early months progressively gave way to anxiety as Belgian refugees begin to arrive in chaos in Paris in spring 1940. Anxiety about the unfolding military conflict did not spur her into leaving the capital with many of her fellow postgraduate expatriates. Her French nationality may have made a hurried departure appear less necessary but complacency – she spent the last days before invasion shopping for trinkets for her parents – meant that she missed the last boat home. In her final letter on 1 June 1940 she told of the boat and train tickets she had bought for the return to Britain as she reassured her parents that she would soon be heading up 'The Great North road' to Yorkshire. It was a journey she did not make. The German advance had cut off the route to the ports preventing her departure and nearly five years elapsed before she saw her parents again.

On 1 October 1940, she began a diary which she conceived as a continuation of the correspondence she had shared with her mother during the Phoney War. Now, unable to send letters other than Red Cross telegrams, she intended the diary to act as their substitute, to mimic 'dialogue' with her mother and to preserve traces of her life to be read, like a delayed letter, when she finally returned home.

A number of factors particular to Madeleine's life influenced the style and content of her occupation diary. Had Madeleine not had French papers she would have been interned, possibly for the duration of the war. As it was, she was one of few British citizens to be at large in occupied territory and quite possibly the only one writing a daily diary of what she was living. Her documentary diary style which favoured description over feelings and impressions reflected a contemporary trend in British journal keeping inspired by the Mass Observation project (as well as harking back to Pepys whom she regularly quotes).[1] It was also a style typical of migrant letter writers, who recorded banal everyday detail which appeared to them and their readers to be novel and extraordinary thereby producing very rich micro-histories of their day-to-day lives.[2] Both these characteristics make the diary a particularly valuable source of information about how civilians lived historical events through an everyday ordinariness which is largely invisible in histories compiled from events deemed retrospectively to be important. In such a descriptive diary, Madeleine's feelings and emotions are inescapably embedded in entries about her everyday life because she invariably gave an opinion about what she was writing down. When this meticulous, descriptive style intersects with major historical and military events like the Liberation of France in 1944, a unique narrative emerges. It is a narrative which presents the civilian experience through the finest grain of domestic detail and weaves it through a range of emotions encompassing the present moment and a future which Madeleine was beginning to glimpse. This chapter tells the story of Liberation in Paris through the eyes of Madeleine Blaess and, in particular, through emotions not commonly accommodated in the commemorative narratives through which these events are largely remembered and sustained. The diary acts as an alternative historical record, documenting the civilian Liberation experience through the emotions of the everyday.

Madeleine's diary runs from October 1940 and finishes in September 1944, a month after the Liberation. When her Canadian student friend Ruth Camp was arrested in front of her at the flat they shared on the rue Rollin on 5 December 1940, a frightened Blaess decided that it was 'better to keep quiet about political matters'.[3] She mostly kept to this until 1944 when the reticence of cryptic allusions gave way to a frenetic account of the military liberation of Paris. For Madeleine, as for civilians across France, the Liberation was more than a military event. It was experienced as hope and expectation from the summer of 1943 when the Allied victory in North Africa, landings in Sicily and Soviet victories on the Eastern front gave the public confidence that the liberation of central Europe was only months away.[4]

This chapter examines the meaning of the Liberation through the emotions stirred by the Allied military campaign to liberate France, from the Normandy landings on 6 June onwards. It took the Allies three months of hard fighting to reach Paris. The uncertainty of an outcome which threatened to embroil civilians in front-line fighting and which, over a two-week period, caused chaos to spill into the streets of the capital, prompted Madeleine to record a range of feelings and emotions which have been largely ignored by commemorative popular narratives of the Liberation. Madeleine's diarized account of Liberation corroborates an emerging historical consensus that the Liberation memory has been distorted in transmission though a selective range of uniquely positive emotions. Jean-Pierre Azéma has described it as a powerfully emotive image-driven narrative: girls climbing onto tanks, cheering crowds, men parading down the Champs-Élysées in their best clothes; a narrative from which the victims of the war have been expunged.[5] Alain Brossat shares this view, pointing out too that a Liberation narrative simplified in this way cannot accommodate the vast range of emotions and experiences recorded in personal testimonies in particular.[6] The definition of Liberation and the moment of its happening have been problematized in recent years. It is no longer seen as a specifically Parisian event which took place in August 1944. However, it is still the case that the military operation of 1944 remains central in the revised narrative. What Azéma writes is typical: 'Should one speak of the Liberation in the singular? I would say not. One must broach it in the plural [...]. A full six months separate the beginning of Operation Overlord on the Normandy beaches and the taking of Strasbourg.'[7] These military narratives of Liberation, whether they centre on Paris or recognize that Liberation took place across metropolitan France well into 1945, are narratives of heroic soldiering, strategy and planning from which women are largely excluded.

Madeleine's long liberation

Between the summer of 1943 and the Liberation of Paris in 1944, Madeleine's diary records her emotional response to the prospect of Liberation. In the same way that the German Occupation provided a backdrop to Madeleine's everyday life and feelings across the four previous years, now the idea of Liberation was articulated in her diary as a stimulus for thinking about her own future. The events so often at the heart of historical and popular representations of the Liberation are obliquely present, in the background of her life or as an imagined future. In the summer of 1943, the Liberation exists – if one can say as much – as the set of emotions that its contemplation provokes.

For Madeleine Blaess, the prospect of Liberation was heartening but it also made her anxious because she feared that the future which lay beyond it would be one of restricted freedoms and frustrated ambitions. Universities had opened their doors wider to women in the wake of the First World War. A generation of men had been killed in the trenches and young women who had grown up in the hey-day of first-wave feminism expecting greater educational opportunity were replacing them. But this abrupt improvement in access to higher education did not sweep away chauvinist prejudice. Blaess encountered sexism and hostility from male teaching staff and students at the Sorbonne and the pages of her diary are troubled by the conflict between her professional ambitions and the self-abnegating domesticity she felt was expected of her. In the 1940s women were still expected to prioritize marriage and children over careers. By the summer of 1943, with Liberation seemingly in the offing, Madeleine was preoccupied with her future and the dilemma of whether to choose career or family. She was now twenty-six years old, the average age at which British women married in the 1940s, but was as committed to her dream of being an academic as much as she had been when she first arrived in Paris in 1939.[8] However, very little progress had been made on the thesis and her university funding had run out. Longer, reflective passages irrupted from the more neutral descriptions of everyday events, and these were fearful about the prospect of surrendering her life of autonomy in Paris for one of financial dependency and limited horizons back in Yorkshire with her parents. Tumbling forth across the passages is an anxious 're-voicing' of the gender prejudice encountered by women in the 1940s which she does not challenge but appears resigned to having to cope with somehow. A good marriage with an academic might save her, she mused before concluding that men tended not to find women with qualifications attractive. On 15 August 1943, woefully foreseeing a future stuck at home caring for her ageing parents she wrote:

> If I stay, I will be dead as a woman and will be doing the same work again; the housework, the gardening, I'll embroider beautiful tapestries and I'll take the dog out with mum and dad. I will have to get married [. . .] But, who will I find to marry? Who would want me? I am not beautiful but I'm not ugly either – but I am fat – and then, of course, the education I have had –! Oh Good Lord!! (15 August 1943)

Hanna Diamond has observed that many women were 'deeply changed by their wartime experiences' and were reluctant 'to pick up their lives as they had been before the war', and Madeleine was one of them:[9] She was reluctant to relinquish the greater freedoms she had known during the Occupation. The struggle of Occupation had raised her expectations and she set this down in her diary in August 1943: 'I have been too close to misery and to death to be how I was before and I do not share the same opinions as my parents. And what about my freedom?? [. . .] A girl, a girl stays at home – well, yes, perhaps but not when she has had to earn her crust all alone for three years dictated to by necessity and with only herself to keep her going' (15 August 1943).

Madeleine's anxiety about what the end of the war might mean for her dominates the diary in the summer and autumn of 1943, which was now focussed firmly on the future for the first time in four years. It was a future about which she anxiously started to seek reassurance in tarot card readings and kinesiology. She also began to write down her dreams and nightmares which seemed to articulate deep-seated fears about the future. On 8 August 1943 she described a dream in which she had had to beg the Franco-British College for a modest grant of £40 a year because her parents had refused her the financial support she needed to finish the thesis. In a particularly violent and vivid dream on 30 October 1943, a brutal and controlling husband burnt her books, kept her incarcerated at home with their child and raped her to impregnate her again when she tried to escape. Madeleine's liberation, the liberation she envisaged from 1943 when she first seriously contemplated its possibility, was beset by fear and anxiety about a future of closed, not open, doors. For many women and men, the Liberation meant getting plans back on track. For some this meant marrying, settling down and having a family. For Madeleine, and no doubt others like her, the Liberation opened a new chapter of uncertainty and struggle.

From the Normandy landings to the Paris insurrection

Antoine Lefébure has attributed the anxiety he found in letters and phone calls intercepted by Vichy ahead of Liberation to fear of civil war, fear of Allied failure and fear of the political aftermath of Liberation. These ephemeral fears were, Lefébure claimed, briskly 'swept away' by the great 'wind of freedom' accompanying the Allied victory.[10] Pierre Laborie has also analysed private letters and concluded that the fears and anxieties dominating the public mood stemmed from the daily struggle to survive rather than from more abstract concerns. He noted that the excitement over the Normandy landings faded quickly as civilians turned their attention back to surviving the worsening conditions of their everyday.[11] Laborie's findings mirror Madeleine's reaction. Initially she was excited when she heard the news on the morning of 6 June: '"They" have landed!!!!!!! [. . .] At 1.30 am at Carenton (near Cherbourg). They are at the mouths of the Rivers Orne and Vire and at the Seine, Le Havre. Parachutists landing in Caen. [. . .] Jacqueline is sticking to me like glue to listen to the radio and getting on my nerves.'[12] By the following day, she was already complaining that there was no bread to be had. Indeed, hopes of liberation were raised and then dashed within days.

On 7 June tanks were present on the streets and Madeleine reported a mass public exodus towards Versailles.[13] The next day she noted the German military out in strength in camouflaged Tiger tanks and lorries, and worriedly wrote that she had heard on Radio Paris that the Allied campaign was in difficulty: 'The Germans are carrying out a stalling offensive which the Allies haven't been able to stop [. . .]. At Falaise, the German troops are pushing the English troops towards the South (??!!)'[14] This seemingly stuttering offensive worried Madeleine and, over subsequent weeks, news of the fierce and bloody battle raging across northern France was frightening and disheartening, not least because it presaged what might await Parisians themselves. News arrived first-hand from refugees fleeing from the front-line in Normandy. A friend's father told of mayhem and death:

> Françoise has just brought some butter and some meat because her father was in Normandy. He's had a nightmare journey back. The Germans are going to battle in everything they can find, even French cars and so the English are machine gunning everything. The lorry that was following them was machine gunned. The teeth of the person driving were found incrusted in the dashboard. It was impossible to get them out.[15]

The following day she overheard a refugee from Normandy addressing a crowd anxious for news:

> At the Gare Montparnasse I saw a woman who had come from Normandy with her dog and two little suitcases. There was a huge crowd around her and she was answering questions. She was hard, fiery and tough, lots of bravado. One could feel her shaking from the struggle to get out.[16]

Thus, the wait for the Allies began to be coloured by dread as the 'Liberation' stretched out across the territory and hopes of a rapid victory diminished. Within a very short time, the euphoria of the Normandy landings had given way to the realization that French civilians in northern France were now in the path of a bloody battle, which risked embroiling Parisians too. Thus, it is hardly surprising that there were few signs of excitement to be found in Madeleine's diary after the Normandy landings.

From the pre-invasion bombing campaign of 1943 through to the 'Phoney Liberation' of 6 and 7 June, and beyond, Mary-Louise Roberts writes, the lives of the Normans had been a litany of horrific 'sights and smells – the rot of animal and human flesh, the stench of death [...] a terrible grammar of sounds, sights, smells and tastes'.[17] The Liberation conducted across northern France during the spring and summer of 1944 was far from exhilarating for those caught up in the fighting. Of the Liberation in Normandy Roberts writes: 'anger, fear and loss stripped the moment of its bliss. Liberation was a harrowing experience in which happiness had to share the heart with sorrow.'[18] Parisians had been trained in civil defence since before war broke out in 1939, but the dreaded aerial bombardment had not arrived for those in central Paris. Yet the news from Normandy in June 1944, and the increasing frequency of Allied air raids on industrial and railway areas of the Paris suburbs awakened Madeleine's fears. Like many people across France, before the spring of 1944 she had experienced air raids only as distant and rather beautiful pyrotechnic displays of tracer bullets, flares and light showers of bursting flak shells, watched from afar on her balcony. By spring 1944, her diary entries frequently made reference to death and near-misses, from both bombs and anti-aircraft fire. Madeleine's friend Madeleine F. had a narrow escape at the Closerie des Lilas on the Boulevard Montparnasse when a flak shell fell from the sky killing two people and injuring many others, an experience which left her 'very shaken up by all the screaming and the blood'.[19]

On 2 August 1944, three weeks before the Liberation of Paris, Madeleine herself was caught in a bombing raid in the Paris suburb of Montreuil. The raid killed 147 people including many children in a convent which had taken a direct hit. Madeleine's description of the raid gives insight into the psychological pressure many French people faced during the most intense period of bombing, as the Allies sought to destroy the rail infrastructure in advance of D-Day, and thereafter as part of the military campaign.[20] Her shocked and shocking account describes the explosion and its grisly aftermath:

> The anti-aircraft guns are firing. Aunt tells me to stay. Then, there is a terrible crash, like thunder and crashing planes at the same time. Impossible to describe. Everything black. A huge flame. The window jumps out of its frame and goes back in again letting the smoke and dust in etc, terrible noise, glass falling, everything shaking. Then our thoughts turn to André who is next to the window but all he is bothered about is protecting René's head and telling him not to be

frightened. We pull the beds to the end of the room and pull down the blind. We hear other bombs but they are in the distance. The electricity has gone off and we can hear screaming. After a bit we pull up the blind and all around seems to be in flames. Aunt says that it is the clinic. Several houses have been hit, some are burning, a school has been flattened. They take away the injured from the street and those injured in the courtyard of the clinic which is in flames. André was remarkably calm. I treat a woman who is in a state of shock (her lips are burnt). Then they send me to the convent. It is difficult to walk in the road, glass, telephone lines down, shutters, bricks etc. Lots of dust and rubble. Lots of houses on fire. The emergency services are trying to rescue as many people as possible. There is no water. The cop doesn't let me through because I haven't got an armband. Help to evacuate a burning house but a tile falls on my head and I haven't got a helmet. I have to get out. Very hot. Dazed people stare. A little girl stumbling holding her doll 'Let's leave here Mummy, I want to go. I am frightened, I want to leave here'. No one knows who she is or where her mummy is. A tall man. Blood running down from his nose and ears his right arm limp, doesn't want to be helped. He wants to see his wife. His friend was killed right next to him. Go back to the stretcher bearers. Piles of rubble in the road. Difficult to walk in wooden shoes. My heel gets caught in a shutter. We requisition a coal truck, whistles are blown, detour because the road is flooded. No water. Carrefour Pleyal. No more wounded. A lot of ambulances. We have something to drink, requisition an empty coal lorry and off we go again.

The young male stretcher bearer gives me his arm band. We go to the convent. The cop wants to stop me. He recognized me but I have an arm band. They don't want to let us in but we break down the door. Luckily our team leader is brilliant. It is 6 o'clock. 40 children and 5 nuns have been killed in the shelter. The fire brigade are super but they have to come up every 5 minutes. They bring out the corpses or limbs in sheets putting them down on stretcher to be identified. There are 2 packets of flesh pieces or two bodies per stretcher. They bring a man from the D[éfense] P[assive][21] to identify his little girl. It takes time to clear a way through, to get back up putting in beams for support at the same time. Finally, at 7.30 I am in front of the hole with my stretcher. Other than the nuns there were three women on the site. Now there is only me. The men send us away. They take my arm band off me but I keep hold of my stretcher. I want to do something. In the end, I have two little girls on the stretcher. Took them to the ambulance. Came home. Very tired. Madeleine F. was lovely, she made dinner etc. I don't think I shall ever cry again.[22]

Madeleine's harrowing account of the bombing raid and its obvious psychological impact are important to bear in mind when examining what Parisians were feeling during the long wait to be liberated. Urban destruction on a mass scale was familiar to them through newsreels of the 1940 Battle of France, the London Blitz and the German campaign on the Eastern front. They had heard the tales from Normandy and were now experiencing regular bombing themselves. The population hoped for liberation but dreaded what they might have to go through to get it.

Intensifying crisis

Jean-Pierre Azéma attributes the euphoria felt by the French at the Liberation to their relief at having survived. He quotes Stanley Hoffman's review of *Le Chagrin et la Pitié* to make his point: 'He who didn't live in a French town or village in the weeks before and following the Liberation cannot understand the sheer pleasure to be still alive at the end of such an unspeakable ordeal.'[23] Madeleine's diary gives the same impression: that the joy and euphoria of Liberation are a release from months of intensifying stress and anxiety. Her meticulous, uninterrupted logging of day-to-day vicissitudes and emotional turbulence is a unique barometer of the public mood as Liberation approached. Just as it seemed that the Occupation was coming to an end, the difficulties which had ground down the morale of the populace over four years intensified.

After the *débarquement*, food shortages instantly became more acute as supply chains were interrupted. On 7 June, there was no bread and 'at the Sorbonne they were appealing for students to help distribute food by pulling carts'.[24] The following day, there was virtually no food at all: 'no bread, not a single vegetable in Paris. No lettuce, nothing.'[25] On 10 June, Madeleine went to the market in Auteuil: 'There was absolutely nothing other than parsley and flowers. That's it. There've been no vegetables, nothing in Paris for a pretty long while.'[26] During the four years of Occupation, food had been routinely pooled and shared, ration tickets sold or bartered and food given as payment in kind for work which, in Madeleine's case, was usually English language teaching, baby-sitting or caring for the elderly and infirm. This saving recourse, reliant on arrangement-making, was badly disrupted from June by a ban on telegrams, telephone calls and, one would suppose, the *pneus* of the widely used Parisian subterranean pneumatic messaging system. The Liberation thus disrupted habitual survival strategies, and by the end of June the mood was desperate. On 26 June Madeleine reported that she could only buy food on the black market. On 6 July she wrote of having managed to get 'half a pound of butter for 200fr [. . .], some rolls, lettuce and peaches – but at astronomical cost'.[27] Before, Parisians had been able to bring food into the city from the surrounding countryside, but now food was scarce there too. Even if they reached countryside – which, by July, was already more difficult with a Sunday-only service, and by August was impossible as all public transport was cut – their journeys met with disappointment.[28] Madeleine describes the pointless 'odysseys' of her friend Denise: '6am she was at St Germain where they refused to sell anything to Parisians. She got back on the train and went to Chatou. She walked across fields and queued for 2 hours for 10kg of carrots (100frs). Went to Montesson on foot, nothing, and got back to Paris at 2pm.'[29] Ironically, Madeleine's only fresh food came from Normandy, brought with stories of death and destruction by her friend's father.

Madeleine's liberation had been difficult from June, but by August it was an ordeal of endurance. By mid-August, two months after D-Day and the beginnings of the pre-Liberation food crisis, she felt perpetually faint and nauseous. On 15 August, she reported worsening living conditions: 'I don't think we have enough to eat [...] The water is cut off and the Germans are saying there will be no food unless terrorist attacks stop.' The situation was so desperate that Madeleine reported the slaughter of a cow in the grounds of the Senate building, chopped into chunks there and then and sold at 100 francs a kilo. By 16 August Madeleine was contemplating her own death. In one of her bleakest entries she wrote:

> The undertakers are on strike. Fine time for it! Let's see where we are with the dead in a few days. Didn't sleep. Nice has been captured. The Germans have announced that there is fighting on the road between Dreux and Chartres. Guns firing all night. At South-South-West there was a continuous glow in the sky with very bright flashes all night. I dreamt that I returned home but it was strange. A night terror – will I ever see my parents again etc. Packed suitcase and wrote a goodbye letter etc. Fell asleep at dawn.[30]

So in the early weeks of August 1944, as the Allies fought across France towards Paris, Madeleine waited anxiously, suffering ever more intensely from shortages and frightened about what would happen when the Allies arrived. It was clear in Madeleine's account that into the information vacuum flooded pessimism and anxiety. She worriedly noted down rumours she heard about the progress of the Allies and her anguish that the Allies might fail was an emotion shared by many. For Parisian Françoise Seligman, failure was unbearable to contemplate: 'A kind of inner panic paralyzed me [...] If they fail, if they leave, the proof will have been made that France has become an impregnable bastion of Nazi power.'[31] Another fear was of the violence the Germans might inflict on the civilian population. On 20 August, Madeleine noted down a directive which she believed to have been issued directly by the SS:

1. Curfew from 9pm to 7 am.
2. All windows to be closed. No one to stand at the windows.
3. All main and side doors to buildings have to be kept open even during the night.
4. All cinemas, theatres, cafes and other going out places are to be closed (a bit late there).
5. Gatherings of more than 3 people are banned.
6. Certain zones are off-limits to civilians who will be shot without warning.
7. Anyone giving information to the enemy will be treated as a spy.[32]

Entries made on 17 and 19 August, written progressively over the course of the days as events unfolded, vividly describe the anxious uncertainty:

> We can hear gun shots. It is worrying. Everybody is restless and anxious. They are saying that the Germans have blown up the power stations, the bridges, the hotels where they have been staying, the Senate building. Meanwhile, the suburbs are well alight. The water came back on this evening. There is a little gas but it takes 1½ hours to sauté potatoes. Explosion after explosion and one which sets the building rocking but I don't know where that one was. Fires near Villeneuve St George.[33]

Madeleine's account of 19 August gives a particularly vivid picture of public fear in the final days before the Liberation. It also betrays a degree of anger and frustration. The Allies were needed to support an insurrection which had begun to look vulnerable and exposed, but they were nowhere to be seen:

> The Préfecture is surrounded. 500 men inside. Nearly out of ammunition. They are worried about bombing. Huge explosions, the Hôtel de Ville and the Préfecture we think. And these God-forsaken allies who don't come. Flags being hung everywhere – then taken down because the Germans are shooting at decorated windows. They are evacuating their injured, piled up in open wagons in the full glare of the sun without bothering. Jacqueline came. She is so tense. Good Lord, if only we knew something, were able to know.

Madeleine's wait for liberation was one of mounting tension and anxiety in a city where, for nearly a fortnight, it was not at all clear what was happening or who was in control. In her diary entries now, there was nothing about hopes and dreams of a life beyond the Liberation: everything was tied up with the present.

Paradoxically, when freedom was so close, she wrote of the fear of not surviving to see it. The wait for liberation was a battle to survive material deprivation. It was also a battle of nerves.

The arrival of the Allies

Rod Kedward drew on the theory of carnival to frame the 'joyful exuberance, anarchy and violence' of the celebrations after the Allied arrival. To do so was not new, he pointed out. Jean-Marie Guillon had explored it in relation to the 'enactment of collective exaltation, excess, transgression and inversion of the social order' in his account of Liberation in the Var. Alain Brossat also invoked it for the retributive head shaving of 'collaborator' women, which he describes as the 'ugly carnival' of misogynist violence running as an undercurrent in popular public celebrations. Kedward also evokes Foucault's ideas that events do not need their immediate historical context to explain them; their causes can be found elsewhere in longstanding cultural rituals. He sees both carnival and Foucault's discontinuities repeatedly in written and oral memoirs which tell of the Liberation as 'a kind of unreality, a vacuum in time, a highly charged present without past or future, a period of dislocation or hyper-action'.[34] We see something of all this in Madeleine's account of the military liberation of the capital. There is sense of carnival and the diligently observed chronological pace of the diary is upset as 'happenings' cascade one after the other through dates which appear, on occasion, to have been written down in advance and for which the allotted space cannot contain the detail. The erstwhile neat longhand script also becomes an untidy scrawl as the diary object itself seems to mediate the emotions of its writer. From 22 August, three days before the military liberation of Paris, excitement and exhilaration displaced anxiety, temporarily at least, as Madeleine finally left her flat to see what was happening on the streets. Ever the *flâneuse* who had previously described the withering decline or blossoming regeneration of the city's flowers and trees as she walked through the seasons, Madeleine now documented every barricade, every chunk of detached masonry, every tract and proclamation stuck up on the walls:

> Went round the barricades to see the damage. Beautiful barricade up at the Panthéon. On the Rue d'Ulm I nearly got myself killed by one of the militia on the roof next to the École normale. I sheltered in a porch for 10 minutes. There are barricades on all the streets. Those on the Rue Berthollet and the Boulevard Port-Royal are fantastic with overturned lorries and everything![35]

By 22 August the civilian insurrection was in full swing. There was a 'magnificent spirit' she wrote, 'volunteers sawing wood for the Free Forces, coming round from door to door collecting sheets, bandages, safety pins etc'. She headed out into the thick of the action, going to see her friend Coutelier at the town hall in the 5th *arrondissement* which had been attacked by 'two big guns'. Now far from anxious, she was caught up in the thrill of pitched battles which raged around her. Impatient with frightened friends, there was now no place for either her own fear or that of other people: 'Jacqueline Eichhorn came over. I want to throttle her. She is such a scaredy-cat and feeble.' The same exuberance was clear when at 7am on the morning of 25 August, General Leclerc's tanks arrived under her window and she raced to greet them in her dressing gown. She returned to her apartment to dress – the soldiers having drawn attention to her attire – and then, still wild with excitement, she followed them to the Luxembourg Palace, putting herself in grave personal danger:

> They fire on the Senate and the Senate fires back with its heavy gun causing the branches of the trees above us to break off. There are two blasts. We go in. Madeleine F is scared stiff. She has to bandage herself because she threw herself down on the ground too quickly scraping her knee and her arm. To be fair, today she hasn't gone on too much.[36]

In Madeleine's account of the morning of the Liberation, we read a very familiar account of joy and exuberance but this mood lasts literally for moments and is interspersed and surrounded by emotions which are much less positive.

Negative Liberation

An examination of how and why emotions have been edited out of official narratives of the Liberation suggests that certain emotions have been judged inadmissible because they cannot be assimilated in a virile and heroic masculine discourse. Keith, Aubert and Roberts all see evidence of the displacement or marginalization of women in the Liberation narrative chiefly reducing them to a symbolic sexual presence over which both Allies and French men could assert (re-assert) their virility.[37] As Aubert notes, citing Ricoeur, there is a need for the story of women's civilian life to be told via a 'kind of parallel history [...] of victimization, which would counter the history of success and victory'.[38] Madeleine's day-to-day account challenges the standard war narrative of the Liberation, in which men occupy centre stage in a positive story and women are marginalized or completely absent. The challenge comes in the form of 'negative' emotions (anger, shame, pity, fear, anxiety and so on) responding to the exclusion of women and male violence towards women, which are disallowed by Liberation narratives foregrounding triumph and joy.

When the Allies reached the outskirts of Paris and the insurrection became visible on the streets, Madeleine, a trained first-aider, went straight to the Red Cross to report for duty: 'took my report to the Red Cross this afternoon and volunteered but it is useless. They don't want women – they only want men for the barricades, to drive and to courier. I am furious.'[39] She was forced into the role of observer and her account was by no means full of cheering, flag-waving, climbing onto tanks, arranging dates with GIs, and posing for the newsreels – even though all of these are present nonetheless. There was a darker, frightening side to the insurrection and she was distracted by the anarchic retributive justice taking place on the streets. The Resistance frightened her. On 19 August she wrote:

> No lesson with Corneau. Too dangerous outside just here in this district. Stormy weather. Listened to the radio. Not a single word about Paris. The Resistance uprising has been premature. These fellows who are walking around without a care with machine guns or grenades in their hands as if they were holding an umbrella or a walking stick. They are still killing. Good Lord, when will it end. I was frightened of the bullets this morning. We don't know where they come from.

Even though Madeleine had contributed to acts of civilian 'passive' resistance at various points over the Occupation she shrank from violence, and had written on 9 October 1943: 'At the office – the parents of M. Delbot (collaborator) and their daughter (17 years old, a collaborator too) received little coffins on which was written "Sentenced to death". I find all that pretty puerile'. She was similarly contemptuous of vengeful excess during the Liberation events, noting on 18 August: 'People are behaving in a dignified way. It's only the rabble who went out to laugh at the Germans moving out of the "Trianon."' Her admiration of the valour displayed at the Senate, the Hôtel de Ville and on the St Jacques barricades quickly gave way to disapproving and worried descriptions of the first malicious (and anarchic) manifestations of the *épuration* (the purge of collaborators).

On 20 August, she wrote that the Forces françaises de l'intérieur (FFI), armed with revolvers, were roaming around the district on their way to execute people at '72 Bd. Port Royal' which was, at the time, the hospital of the Val-de-Grâce. Criticisms of Resistance violence are also accompanied by descriptions of the abuse of women suspected of having collaborated. Fabrice Virgili states, somewhat over-confidently, that the public supported this violence perpetrated against women despite their distrust of the Resistance itself. Brutalizing these women was, he claims 'an opportunity for the public to share with the Resistance an act of hostility against the Occupier' and 'if disputes took place then they were between different Resistance groups, the priest, the mayor or the police'.[40] However, there was nothing gleeful about Madeleine's descriptions of the suffering of the victims of Resistance vigilantism. She was discomfited by the aggression, felt pity for the victims, contempt for their aggressors and a generalized distrust and disdain for the mob violence is as prominent in her account as the glad-handing joy and exuberant camaraderie running alongside it. There are several examples:

> Saw German women with huge letters F.F.I attached to them. Everyone was clapping. Saw a prisoner who they were bringing in with his left hand behind his neck, his right wrist was being held behind his back and there was a revolver stuck into his waist. He looked wretched.[41]

On Saturday 26 August, there are more examples of this same concern for women attacked by the Resistance and supporters:

> In front of the Lycée Montaigne a German lorry full of paper is still burning. Five women go by, their heads have been completely shaved and a swastika stuck on them. They are wearing a Nazi flag around their necks and are making the Nazi salute. They are ashen with hatred and with rage. The crowd just says 'ha ha' but doesn't do anything else.

And, later that same day, the most moving description of their suffering:

> In the afternoon I went out with Madeleine F. On the corner we saw another woman, bare feet, hair shaved off, a red cross on her head, left to make her way through the crowd heckling at her. She looked to be suffering terribly with the shame of it all. People who looked as if they knew her said that she deserved it. I worry that she will be so terribly poorly after that. I saw a portrait of Hitler hung from a lamppost.

Madeleine's descriptions of newly liberated Paris do not fit, therefore, with the exhilaration narrative, at least not in any sustained way. The moments of joy are soon overtaken by fear, doubt and concern. Within days, the Liberation moved away from centre stage and Madeleine became, once again, concerned with her own everyday life. On Tuesday 29 August, four days after the arrival of Allies, she was back at work:

> Was up at 6 am. 7.30 I was en route to work in the drizzle and in new shoes. They don't hurt me as much I had feared they would but they hurt enough. Furious with Kort. There is nothing to do at the office but he makes me come in on purpose and I will have to come in tomorrow afternoon for my pay and Thursday as usual.

Conclusion

Disgust, fear, anxiety, horror, gloom and pessimism characterized Madeleine Blaess's Liberation, through which she had lived in fear of starvation, bombing, illness and violence from both the Germans and from Resistance fighters. The future beyond the Liberation was not yearned for. Rather, it was feared because, for the scholarly, career-minded woman that Madeleine was, it seemed to offer little prospect of the freedoms she craved. Within days of the German capitulation, the diary entries shortened to become, once again, the routine, workaday observations typical of the first three years. They ceased on 17 September even though she stayed in Paris until February of the following year. Two years after the Liberation, in September 1946, Madeleine returned to Paris and for three weeks she kept a diary which is a frenzy of descriptions of restored relationships and reformed families, of people making children and making futures in a country racing to recoup a lost four years. This zest for the future is a distant echo of August 1944 but her diarized record of aftermath also showed very keenly the grief and the psychological pain for which there had been no place in the carnival of Liberation. In the three weeks she notes down, Madeleine visited the grave of a close friend who had died of influenza in 1943: 'Godmother's grave was alright, just about. I didn't get the feeling that she was waiting for me to come like Cécile who hasn't left me since. She is with me everywhere I go. May she rest in peace.'[42] And of her sister's fiancé, labour camp survivor Michel, Madeleine wrote:

> Normally he only speaks about things which are amusing and funny [...] Terrible things have happened to him. [...] When he speaks about it, he was like a caged monkey. Normally it doesn't show. It did this time. Not being able to move or to say a word without permission. How awful.

These 1946 entries, as fiercely observant as those in the war diary, are a logical appendage to Madeleine's Liberation account, in that they countenance a parallel narrative of pain, and hint at new narratives opening up around the conflicting needs to forget and to remember.

Notes

1 Joe Moran locates the vogue for documentary diaries in the 1930s as coming from the Mass Observation project which valorized this form through its national appeals through the media for contributions. The project sought descriptive diaries and not diaries in which everyday life was abstracted and mediated through the writer's thoughts and feelings (J. Moran, 'Private lives, public histories: the diary in twentieth-century Britain'. *Journal of British Studies* 54.1 (2015), 138–62).

2 An excellent example of this can be found in Alistair Thomson's *Moving Stories: An Intimate History of Four Women Across Two Continents* (Manchester: Manchester University Press, 2011); see particularly Chapter 6, 'Letter Stories'.

3 University of Sheffield Library, Special Collections and Archive, MS296/3/40: M. Blaess, Documents, Letters; and MS296/3/42: M. Blaess, Journal (hereafter Blaess, diary). Blaess, diary, 10 January 1941.

4 P. Laborie, *L'Opinion française sous Vichy: les Français et la crise d'identité nationale 1936–1944* (Paris: Éditions du Seuil, 2001), pp. 289–90.

5 J.-P. Azéma, 'Les Libérations de la France: prologue', *French Cultural Studies*, 15.5 (1994), 223–6, p. 223.

6 A. Brossat, *Libération, fête folle, 6 juin 1944 – 8 mai 45: mythes et rites ou le grand théâtre des passions populaires* (Paris: Éditions autrement, 1994), p. 62.

7 Azéma, 'Les Libérations de la France', p. 224.

8 J. Fulcher and J. Scott, *Sociology* (Oxford: Oxford University Press, 2011), p. 275.

9 H. Diamond, 'Women's aspirations, 1943–47: an oral enquiry in Toulouse', in H. R. Kedward and N. Wood (eds), *The Liberation of France: Image and Event* (Oxford and Washington DC: Berg, 1995), 93–101, p. 93.

10 A. Lefébure, *Les Conversations secrètes des Français sous l'Occupation* (Paris: Plon, 1993), pp. 363–4.

11 Laborie, *L'Opinion française sous Vichy*, pp. 314–15.

12 Blaess, diary, 6 June 1944.

13 There has been little scholarly research about the exodus from Paris in 1944 but it is clear from Madeleine's diary that there was a repeat of the panic and flight of civilians in 1940.

14 Blaess, diary, 8 June 1944.

15 Blaess, diary, 22 June 1944.

16 Blaess, diary, 23 June 1944.

17 M.-L. Roberts, *What Soldiers Do: Sex and the American GI in World War II France* (Chicago and London: University of Chicago Press, 2013), p. 17.

18 Roberts, *What Soldiers Do*, p. 18.

19 Blaess, diary, 22 June 1944.

20 See, on bombing, A. Knapp, *Les Français sous les bombes alliées, 1940–1945* (Paris: Tallandier, 2014); on civilian experience of bombing see L. Dodd, *French Children*

under the Allied bombs, 1940–45: An Oral History (Manchester: Manchester University Press, 2016).

21 The Défense Passive was the civil defence organization which presided over local air raid precautions, including blackout, first aid and bombsite clearance.

22 Blaess, diary, 2 August 1944.

23 Azéma, 'Les Libérations de la France', p. 225.

24 Blaess, diary, 7 June 1944.

25 Blaess, diary, 8 June 1944.

26 Blaess, diary, 10 June 1944.

27 Blaess, diary, 6 July 1944.

28 Blaess, diary, 9 July 1944.

29 Blaess, diary, 26 June 1944.

30 Blaess, diary, 16 August 1944.

31 Seligman's diary, cited in Roberts, *What Soldiers Do*, p. 20.

32 Blaess, diary, 20 August 1944.

33 Blaess, diary, 17 August 1944.

34 H. R. Kedward, 'Ici commence la France libre', in Kedward and Wood (eds), *The Liberation of France*, 1–11, p. 6.

35 Blaess, diary, 24 August 1944.

36 Blaess, diary, 25 August 1944.

37 S. Keith, 'Collective memory and the end of Occupation: remembering (and forgetting) the Liberation of Paris in images', *Visual Communication Quarterly*, 17.3 (2010), 134–46; M.-L. Roberts, 'La photo du GI viril: genre et photojournalisme en France à la Libération', *Le Mouvement social*, 219 (2007), 35–56; N. Aubert, '"We have nothing better than testimony": History and memory in French war narratives', *Journal of European Studies*, 45.5 (2015), 287–300.

38 Ricoeur as cited in Aubert, '"We have nothing better than testimony"', p. 295.

39 Blaess, diary, 22 August 1944.

40 F. Virgili, *Shorn Women, Gender and Punishment in Liberation France* (Oxford: Berg, 2002), pp. 89–93.

41 Blaess, diary, 20 August 1944.

42 Blaess, diary, 1 November 1946.

11

Counter-Revolution? Resisting Vichy and the National Revolution

Mason Norton

In 1974, the former resister and journalist Pascal Copeau wrote about resistance not as an organized structure, or even an army of the shadows, but 'a spider's web', a set of threads which, when woven together, constituted the Resistance.[1] This idea grounded resistance as a struggle that encompassed all forms of life – cultural, social and the everyday. The potential for everyday life to be a realm within which resistance could operate or even prosper has been an important aspect of works in resistance studies, not just in the case of occupied France, as shown by H. R. Kedward, but also for example in Fanny Gallot's more recent work *En Découdre* about resistance in the workplace, or more famously, James C. Scott's *Weapons of the Weak*.[2] Olivier Wieviorka and Jacek Tebinka have acknowledged its potential within a transnational context, right across occupied Europe.[3]

Most works on the Resistance in France focus on the fight against the Nazis, even if the historiographical school of the 'Second Thirty Years War' has long since been left behind.[4] That focus can also be seen, for example, in Wieviorka's and Tebinka's study, with its emphasis on the regimes of Hitler and Mussolini. This chapter considers resistance in France from a slightly different angle – resistance against the Vichy regime within the sphere of the everyday, asking how resistance functioned when the enemy was not just Nazi Occupation, but also the Vichy regime of Marshal Pétain, and other French people who chose to collaborate.

Defining the everyday and the political

In the 1970s in West Germany, the historiographical school of *Alltagsgeschichte* (the history of everyday life) showed that a study of everyday practices, even at the smallest scale, could be revealing about national politics in a particular era. A historiographical review by Alf Lüdtke concluded that ordinary Germans were complicit in perpetuating the values of the Third Reich and the formation of the *Volksgenosse*.[5] Lüdtke argued that the history of everyday life was in fact a very political undertaking.[6]

In France, René Rémond argued for a distinction between a narrow, power-based conception of electoral politics and a broader, daily-life, socially-based conception of politics that encapsulated all walks of life – he called the former *la politique*, and the latter *le politique*.[7] This conception of *le politique*, or the political, has been further broadened by Vincent Peillon, whose 2011 *Éloge du politique* drew upon Aristotle's conceptions of the political as a form of civic engagement, a search for the common good.[8]

Such ideas about the political dimension of everyday activity are important for a study of resistance because resistance encompassed so much more than armed struggle and military action. In the Seine-Inférieure, for example, resisters tended to unite only for their resistance activities, and then dispersed again back to their homes in their own communities. For even the most established *maquisards*, much of the time prior to the landings in 1944 was spent trying to keep warm, keep healthy, well-fed and watered, and only occasionally engaging in activity. The accounts of Georges Guingouin in the Limousin and Yves Pérotin in the Vercors demonstrate that the *maquis* was rarely about gunfire and explosions prior to 6 June 1944.[9] Equally, a large number of resisters never bore arms. Their resistance was grounded within daily life, and sometimes in mundane activities.

So this is what is meant by 'the everyday': daily practices that may at first seem far removed from the theatres of war and politics. Yet these practices were firmly anchored within both, a society that was shaped by war, what Alya Aglan and Robert Frank have called *la Guerre-monde*.[10] In Vichy France, the everyday and the political were intertwined, because the everyday was inherently political.

Henry Pickford has suggested that resistance has three defining characteristics: 'resistance against', or its opposition; 'resistance towards', or its aims, and 'resistance as', or how resistance is manifested.[11] Clearly, much of 'resistance against' aimed at ridding France of the occupier, yet a further dimension is clear in 'resistance against' Vichy itself. Equally, what about the other two criteria, namely 'resistance towards' and 'resistance as'? The former defines most broadly the different strands and groupings of anti-Vichy resistance, which can be discerned by applying Reinhart Koselleck's theory of 'horizons of expectation', or *Erwartungshorizont*.[12] What were the goals of resisters? What were they aiming towards? The latter defines the manifestation of resistance against Vichy, which could be as varied as a resister's ingenuity and agency allowed. These criteria of resistance will help us to understand the nature of resistance specifically against Vichy, by looking at how resisters reacted to the two principal elements of polity in Vichy France: hegemony and collaboration.

Combating hegemony

Vichy's National Revolution was intended as an ideological programme of reform which underpinned the new regime and attempted to give it substance. It aimed to create the conditions for the national 'renewal' of French life following the traumatic defeat of 1940. Its policies revolved around three central tenets of the regime, *Travail, Famille, Patrie* (work, family, fatherland). To understand the Vichy regime, its internal workings and how it managed to govern with the consent – or perhaps the indifference – of the population, and to understand the difficulties faced, the concept of 'hegemony', as defined by the Italian anti-fascist thinker Antonio Gramsci, needs to be understood. Gramsci used this concept to explain a position of dominance by an elite not just from a political perspective, but also considering cultural, economic and social factors.[13] Vichy never created a single governing party in the way that other fascist and totalitarian regimes did. Instead, the regime rested entirely upon *le culte du maréchal*. This personality cult saw Pétain everywhere – street names, currency, stamps, busts, sports trophies, to name but a few.[14] Every morning at school, children had to sing the anthem '*Maréchal, nous voilà!*' Pétain appointed not just all ministers, and had the right to name his successor, but also all civil servants, who pledged allegiance to him. The regime had a degree of cultural hegemony that was almost unprecedented in living memory. *Le culte du maréchal* was the myth upon which Vichy built its political, social, cultural and moral legitimacy.[15]

One of the ways that Vichy could be resisted was by engaging in a critique of this personality cult. André Pican was a primary school teacher in Le Houlme, near Rouen, whose involvement with the French Communist party (PC) pre-dated the Occupation, and for whom Communist ideology represented the best critique of the state that France was in.[16] However, for Pican, it was an approach that addressed the everyday as much as the elevated. The roots of Pican's resistance were through what the French might term *éducation populaire*. He gave classes firstly at the Rue des Tranchées in Rouen (which according to Jean Basille, were ironically known as 'catechism classes'),[17] then in private homes in Sotteville.

Whereas many Communist-organized classes were about explaining the party line to a wider audience, Pican's were about political awareness more generally.[18] In his classes, he outlined the nature of Pétain's personality cult. If Vichy, and with it Nazism and Fascism, were to be defeated, then it would have to be done by firstly deconstructing, and then breaking, the cultural hegemony that it had established over the summer of 1940. Only then could the Communists begin to construct their vision of the future.[19] From then on, revolution could begin. It is telling that for Pican, the idea of Communist uprising was envisaged in the terms and language of 1789 – he made reference, for example, in his diaries to an 'assault upon the Bastilles [sic]'.[20] His diaries take a form that uncannily reflects his resistance – a passage from cultural critique to action. This action initially took the form of working to free Communist prisoners. As Pican wrote 'COMMUNISTS IN PRISON, FRANCE IN CHAINS!'[21] In Pican's eyes, the fate of France was irrevocably intertwined with the fate of Communism, because, for him, the Communist mode of production was the final destination, towards which progress would be made once the old regime had collapsed.[22] Pican saw the ideological anti-Communism of the authorities, and their supposed opposition to the 'people', as being to blame for the defeat of 1940 – in his eyes, the Third Republic, and subsequently Vichy too, was a regime of elites rather than the people. The first part of Pican's work analyses what took place in 1939–40, the second part looks at the present time (1941), and his conclusion envisages the day of the uprising.

Pican's account only had a limited audience contemporaneously, but this account is indicative of the teaching and inculcation within the underground Communist scene at this time, of Communist thinking about Vichy in a period whereby, in the wake of the Nazi-Soviet pact, their position collectively was severely compromised. Yet as is well known, not all Communists waited until the events of Barbarossa in June 1941 to start their resistance, including anti-Vichy propaganda. Valentin Feldman, a secondary teacher of philosophy who had been at one time the youngest *agrégé de philosophie* in France, along with another young teacher at Avremesnil near Dieppe called Marie-Thérèse Lefevre, started in November 1940 a resistance paper whose title evoked the Communist horizon, the movement towards: *L'Avenir Normand*.[23] Meaning 'The Norman Future', it strove to broaden the messages put across in Pican's political lessons, and offered an alternative commentary on the war and on current affairs, a perspective found neither in the Vichy-controlled press nor on the BBC French Service broadcasts of the time: a critique of both Vichy and the Nazis.[24] Even before Barbarossa, it was clear that these Communists were rejecting not only Nazism, but also Pétainism and Gaullism. To this extent, the combat against Vichy's cultural hegemony marks the origins of the relationship between the PC and resistance. Indeed, given the fact that as an organization, the PC did not enter into resistance until after Barbarossa, it is more accurate at this stage to talk about 'resistance by Communists' than 'the Communist Resistance'.

Not all challenges to Vichy and its hegemony in the clandestine press emanated from the Communists, however. In the autumn of 1940, a group of non-Communist students at Lycée Pierre Corneille in Rouen, amongst them a young trainee teacher, or *normalien*, called Georges Brutelle, began to meet to discuss the political situation, and how to construct some kind of critique of Vichy. They began to produce a newspaper called *Jaurès*, which appeared for the first time in February 1941.[25] The editorial line of *Jaurès* was not one that reflected the majority of French opinion in 1941. Those who contributed were almost exclusively *instituteurs* or training to join the teaching ranks.[26] In some ways, its outlook was quite parochial: much of its writing was dedicated to attacking not the German occupation, or even Nazism, but the Vichy regime and the National Revolution.[27] From the outset, the language of *Jaurès* was not only disrespectful, but violent, making disobliging references to Pétain's age, and pouring scorn on the social conservatism of the time.[28] The virulence of these attacks may well have shocked many readers who did not belong to the social circles in which many of these resisters moved however, and it is difficult not to conclude that much of the paper's content was a mixture of crude rhetoric, meant deliberately to shock and preaching to the already converted. This, along with a shortage of paper and money, meant that the paper never reached a wide audience, and folded in 1942, in part affected too by Brutelle taking up a teaching post and leaving 'Corneille'.

Undermining Vichy's hegemony also happened beyond print propaganda. In the small Norman village of Nesle-Hodeng, Roger Cressent was the teacher of the boys' classes at the village school, and was also *secrétaire de mairie*. He would go on to be one of the main organizers in the district of Gournay-en-Bray of the *Bureau des Opérations Aériennes* (BOA), a resistance network whose principal activity was the recuperation of Allied airmen. But in the early years of the war his acts of defiance were more firmly grounded in his everyday teaching practice; for example, he refused to enforce the *liste Otto*, which although emanating initially from the German embassy in Paris, was enlarged by Henri Filippachi, an editor working at Hachette,[29] and enforced in French schools by the *inspecteurs d'académie*. Such an offence could have led to his dismissal, but teaching in a remote village school where the only other teacher was his wife Madeleine meant that he was also far away from the prying eyes of the *rectorat*, or local education authority. He also refused to engage in many of the other activities that were encouraged by the authorities, such as obliging children to write thank-you letters to Pétain.[30]

The direct success of such challenges is debatable. Even in May 1944, when Pétain visited Rouen after the city had been heavily bombed, he was greeted by cheering crowds.[31] The popularity of Pétain and that of his regime are two separate questions, and it would appear that the former lasted longer. Yet what such resistance shows is that not everyone was accepting of *le culte du maréchal*, and that rejection of Pétain's personality cult was often the starting point for more significant and substantial resistance, as was the case for all of the resisters examined here,[32] and was therefore an important point in the individual trajectories of resisters as they passed from a stance of rejecting Vichy to a stance of actually resisting both it and Nazi occupation more generally – or, to use the terms of Albert Hirschman, the passing from 'exit' to 'voice'.[33]

There was also, at this time, a diversity and a lack of coordination in terms of 'resistance towards' – one of the issues that Brutelle encountered was the formulating of a concrete aim, beyond the slightly redundant idea of a 'new Popular Front', which was in any event a non-starter given his hostility towards the Communists.[34] So using Pickford's three criteria of resistance, we can see that much of the resistance against Vichy at this time was hindered by dint of the fact that goals were not always clear, the critique not always well-received and the forms of resistance limited. As such, the beginnings of resistance against Vichy were difficult, because finding a receptive audience, and formulating an effective message, were difficult for the resisters to achieve.

In 1942, the return of Pierre Laval and the marginalization of organizations such as the *Légion française des combattants*, which had been an important vector of Vichy's hegemony, marked what Jean-Marie Guillon has called 'the crisis of orthodox Pétainism'.[35] From this point on, the emphasis in Vichy's polity shifted from hegemony to collaboration.

Combating collaboration and the Vichy state

If the National Revolution was the ideological context to the early years of Vichy, then the *État français* – the French State – was its state apparatus. Designed to be a conscious break with the Republic, without actually promising a restoration either of Empire or the monarchy, it represented the body of law and order, and the functioning of the new French state. Now, it seemed, the discrediting of Vichy could only be achieved via actions that showed the regime's inability to govern rather than its unsuitability.

Everyday life was at the heart of this battle. One of the earliest examples came with the Miners' Strike in the Nord-Pas-de-Calais in 1941. The right to strike had, in theory, been guaranteed for French workers since 1864. It had been a wave of strikes that had brought the Popular Front's labour reforms to fruition in 1936. Yet a series of measures, beginning under Daladier's government in 1938, sought to repeal these measures, and what remained was clearly targeted by Vichy. This was the case in the mining areas of the Nord-Pas-de-Calais where the decline in working conditions and the collaboration of the mine-owners led to a large demonstration on 1 May 1941, in contradiction of an explicit interdiction emanating from the authorities. On 27 May, at the Dahomey pit in Montigny-en-Gohelle, an indefinite strike broke out, followed across the region until, by 4 June, almost 100,000 miners were on strike. The strikes were linked into the national struggle of the Resistance thanks to the propaganda of the local Communists, despite the still ambivalent attitude of the PC's national structure. But at their origin, the demands of the strikers targeted everyday working conditions, namely opposition to the reintroduction of streamlining measures, opposition to bullying by bosses and management, and better rationing, including the reintroduction of soap at the pit showers.[36] The strike was ruthlessly crushed by the Nazis, and on 4 October 1941, Vichy passed its new *Charte du Travail*, or labour agreement, which criminalized striking. Yet such industrial action, although not common, was not totally eliminated, and periodically occurred in reaction to perceived collaboration in the workplace.[37]

One of the most notorious areas of Vichy's collaboration was in its introduction of the *relève*, the (initially voluntary) call for French workers to go to Germany. With insufficient numbers signing up, it became a compulsory labour draft (the *Service de Travail Obligatoire* – STO). Contrary to one of the popularly-held myths of the Resistance, it did not spark a flood of recruits towards the Resistance, but resistance did help, both formally and informally, those who wished to avoid the draft from going. One case study in the Eure demonstrates the persistent chipping away of Vichy authority around the forced labour draft. René Gérard, a railwayman in Évreux, was officially designated as 'skilled' (he held a *Certificat d'Aptitude Professionnel* in mechanics) and his skills and domestic situation (young, in good health, of the age of majority and without children) drew him to the attention of the labour inspectors and the *Reichsbahn*.[38] In September 1942, he was requisitioned for work in Nazi Germany. The next day, he did not turn up for work, providing a medical certificate stating that he had bronchitis. He then requested a year's exemption, which the Vichy administration granted. This, however, did not satisfy the *Feldkommandantur* which sent him to see a doctor in Évreux, and from there, to the dispensary of the city infirmary. Both the doctor and the nun administering the dispensary could see that he was not truly suffering from a severe pulmonary condition, but provided a forged radiography, and a report stating a catalogue of bronchial and cardiac complaints, which sufficed for the *Feldkommandantur*. This was not only enough to ensure that he avoided being sent to Germany, but was also enough that he was sent home to his family in Conches-en-Ouches in the rural south-west of the Eure, no longer able to work for the SNCF.[39]

There, he found alternative employment as a lumberjack, which would have been the end of his difficulties, until a law of February 1943 further widened the eligibility for the STO to include unskilled workers. He received papers requisitioning his labour, and requesting that he be examined again. However, the doctor charged with examining him was Dr Mathieu, the family doctor who had initially provided him with a sick certificate for bronchitis, and so again, he avoided going to Germany. But in July 1943, his exemption was cancelled after a review, and the next day, along with 247 others, he was herded onto a train at Rouen, and sent to Paris. It was at Saint-Lazare station in Paris that he escaped:

> We were waiting to be escorted into the vans, and we were gathered in the courtyard. I saw someone I had worked with (I knew St-Lazare well from my time in the SNCF), and we got talking. In the confusion, I escaped, and ran up the hill to a barber's shop for a haircut. Then, I went back to the station, hid for a few hours, and then smuggled myself onto a train back to Normandy. When I got back to Conches, I went to see Monsieur Dagiral, the town pharmacist, who I had heard could help you if you wanted to flee.[40]

René Gérard found a farm nearby, where he worked on the harvest, but afterwards, worried about the risk of being denounced, fled to the department of Mayenne, where he spent the rest of the Occupation working as a farmhand, and working with the Resistance as an auxiliary railwayman in the summer of 1944.[41]

Considering that manpower is a crucial factor in any economy, it is easy to see how the STO was the most blatant example, along with the payment of occupation costs, of Vichy's economic collaboration with the Reich.[42] By facilitating forms of evasion and 'draft-dodging', resistance was operating at two levels. First, there were the individual acts of resistance which subverted the functioning of Vichy's state machinery. These collectively undermined the reputation of Vichy as a competent regime able to be a fully operating collaborative partner in Hitler's Europe, one of the aims of the more committed collaborationists at Vichy.[43] But there was also another form of resistance going on – that of a resistance economy, a 'black' economic system that served to not only undermine collaboration and facilitate refraction, but which also functioned entirely outside of Vichy's control; a system that served, and made possible, an entire clandestine society. This could be interpreted less as economic resistance, and more as the resistance economy.

A further example of this resistance economy was in the Limousin, where Georges Guingouin gained the nickname of *le préfet du maquis* (the Prefect of the *maquis*) for his blatant ignoring of official food prices imposed by Vichy, and his enforcement of *maquis* control. From 1943 onwards, shops in the area of the Haut-Limousin where Guingouin and his *maquisards* were most active had to sell at '*maquis*' prices; anyone caught selling at 'Vichy' prices had fines imposed upon them.[44] Meanwhile, farmers were ordered to ensure that their produce did not go to the occupier. Here we see the hidden economy of resistance functioning as a 'just' economy, along the lines of a 'moral' economy as envisaged by E. P. Thompson.[45] There was both the idea of a 'just' price, which undercut both the excessive official pricing of Vichy and the exorbitant pricing of the black market (black marketeers were also targeted by Guingouin's men), but also an economic system that was designed to serve a just cause: the fines levied helped fund *maquis* activity. At the same time, Guingouin's men received goods, shelter and assistance from many living in surrounding hamlets and farms, and *la Première Brigade*, as it was sometimes referred to, became a destination for those either fleeing the STO or those wanted for resistance activity by the French police.[46]

Guingouin's *maquis* showed that the *État français* could be undermined not just by targeting its policies of collaboration, but also by sabotaging its cultural showpieces. The Tour de la Haute-Vienne was a one-day cycle race starting and finishing in Limoges, which took in the hills that lie in the Haute-Vienne countryside. In 1944, the route had been supposed to take in the hills in the far south-east of the department, but continued *maquisard* activity meant that most of the climbs initially scheduled were left off the route, with the race instead only touching the fringes of the Forêt de Châteauneuf. This still did not prevent the race, held on 4 June, from being sabotaged. A group of *maquisards* blocked off the crossroads of the D12 and the D16 roads in the commune of Saint-Méard, bringing the race to a halt. All of the competitors, officials, and journalists following the race by car were escorted at gunpoint into a field, where one of Guingouin's lieutenants said to them 'the time is no longer for sport, but for the struggle for Liberation [. . .] you can fight with us, or you can return to Limoges in the *camion-balai*.'[47] It seems that no-one took the *maquisards* up on their offer, so the bikes and cars were confiscated in order to be used by resisters, whilst everyone was herded onto the wagon, where they arrived in Limoges a considerable time later. The reaction of the crowd gathered in Limoges, eagerly awaiting the finish was, needless to say, one of astonishment when the wagon arrived first, complete with cyclists, but without bicycles.[48]

The effect of this sabotage was two-fold. Ostensibly, it permitted the mass requisition of bicycles for use by resisters, in preparation for the forthcoming fight for liberation – D-Day had initially been scheduled for the following day, and eventually occurred two days later. But it also permitted a propaganda coup; namely that the rumours circulating in Limoges about the strength of the *maquis* in the countryside were not so ill-founded after all. It showed that if Vichy could not even organize a cycle race without incident, it had become a regime that come June 1944, although in office, was not in power.

The shift in emphasis from hegemony to collaboration not only made the necessity for resistance against Vichy more acute, but it also gave resisters a greater focus. The defeat of both Vichy and Nazism helped to define both 'resistance against' and 'resistance towards', and the targeting of institutions, systems and events at the heart of everyday life became the focus of 'resistance as' in the fight against Vichy. As a consequence of these three criteria of resistance becoming more clearly identifiable, resistance against Vichy was more effective, and achieved more. The regime was increasingly undermined, and became more and more ineffective – a contrast to the desired aim of collaboration.

Beyond the screen? Conclusion

The myth of *résistancialisme*, along with cultural vectors such as commemoration or the cinema, allowed for the emergence of what Freud termed a 'screen memory', or *souvenir-écran*, a recurrent memory that whilst not totally false, is usually far from accurate.[49] Yet beyond this lies the reality of resistance in the everyday. Not all resistance struck out against the grey uniforms of the Wehrmacht – it sometimes targeted fellow Frenchmen and French policies. Equally, armed struggle was only a part of the resistance experience; for many, there was no violence and no arms involved at all.

With Vichy's accession to power in the summer of 1940, the norms of democracy were suspended. Resistance against Vichy was the expression of dissent in this society, or *guerre-monde*. To this extent, resistance can be seen as political, but within the more heterogenous conceptualization of *le politique* – the political of the everyday, rather than the politics practised in the corridors of power.

Similarly, it is important to state that most resistance against Vichy was conceived and performed at a local level, and can only be discerned through the lens of 'history from below' and that of *Alltagsgeschichte*. Instead of being seen through the prism of organized, military resistance, thereby taking a 'top-down' approach, many acts can be seen as acts of resistance against Vichy rather than acts against Vichy by the Resistance. Resistance against the Nazi Occupation became increasingly organized as the war progressed, and by 1944, was mostly coordinated under the auspices of *comités départementaux de libération*, the *Conseil National de la Résistance*, and the *Forces Françaises de l'Intérieur*. In contrast, resistance against Vichy was usually conceived and enacted within the everyday, and therefore on a much smaller scale than resistance against the Nazis. As a consequence, examining resistance against Vichy also points towards the ways in which the regime was facilitated and put into practice at a local level – a history that, to a certain extent, remains to be written.[50] If Vichy functioned as a regime, then it was not just as a result of directives emanating from the hotels of that faded spa town; it was also a result of the willingness of those at a local level willing to advance either or both the cult of Pétain and the policy of collaboration, such as the school inspectors in Normandy, the mine managers in the Nord-Pas-de-Calais and civil servants in the Limousin.

This smaller scale may explain in part why resistance against Vichy has tended to be omitted from the 'screen memory'. As Sandrine Kott has argued, *Alltagsgeschichte*, and the everyday more generally, is firmly anchored at the scale of the local, and cannot really be practised on a macroscale.[51] This creates a greater capacity for it to be overlooked in an era where the 'screen memory' was forged on a national scale, influenced by powerful cultural vectors as well as the state (and state-funded historical research, such as the case of the *Comité d'Histoire de la Seconde Guerre mondiale*), and designed, in the shape of *résistancialisme*, to serve an explicitly national narrative.[52]

So can we define resistance against Vichy using the criteria suggested by Henry Pickford – that is 'resistance against', 'resistance towards' and 'resistance as'? The 'resistance against' is indicated by the title of this chapter, but more fully, it was resistance against a regime that established a pervasive hegemony and pursued a policy of collaboration, both of which oppressed and repressed everyday freedoms. The everyday was the front line for Vichy's war of hegemony and conquest in French society, and that was where resistance had to be grounded. The 'resistance towards' took several different forms, from the dream of *le grand soir* in Pican's writings to the preservation of individual freedom for René Gérard; yet ultimately, it focused on the immediate aim of defeating the *État français*, and re-establishing the Republic. Which leads us to the 'resistance as': again, a variety of forms, but all of them intended to support both the 'resistance against' and the 'resistance towards'. As such, this resistance should be considered as political, if not necessarily politicized or belonging to any one party. If *le politique*, as Peillon suggested, is the search for the common good, then we can interpret anti-Vichy resistance as political action within the everyday in an undemocratic society.

The 'screen memory' of wartime France is one of violence and drama, a mixture of the shameful defeat of 1940 and the dramatic liberation of 1944, and everything those events drew on or engendered. Likewise, the 'screen memory' of the Resistance is also one of violence and drama in its growing war against the Nazis. We can see that both of these memories are not fully accurate, and perhaps even guilty of generating 'alternative facts'. Beyond the screen memory of defeat and liberation, of violence and drama, lies the everyday, where the realities of wartime society were most often forged. And likewise, beyond the image of *résistancialiste* combat against the Wehrmacht lies resistance against Vichy, in which the actions of individuals and small, localized groups are more discernible. Just as Alf Lüdtke and his colleagues made use of the everyday to reveal deeper complexities about how the *Volksgenossen* was formed, so a study of resistance against Vichy in the everyday reveals a picture of resistance which goes beyond the screen formed in, and by, memory.

Notes

1 P. Copeau, *La Libération de la France, actes du colloque international tenu à Paris du 28 au 31 octobre 1974* (Paris: CNRS, 1976), pp. 951–2.

2 H. R. Kedward, *Resistance in Vichy France* (Oxford: Oxford University Press, 1978); H.R. Kedward, *In Search of the Maquis* (Oxford: Clarendon Press, 1993); F. Gallot, *En Découdre* (Paris: La Découverte, 2015); J. C. Scott, *Weapons of the Weak* (New York: Oxford University Press, 1985).

3 O. Wieviorka and J. Tebinka, 'Resisters: from everyday life to counter-state', in R. Gildea, O. Wieviorka and A. Waring (eds), *Surviving Hitler and Mussolini: Daily Life in Occupied Europe* (London: Bloomsbury, 2006), p. 155.

4 A. Muller, *La Seconde Guerre de Trente Ans* (Paris: Édition Universelle, 1947). For a more detailed look at the historiography of resistance in France, see L. Douzou, *La Résistance française – une histoire périlleuse* (Paris: Seuil, 2005).
5 A. Lüdtke, 'What is the History of Everyday Life and who are its practitioners?', 3–41, in A. Lüdtke (ed.), *The History of Everyday Life* (Princeton: Princeton University Press, 1995; transl. W. Templer), pp. 4–5.
6 Lüdtke, 'What is the History of Everyday Life ...?', p. 28.
7 R. Rémond, 'Du politique' in R. Rémond (ed.), *Pour une histoire politique* (Paris: Seuil, 2nd edn, 1996), pp. 385–7.
8 V. Peillon, *Éloge du politique* (Paris: Seuil, 2011).
9 G. Guingouin, *Quatre ans de lutte sur le sol Limousin* (Paris: Hachette, 1974); Y. Pérotin, *La vie inimitable* (Grenoble: Presses universitaires de Grenoble, 2014).
10 A. Aglan and R. Frank (eds), *La Guerre-monde* (Paris: Gallimard, 2015).
11 H. Pickford, 'Conceptualizing resistance', workshop at the Centre of Resistance Studies, University of Sussex, 18 November 2015.
12 R. Koselleck, *Vergangene Zukunft: Zur Semantik geschichtlicher Zeiten* (Frankfurt-am-Main: Suhrkamp, 1995), pp. 349–75.
13 A. Gramsci, *Prison Notebooks*, J. A. Buttigieg (ed. and transl.) (New York: Columbia University Press, 1992), pp. 233–8.
14 G. Miller, *Les Pousse-au-jouir du maréchal Pétain* (Paris: Seuil, 1975).
15 D. Rossignol, *Histoire de la Propagande en France de 1940 à 1944* (Paris: Presses universitaires de France, 1991).
16 Private archive: interview with Germaine Pican by Thierry Lamiraud, 1984. The PC changed its name to the PCF (Parti communiste français) in 1943.
17 Archives départementales de Seine-Maritime (ADSM), AV09/165: interview with Jean Basille (1983).
18 ADSM: interview with Jean Basille.
19 Interview with Germaine Pican. See also 'Journal d'André Pican' in J.-C. Vimont (ed.) *TRAMES* (no. 8, 2000), pp. 169–96.
20 'Journal d'André Pican', p. 195.
21 'Journal d'André Pican', p. 195.
22 'Journal d'André Pican', pp. 191–6.
23 ADSM, AV09/102: interview with Marie-Thérèse Fainstein (née Lefevre) (1982).
24 ADSM, AV09/107/220: interview with Yvonne Dissoubray (1982).
25 G. Touroude, *Les Braconniers de l'espérance* (Royan: Éditions de la Langrotte, 1995), pp. 48–9.
26 Letter from Georges Brutelle to Claude-Paul Couture, 3 August 1987. Cited in Couture, *Les Écrits de la Presse Clandestine en Seine-Inférieure et leurs emprunts à la Révolution française* (Luneray: Bertout, 1986), p. 11.
27 Couture, *Écrits de la Presse Clandestine*, p. 11.

28 Couture, *Écrits de la Presse Clandestine*, p. 14.
29 S. Corcy, *La Vie culturelle sous l'Occupation* (Paris: Perrin, 2005).
30 ADSM, AV09/100: interview with Roger Cressent (1983).
31 R. O. Paxton, *Vichy France: Old Guard and New Order* (New York: Columbia University Press, 2nd edn, 2001), p. 326.
32 See M. Norton, 'Resistance in Upper Normandy, 1940–44' (unpublished PhD thesis, Edge Hill University, 2017).
33 A. O. Hirschman, *Exit, Voice and Loyalty* (Cambridge, MA: Harvard University Press, 1970).
34 Private archive: interview with Georges Brutelle by Thierry Lamiraud (1984).
35 J.-M. Guillon, 'La philosophie politique de la Révolution nationale', in J.-P. Azéma and F. Bédarida (eds), *Vichy et les Français* (Paris: Fayard, 1992), p. 178.
36 Y. Le Maner, 'Les grèves dans le bassin du Nord-Pas-de-Calais, 1941', in F. Marcot et al. (eds), *Dictionnaire historique de la Résistance* (Paris: Robert Laffont, 2006), pp. 603–5.
37 An example of this is found in Rebecca Shtasel's analysis 'The Bréguet factory in Le Havre: a site of trade unionism from the Popular Front to the Liberation', in O. Feiertag (ed.), *Histoire et Mémoire de la Résistance en Seine-Inférieure* (Rouen: Presses universitaires de Rouen et du Havre, 2017).
38 Interview with René Gérard by Clément Met, 16 December 2002. Cited in C. Met, 'Le Service du Travail Obligatoire dans l'Eure' (unpublished mémoire de maitrise, Université de Rouen, 2003), p. 107.
39 Met, 'Le Service du Travail Obligatoire', p.107.
40 Interview with René Gérard.
41 Interview with René Gérard.
42 For more on the policy of occupation costs, see M. Boldorf and J. Scherner, 'France's Occupation Costs and the War in the East: the contribution to the German war economy, 1940–44', *Journal of Contemporary History*, 4.2 (2012), 291–316.
43 See P. Ory, *Les Collaborateurs* (Paris: Seuil, 1976).
44 F. Grenard, *Une Légende du Maquis: Georges Guingouin, du mythe à l'histoire* (Paris: Vendémiaire, 2014), pp. 191–2.
45 E. P. Thompson, 'The moral economy of the English crowd in the eighteenth century', *Past & Present*, 50 (1971), 76–136.
46 Guingouin, *Quatres ans de lutte*; '*Femmes résistantes*', brochure by Comité de l'Association Nationale des Anciens Combattants et Résistants (ANACR), Châteauneuf-la-Forêt (2010); *Première Brigade* (dir. François Perlier, 2006).
47 Quoted in Grenard, *Une Légende du Maquis*, p. 223. The *camion-balai* refers to the 'brush wagon' used to collect cyclists who have fallen too far out of contention, and who are no longer eligible to compete in the race.
48 Grenard, *Une Legende du Maquis*, pp. 223–4.

49 S. Freud, 'Sur les souvenirs-écrans', in S. Freud, *Nevrose, Psychose et Perversion* (Paris: Presses universitaires de France, 1973), 113–32.

50 See, for example, C. Malon 'Derrière l'écran: collaborations, vichyisme et confiscation de l'humanitaire', in J. Barzman and C. Malon (eds), *Les Enjeux des bombardements du Havre: résultats et nouvelles pistes* (Le Havre, Presses universitaires de Rouen et du Havre, 2016). Malon talks about the need to write about the local history of collaboration, and more precisely, the idea of 'Vichy-sur-Seine' in order to understand how Vichy worked at a local level beyond the machinery of the state based in the town of Vichy.

51 S. Kott, 'Alltagsgeschichte', in C. Delacroix et al. (eds), *Historiographies, I: Concepts et débats* (Paris: Gallimard, 2010), pp. 25–31.

52 For an examination of the vectors that have formed this 'screen memory', see H. Rousso, *Le Syndrome du Vichy* (Paris: Seuil, 2nd edn, 1990) and for the Resistance more specifically, Douzou, *La Résistance française*.

12

Vichy Cinema and the Everyday

Steve Wharton

During the Occupation, French cinemagoers had the chance to view Christian-Jaque's film *La Symphonie fantastique*, produced by the German-owned but apparently French company Continental Film, and telling the story of Berlioz and his work. Premiering at the Normandie *Soldatenkino* – a cinema reserved for German soldiers – on the Champs-Elysées on 2 April 1942, it was hailed as 'the first film of France's cinematic renaissance'. Such patriotic feature film fervour did not, however, please Goebbels, who reminded Continental's boss Alfred Greven that it was the purpose of the company to produce films which were 'simple, entertaining but anodyne' – bland entertainment rather than a call to cinematographic or other arms.[1]

But was Vichy cinema so really bland, so banal, so *quotidien*? Over 200 feature films and 550 documentaries were produced between 1940 and 1944, and the percentage of French filmic material in programmes rose from roughly 45 per cent in 1939 to 85 per cent in 1944. Cinema was certainly an everyday practice in 1940s France: following the Armistice, overall numbers of cinemagoers rose from 255.6 million in 1940 (a drop from 1939's figure of 373.3 million, though understandable with cinema closures as France entered the war and due to the disruption of exodus and the events of May 1940) to 281.5 million in 1942 and 304.5 million in 1943.[2] In terms of the simple definition, then, such prolific figures in terms of both production and attendance demonstrate the everyday presence of film. By the same token they also meet the other interpretation of the everyday: the way in which people adopt and adapt their daily practice such that innovation and change become natural and taken for granted. The public's input to the everyday practice of cinemagoing was adopted and adapted by Vichy to provide opportunities to render its policies everyday through the regular projection of documentaries which subtly underscored the *Travail, Famille, Patrie* (work, family, fatherland) motto of the État Français. Perceived as a truthful and didactic medium by the public, documentary film could be harnessed to the contextual benefit of the regime, as production structures and subsidy were refashioned to provide a suitable framework within which this could be achieved. What was this framework, and what were the everyday messages the regime sought to communicate through these forms? These are the questions I seek to answer here, with an accent on documentary film and newsreel, staples of the daily film programme of the period.

Key to this refashioning of cinema's poor relation – documentary – were the structures within which cinema (was) operated. The aftermath of war offered a cinematographic *tabula rasa* which was quickly seized upon by the Vichy authorities, setting about the establishment of new administrative frameworks for the propagation of new policy in the area of film. In terms of the general physical infrastructure in which films were shown, very many cinemas had been damaged in the battle for France in 1940, having had to close both for reasons of public safety and indeed for lack of materials (electricity to light and run, number of films available).[3] Force of circumstance meant that any slow return to 'normal' post-Armistice, would require some changes.

The publication on 24 October 1940 of the 'Law on the Regulation of the Cinema Industry' was the first step towards such change, abolishing the double bill and preventing cinemas from screening more than one film of a length greater than 1,300 metres at any one showing.[4] The main intention of this new legislation was to give the French industry a breathing space to get production on its feet again. An earlier move banning American films (perceived by the regime as ideologically suspect) from screening in France meant that a large amount of material previously available for cinema programmes was lost. The debilitated French industry could not fill the gap, so the removal of the need for two feature films per screening halved the deficiency to be made good. Documentary and newsreel accompanied the main feature within a new regular format for cinema programmes: documentary, newsreel, and main feature.

Such direct interventions in the industry were a departure from the *laissez-faire* attitude of governments which was prevalent before 1940, even though the Popular Front government of 1936 had commissioned a report on the film industry but had never implemented any of its recommendations. Yet it was the author of that report, Guy de Carmoy, who was to become the first Director of the Organising Committee for the Cinema Industry (COIC) established on 2 November 1940, with a budget of 66.5 million francs. No time was therefore lost in ensuring that cinema too was treated as an industry rather than an art form; the impulsion for this was not necessarily simply a product of the Vichy regime, as surviving documents indicate that 'The particular interest in the film industry shown by the German Authorities requires that [the body established to run it] is able to operate as soon as possible'.[5] We know from David Welch's *Propaganda and German Cinema 1933–1945* that Germany's interest in film and its production in the promotion of policy had been clear since the rise of the Nazis to power. Within a French context this German inspiration was a recurrent interest and indeed trope; for example, industry publication *Le Film* saw another decision, the withdrawal from projection of films produced before 1937 announced in May 1941, as evidence of 'the extreme interest that the Organising Committee and the German Authorities currently have in cultural film'.[6]

Another legislative move was May 1941's 'Law in Relation to Financial Advances to the Film Industry'. Based on pre-existing industrial subsidy legislation, the law allowed film producers to raise loans from the national loans body the *Crédit national* at an interest rate of 5 per cent within an overall ceiling of 50,000,000 francs.[7] The sum borrowed was to be repaid within three years of the loan being taken out, and was not to represent more than 65 per cent of the cost of the proposed film (in practice, up-front funding for half of the production costs was expected before any application, and an undertaking that the producer cover excess expenditure). Seventy-five per cent of box office receipts went to the producer with the balance to the *Crédit national*, thereby ensuring steady repayment of the loan. This arrangement for the financial security of the film industry was the latest in a series of moves made soon after the establishment of COIC to increase the documentary's chances of commercial success. Regarded as a 'filler' or *film de complément* making up the programme – often scheduled first on the programme in pre-war screenings so that latecomers missed nothing 'important' – documentary had an additional advantage for its producer and backer in that it could be made with cheaper fast film stock and required fewer or no professional actors. Studios were rarely needed as filming took place 'on the spot', with dubbing, editing and the addition of a soundtrack being the only technical requirements. So it was that documentary flourished under Vichy, providing a steady flow of films on subjects as varied as apiculture, boxing and yachting.

This flourishing enabled documentaries to become a staple part of the everyday cinemagoing experience for the French, though further means other than the simple obligation of the inclusion of a documentary in the box office mix were also used. One man in particular, André Robert, worked tirelessly to promote the genre between 1941 and 1944, his efforts culminating in a government-sponsored First Documentary Film Congress or *Premier congrès du film documentaire* in April 1943. I shall return to him later.

Newsreel

Before that, however, having looked briefly at the structural framework within which the film industry operated I turn now to newsreel, a vital element of the restructured cinema programme. Cinemas used the newsreel as a staple within their programmes, providing a weekly digest of key events[8]. Before the war there had been three French newsreels – *Pathé-Journal, France-Actualités-Gaumont* and *Éclair-Journal* – produced by three separate companies. With France divided and occupied, the rules of the game clearly had to change, and at first the Germans allowed only the screening of their newsreel *Actualités mondiales*, made by the company Deutsche Wochenschau and shown in the Occupied Zone. In September 1940 the Germans proposed the extension of this across France through the creation of a news organization which would have a majority German shareholding. Naturally, the Vichy government was opposed to the suggestion, countering with a proposal for its own company in the unoccupied zone with French majority shareholding, effectively replicating in cinemas the political situation on the ground: a nation divided into two parts, each with its own modus operandi. Such a situation was clearly undesirable to both occupier and occupied, since national propaganda through two potentially competing newsreels – or at least, two newsreels which did not always operate the same selection criteria – could be problematic, as we can see from the following memorandum of a conversation held on 17 February 1941 between the man in charge of the Deutsche Wochenschau [Teitz] and COIC's Guy de Carmoy:

> The German and French Governments, each recognising the influence which the News can have on public opinion, have come to the conclusion that it is necessary to end the current state of affairs and to establish a single newsreel which can be shown in both Zones. In a spirit of collaboration, the German government wishes to support the French government in the establishment of a single National News [Service] which will in turn serve as an efficient means of bringing people together. [...] The French government wishes to make known to all Frenchmen and women, be they [in France] or in the Colonies, a sense of its actions and achievements. It wishes its newsreel to show its character to the world, thereby making it truly attractive as well as efficient on all fronts.[9]

Discussions continued, and in September 1941 the Cinema Service – the part of the Ministry of Propaganda charged with oversight of the industry – noted that:

> The protocol envisages that the French newsreel will make sufficient room for German newsreel items as well as from those countries under German influence.

> It leaves to the German Government the selection and provision of the international elements to be inserted, whilst imposing no obligation to do so. However, the [new] Company has the complete freedom to choose what is to be filmed in France with the natural proviso that such filming be not troubling to the German government. *It is self-evident that as long as the Occupation is in force the Company will not enjoy freedom owing to the presence of German troops* [my emphasis], but no obligation may be placed on it in respect of the editing of the news.[10]

Despite this last sentence, the Germans expressed a certain 'displeasure [...] at Vichy's attitude which does not really use the items offered as part of the agreed exchange save for anodyne and sporting subjects.'[11] So entertaining, certainly; but anodyne (to quote Goebbels earlier) in terms of German propaganda impact.

The new company – which had 60 per cent French and 40 per cent German ownership – was known as France-Actualités-Pathé-Gaumont, the name itself bringing together those of predecessor organizations. And so the Vichy regime continued with its aim of taking the past and applying it to the present to forge the future, even in nomenclature. And we shall see later how this symbiosis enabled newsreel to be harnessed to serve documentary promotion.

All of this demonstrates clearly that newsreel was seen by the government and its agents as a means of engagement with, and influence over, the people. This perception was the motivation for collaborative moves over newsreel, and legislation for the compulsory screening of a documentary with each feature film was further supported by government subsidies to the private sector in order to increase documentary output. Statistics show clearly how the documentary branch of the industry gradually became more able to fend for itself,[12] whilst the feature film required ever more money.

André Robert and documentary

However, as suggested above, documentary achieved a presence in the cinemagoing everyday through more than its inclusion on the cinema bill: specific, tailored screenings of documentary programmes designed to change the perception of audiences shown high-quality products also played their part. The Vichy government and the German authorities were fortunate that a cinema journalist with an interest in documentary, André Robert, provided them with a foil for promotional activities. Born in 1912 and abandoning his law degree to concentrate on cinema journalism, Robert set up and promoted special screenings of documentaries in the Cinéma des Champs-Elysées (at 118 avenue des Champs-Elysées, next door to the Normandie *Soldatenkino*). From 1942 to 1944, thirteen programmes dedicated exclusively to documentary were arranged by him under the title 'Arts, Sciences, Voyages', melding French and German films together into programmes which were both complementary in their content and quality whilst also providing a subtle underscoring of the *Travail, Famille, Patrie* motto of the Vichy regime. In addition, the programmes provided a concrete demonstration of how Franco-German collaboration in matters filmic could bear fruit, offering the opportunity for the French to transpose their understanding of the benefits of collaboration observed in their cinematic everyday, to the wider sphere. André Robert's organizational skills were not limited to the screenings themselves: many of these programmes were preceded by press previews at venues which suggest a certain proximity to the machinery of government and to occupier. Be it through arranging with the Occupying Authorities for a press tour of Rouen prior to a programme containing the film *Rouen, naissance d'une cité* in August 1941, to a banquet hosting Geneviève Chaumel-Gentil – the first woman to be decorated with the Légion d'Honneur by Pétain – prior to an 'Arts, Sciences, Voyages' series featuring her film *Sortilèges exotiques* in November 1942, André Robert showed that he was an able promoter of the genre whilst also providing a clear example of the benefits of working with the regime.

This collaboration was to the fore when he organized April 1943's First Documentary Film Congress or *Premier congrès du film documentaire* which took place in Paris with the support and participation of key Vichy and German players. The Congress, held under the auspices of the Ministry of Information, the General Directorate for Cinema and the Ministry of Education with the support of the COIC and also showcasing the latest 'Arts, Sciences, Voyages' programme, marked official recognition of the status of documentary. For the first time in its history, the work of documentary producers in France was openly celebrated, and rewarded with the Grand Prix for documentary decided by a jury whose honorary president was none other than Louis Lumière, pioneer of cinema.

The scheduled daily events of the Congress were detailed in a 114-page brochure in which, after a series of introductions by Abel Bonnard (Minister of Education), Louis-Émile Galey (Director of the Cinema Service) and André Robert himself, the reader is given details of 'Arts, Sciences, Voyages' programmes to date, a timetable of the events of the Congress, and a breakdown of the Jury for the Grand Prix to be awarded for the first time at the end of the fortnight's events. As Robert's work clearly provides a subtle promotion of Franco-German collaboration as everyday in matters filmic, two articles from the brochure are of particular interest. Leni Riefenstahl, director of the film reports on the 1936 Berlin Olympics made expressly for the Nazis and whose work was also to feature in the screenings of the Congress, contributed an article entitled 'Sur la raison d'être et la conception du documentaire' ('On the purpose and conception of documentary'). In it she explained the motivation behind the making of a documentary: to put across an 'ideal, be it the FAITH of a party meeting or the themes of struggle and victory in films as in the Olympics'. In another article, on German documentary, Karl Melzer, the General Secretary of the German International Film Chamber, argued for this ideal and faith to be channelled in a particular way:

> Film becomes a powerful vehicle for educative ideas [. . .] In all German cinema programmes, Documentary and the News [form] a solid base for the education and edification of the people.

The occupied French authorities were therefore taking what had become everyday for the Germans – an educative newsreel and documentary film programming used to support the regime – and transposing the concept to the French context in order to render it everyday for their own people. Indeed, closer inspection of the events of the Congress and its films can show us how this influential education (or educational influence) might work within a framework of Franco-German collaboration so much part of the everyday in Occupied France. A ceremony held in the *Conservatoire national des arts et métiers* on 5 April 1943 presided over by André Debrié of COIC's Management Committee – responsible for the elaboration and implementation of policy – opened the proceedings, and after his speech guests toured the Conservatoire's collection of old cinema equipment: an example of the familiar Vichy trope of the lessons of the past applied to the present to forge the future. The present-day Congress thus became the latest event of a long historic tradition. Just as the French have become accustomed to the cinema and cinemagoing in their everyday lives, the argument ran, they should assimilate the subtle message of the everyday nature of the regime and its policies as depicted in the films they see. The key point of Debrié's speech makes the government's intentions with regard to its support of cinema quite clear:

> You know what an amazing power the Cinema represents as an instrument of national and internal propaganda, as a means of dissemination. More than all other arts, more than other means of expression of human thought, it reaches the masses, all the people.[13]

With its mention of 'all the people' Debrié's speech also makes clear the view of those in authority in France that film – through its wide-ranging power and potential influence – should be used as a (motivational) rallying point, its everyday presence providing a dual act of normalization and realization of its propaganda role. Just as the Congress began with an evocation of the historical presence of film, the first day of the programme proper, held on 7 April, was devoted to a retrospective of works officially dubbed 'masterpieces of documentary film'[14] as if to anchor this sense of legacy in the minds of the public. Alongside French classics and more recent high-quality documentaries, UFA's *Rayons X* – 'magnificent film'[15] – figured here just as it had launched the 'Arts, Sciences, Voyages' series in 1941, then as now deployed in the interests of underscoring Franco-German collaborative duopoly. Sponsored by the Ministry of Education, the screening's events were presided over by Minister Abel Bonnard himself, thereby lending the official government cachet to proceedings. Reprising their presence in this initial Congress programme event, a specific screening of German-language films was arranged for 13 April in the Le Français cinema, and was prefaced with a speech from Kaufman, head of UFA's scientific film section and responsible for German cultural films. He reminded the audience that documentary offerings had to differ from those of feature film programmes:

> He insisted on the fact that documentary needs to be both instructive and recreational as it is aimed at a public which is used to *going to the cinema for entertainment* [my emphasis] and would be repelled by films coming across as too pedagogical.[16]

So we see the Congress and its events emphasizing both the educational and historical role of documentary, and its everyday nature ('used to going to the cinema for entertainment'). And with the historical framing of documentary thus established in the immediate present, attention turned to the future, and children. An event for Parisian children was arranged for 15 April, at which Vichy's healthy youngsters present in the cinema were contrasted with the German model of *mens sana in corpore sano* thanks to Nazism, courtesy of two films by Leni Riefenstahl, cinematographer of the Reich quoted earlier. *Le Saut* (1937), from her film of the 1936 Olympics, showed Aryan youths performing gymnastically, and their prowess passed from air to water with *Comme un poisson dans l'eau* (1937). Cinemagoers were able to observe how history had been called upon to illustrate both the presence of cinema as part of everyday life, and the ways in which policies aimed at making German youth more healthy had borne fruit. The Parisian children invited to the event had seen their healthy

German counterparts on screen. The inference that these *jeunes parisiens* could not but benefit from Vichy policies in health and fitness which were aimed at them is clear, just as we have seen parallels of the benefits of learning from German innovation and collaboration in the field of film elsewhere.

The Evening of the Filmed Press or *Soirée de la presse filmée* at the Palais de Chaillot on 15 April, courtesy of France-Actualités-Pathé-Gaumont, brought together newsreel and documentary. Opening with a compilation of news items from 1905 to 1909 – yet again underscoring the idea of tradition – the event came right up to date with France-Actualités-Pathé-Gaumont's documentary *La machine à écrire l'histoire* telling the history of newsreel (present also in the concurrent thirteenth 'Arts, Sciences, Voyages' screening), and that day's newsreel itself. Such a programming of the films provided for the direct implication of the audience in the process they had just seen in action – they became involved in the newsreel-making process by watching it on film, and then saw the finished product immediately afterwards. In the interests of balance there was also a screening of the Deutsche Wochenschau, a selection which, according to *Le Film*, 'made quite a splash and was applauded for a long time'.[17] No other event of the Congress is reported on from the point of view of audience reaction, and such a comment in the trade press therefore takes on a particular significance, especially since, as the organ of COIC, *Le Film* was the indirect mouthpiece of the government. Since the Congress provided, in its concentration of the best of French documentary, a symbol of French success, there was thus a slim but potential danger of its serving as a means of increasing the potential for nationalism of a kind that could be turned against the occupying forces (as we have observed in the opening remarks about *La Symphonie fantastique*). As such, it had to be diluted; so we could see these reports of applause a means of toning down any implicit anti-German feelings by stressing the Germans' popularity at what was an otherwise French event.

Le Grand Prix du film documentaire français

The culmination of this fortnight's display of 'everyday'[18] documentary, duopoly, tradition and programming came on 20 April with the award ceremony for the *Grand Prix du film documentaire français*, itself presented at the end of a Gala Evening at the Palais de Chaillot the following day, 21 April (with a catering bill of 65,605 francs).[19] This government-funded prize was the first to be given in the documentary field, awarded by a special jury of thirty-two men representing all branches of the industry and government. Before this announcement and the prize-giving, the General Directorate for Cinema screened a series of films. Opening with *Images et pensées du Maréchal* (1942) – despite the total occupation of the country, the myth of Pétain as mainstay of society had to be maintained – the first half of the programme then passed to films from each of the foreign countries (including Germany, Italy and Romania) whose outputs had been on display during the fortnight. After the interval, André Robert presented the five Grand Prix winners to the audience before showing the films that won the joint first prize: Louis Cuny's *Hommage à Georges Bizet*, and Georges Rouquier's *Le Tonnelier*, which had featured in the tenth and eleventh 'Arts, Sciences, Voyages' screenings respectively. This screening of prize-winning films provided a fitting climax to the events of the *Congrès*, and the following day, Galey declared it closed at a simple ceremony in the Mairie de Paris, followed that evening by a Gala Concert at the Palais de Chaillot. Whereas the arts were clearly intended to be seen as the inspiration for the fortnight's activities – underlined by the use of such venues as the Conservatoire and the Archives nationales in the opening days as well as the closing concert – the shift towards the political use of the documentary and indeed the politicization of the medium was apparent as the *Congrès* progressed. Use of the Mairie de Paris betrayed a wish for the nominal seat of local government to be perceived as representative of the role of the administrator, the central driving force behind the administration and implementation of policy. The Hôtel de Ville thus arguably became a local manifestation of the authority of Pétain himself, described in the *Brochure* for the Congress as 'The Thought we serve'.

Conclusion

What, then, have we learned about the service of Thought and its manifestation in the everyday in cinema – and particularly documentary and newsreel – under Vichy? As well as the specific reworking of cinema programmes and direct collaboration in newsreel production, we have observed how documentary was reorganized under Vichy to ensure its financial stability, with the resultant films deployable to help underscore the tenets of the new regime. Such deployment aided the rendering of those themes as much a part of the everyday as documentary film was an everyday part of film screenings. As film historian Jean-Pierre Berthin-Maghit puts it:

> Documentary is judged by the Vichy regime [to be] one of the most powerful means of exercising a certain influence on the public [. . .] As part of the National

> Revolution, [its discourse] aimed to create the structures of a new society and to denounce those responsible for the collapse [of society that saw France defeated in 1940].[20]

In terms of that influence, Henry Rousso is also clear that:

> We need not see the absence of *direct* links between the regime on the one part and social practices on the other to conclude definitively that it did not have a profound effect. Any such effect was stronger in people's minds than in public bodies or institutions, especially since, in certain cases, it was precisely in sync with the mindsets of a part of French society – whether it was in the minority or no, is another question.[21]

And it is precisely this idea of being 'in sync with the mindsets of a part of French society' that is at the nub of our engagement here with the role of film (and in particular documentary) in Vichy's everyday – both the day-to-day lives of the population, and the regime's intention to control and run the state. In terms of a contestational framework for the reading of events (rather than the simple blank canvas on which things were written), therefore, documentary under Vichy was an ideal tool, clearly belying its simple interpretation as a truthful and didactic medium through the selection and commentary of its scenarii and setting (of subject and projection) and showing us the screening of reality in the everyday: screening not only in terms of the projection of the films themselves, but also in the way that those very projections and programmes, to an extent, obscured the reality of the everyday from the cinemagoing public through offering or inviting their alternative, regime-friendly, interpretations.

Notes

1 Diary entry for 13 May 1942, cited in R. Régent, *Cinéma de France* (Paris: Editions Bellefaye, 1948), p. 168.

2 Centre national de la cinématographie, 'Fréquentation des salles' (available online at http://www.cnc.fr/c/document_library/get_file?uuid=083ec13f–8f23–4c2d-af55-c524788683f2&groupId=18).

3 Interestingly, electricity continued to be a problem in 1942, when Reidinger of the Cinema Service (*Service du cinéma*) wrote on 15 December to the German authorities: 'The Secretary of State respectfully points out once more to the High German Authorities the serious difficulties which the programme of electricity restriction is bringing to the French film industry. It takes the liberty of once more drawing to the

attention of the German Authorities the great importance the French Government places on film at the current time *as it represents the only means of entertaining the masses* as well as remaining a propaganda tool of inestimable importance' [my emphasis] (Archives Nationales de France [AN], F/42 123: Note de service).

4 Most cinemas had tended to follow the A movie/B movie feature film screening format before the war.

5 AN, F/41 21: 'Note on the establishment of preparations for the Professional Cinema Organisation', 18 December 1940.

6 *Le Film*, 'Le film documentaire va enfin avoir sa place dans les programmes cinématographiques', 21 June 1942, p. 33.

7 P. Léglise, *L'Histoire de la politique du cinéma français* (Brive: Filméditions, 1977), p. 55.

8 For another discussion of newsreel in France in this period, see, for example B. Bowles, 'German newsreel propaganda in France, 1940–1944', *The Historical Journal of Film, Radio, and Television*, 24.1 (2004), 45–67.

9 AN, F/42 118: Note de service (anonymous), March 1941.

10 AN, F/42 118: Summary of discussions (anonymous), 26 September 1941.

11 AN, F/42 118: Summary of discussions (anonymous), 26 September 1941.

12 Of the 8,124,820 francs paid in documentary subsidy between 1941 and 1944, 3,426,911 (some 42 per cent) had been repaid by 1944 compared to respective figures of 53,800,000 and 5,492,687 (some 10 per cent) for feature film in the same period (calculated by the author from data located in AN, F/41 369).

13 *Le Film*, 17 April 1943, p. 5.

14 *Le Film*, 17 April 1943, p. 5.

15 *Le Film*, 17 April 1943, p. 5. Interestingly, this German contribution, on the development of X-rays and their application, was the only film to be commented upon in terms of its quality throughout the reporting of the Congress. UFA was Universum Film Aktiengesellschaft, the German film production and promotion organization.

16 *Le Film*, 8 May 1943, p. 5.

17 *Le Film*, 8 May 1943, p. 5.

18 Both in terms of the day-to-day presence of documentary in cinema programmes, and the assimilation of cinemagoing into the lives of the French, before and during Occupation.

19 AN, F/42 124: bill dated 25 May 1943.

20 J.-P. Bertin-Maghit, 'Le cinéma et les actualités filmées' in L. Gervereau and D. Peschanski (eds), *La propagande sous Vichy* (Paris: BDIC, 1990), 195–204, p. 200.

21 H. Rousso, 'L'impact du régime sur la société: ses dimensions et ses limites', in J.-P. Azéma. and F. Bédarida (eds), *Vichy et les Français* (Paris: Fayard, 1992), 573–660, p. 590.

13

Defining Everyday Frenchness under Vichy

David Lees

In the summer of 1942, just as the infamous Relève work scheme was launched by the Vichy authorities,[1] cinema audiences across France were shown a documentary film dedicated to the theme of food. Jean Masson's *Nourrir la France* was a cinematic feast for the eyes.[2] Combining a focus on hard work in the countryside with the very real fruits of the labour of men and women in an unknown rural French setting, the film's message was clear: work hard, be rewarded and take note that France continues to eat well and prosper.

The moral of *Nourrir la France* was one taken up in many of the 550 documentary films commissioned, sanctioned, funded and produced by the cinema section of the Vichy propaganda ministry, the Secrétariat Général à l'Information (SGI), during the four years of Occupation.[3] Scenes of hard work were nearly always complemented by subsequent scenes of reward of one kind or another.[4] Food was frequently used by directors as a way of enticing the audience into joining in the collective work effort.

Yet the images of agricultural abundance in *Nourrir la France* were far from the lived realities of everyday life in wartime France. For some, of course, living in rural areas assured a continued supply of food. For others, especially though not exclusively urban-dwellers, rationing was strict, supplies limited and trips to black market providers common. As Sylvère Aït Amour's chapter in this volume emphasizes and all others attest, there was no standard experience of everyday life in this period, yet food has featured as a common thread across the preceding chapters. From playground games and teachers' canteen innovations, to the charitable aid provided by the Secours National and the American Quakers, to anxieties over malnourished urban children's health which prompted evacuation schemes; from the importance of social networks to provide for a family's needs, to the interactions around food between colonial prisoners of war and French civilians, to the rural *maquis*'s implementation of localized rationing systems, and French women turning to prostitution at times in desperation over scarce resources: everyday life in wartime France revolved around food.

Despite the changes that war and Occupation brought, Vichy's cinema authorities consistently produced, developed and encouraged documentary film which set out a vision of the everyday that appeared to suggest that life from before the war continued as normal. There are few, if any, references in Vichy documentary film to aspects of the Second World War that have since come to define it in the Western European context, such as rationing, the exclusion of minorities, violence and trauma, many of which are clear in the research in these chapters, as well as in recent historiography.[5] Instead, cinema-goers in first the 'Free' Zone and North Africa, and then the entire nation after the German 'invasion' of the south in November 1942, were presented with an image of everyday life in documentary film which grappled neither with the macro-experiences of wartime, like rationing or bombing, nor with the micro-experiences on localized levels.

This chapter uses the representation of food in Masson's *Nourrir la France* as an example of the way in which documentary film defined an everyday Frenchness which consistently refused to acknowledge realities. For Vichy's propagandists, it was vital to project an image of continuity and stability under Marshal Pétain, which was not only at odds with lived experience, but which differed from other forms of contemporary French propaganda. I argue that the consistent ignoring of shortages, privations and discomfort in Vichy documentary films can be explained in two ways: first, there was a pre-established expectation that documentary film would provide escapism and interest, not a confrontation with reality; and second, the traditional function of documentary film as primarily educational, which developed during the Third Republic, became skewed by the demands of supporting and propagating the values of the new regime. Divided into three sections, the chapter first traces the development of documentary film and propaganda before and during the Vichy years. It then moves on to discuss how other media treated the subject of food in wartime France, before analysing in more detail Masson's *Nourrir la France* and its highly selective and far from representative portrayal of food. In its refusal to acknowledge many of the difficulties faced by its audience, documentary film trod a fine line between the persuasiveness which such comforting scenes might offer, and potential rejection because of their sheer unrepresentativeness. The definition of everyday Frenchness which Vichy documentary films proposed was one which eschewed both the chaos and much of the mundanity of everyday life, as examined across the preceding chapters.[6]

Documentary film and propaganda

The development of documentary film in France before and during the Occupation provides vital clues to understanding why Vichy's documentary films so frequently presented such a narrow view of daily life when other media acknowledged difficulties or hardships, often with the intention of increasing national solidarity. This development was a gradual process which began under the Third Republic and culminated in the eventual self-sufficiency of the documentary film industry under the Vichy regime. Such was the commercial success of these films that by 1944 'seed' funding from the state was no longer necessary to enable films to get off the ground.[7] Yet while the vast majority of documentary film produced, sanctioned, funded or otherwise agreed by the cinema section of the SGI were financially successful, even in the early years of Occupation, it should not be forgotten that they were tied to a wider screening programme which included the weekly newsreel and the feature film: the main draw for the viewing public.[8] Thus their financial success depended as much on the quality of the feature as the interest in the accompanying documentary. However, the final years of the Vichy regime marked what could be called a glorious period for documentary film, both in terms of output and financial success.

How, then, did the genre become so prolific and how did this shape the context for Masson's selective portrayal of food in his 1942 work? Largely neglected as a medium in comparison to feature film, documentary and its makers were left much to their own devices until the intervention of the Popular Front government of 1936, when the writer and academic Guy de Carmoy produced a damning report on the state of documentary in France; this led to the state funding a special school to encourage an increase in quality filmmaking.[9] The process of making documentary film was thus professionalized, but the understanding remained that documentary was essentially an educational medium designed to communicate facts. This vision accorded with that of pioneering British documentary filmmaker John Grierson, who styled the genre as one in the service of reality:

> This contact with reality lies, as we know, in using the medium, with every disciplined effort possible, as intensively and imaginatively as possible, and on as wide a scale as possible, in both aiding the public enlightenment and, through the great images of creative action of which our medium is capable, firing the public will.[10]

Steve Wharton has likewise demonstrated in this book and elsewhere that from its origins in the 1920s, documentary film in France was widely perceived to be 'educational' and 'informative', perceptions which were not altered by de Carmoy's professionalization of the medium.[11]

By the outbreak of the Second World War in 1939, the way that the public received documentary film had not changed. Yet what Édouard Daladier's government did begin to change was the purpose of documentary: though the viewing public may not have perceived that the films they were watching were any different in approach, in reality documentary was increasingly politicized. What had been a tool for education was becoming a tool for propaganda. Not only did documentary come under heavy government scrutiny, notably by the first Minister for Information, Jean Giraudoux, but many of its themes shifted to political activities, such as the Munich Agreements of 1938 and then, as France went to war, to military preparations.[12] The increasing influence of the Service cinématographique de l'armée on cinema production during the Phoney War was such that documentaries followed the pre-war newsreel series in documenting the war effort, though of the two genres it was newsreel that remained the more overtly political.[13] There was thus a tangible shift in the production and focus, if not the reception, of documentary film under Daladier, his successor Paul Reynaud, and beyond that into the Vichy years.

To that end, documentary moved away from the educational and the focus on reality, as defined by Grierson in his influential writings, and towards the task of influencing the thoughts and actions of its audience with a view to changing or increasing the standing of the propagandists (the documentary makers) and their 'masters' (the Daladier and Reynaud governments). Indeed, by the time the Vichy regime created its own Ministry for Propaganda, initially controlled directly by Prime Minister Pierre Laval with some delegation to Jean-Louis Tixier-Vignancour,[14] documentary film in France reflected the definition of propaganda advanced by Garth Jowett and Victoria O'Donnell: 'Propaganda is the deliberate, systematic attempt to shape perceptions, manipulate cognitions, and direct behaviour to achieve a response that furthers the desired intent of the propagandist.'[15] Vichy's documentary had cast aside the tenets of 'truth' and 'fact' associated with the genre today (shaped in many ways by Grierson's work), and now sought to distort realities in order to reflect well upon successive governments: 'firing the public will' was now skewed to obtaining consent for the leaders of France.

The important difference between documentary under the Third Republic and under Vichy is the level of acknowledgement of wartime realities in France and the Empire. Whereas documentary and newsreel were initially key tools in the battle to raise morale and boost the French war effort, after the 1940 defeat the realities of wartime were systematically ignored. Although shots of troops manning the Maginot Line before June 1940 were selective, they did nonetheless depict reality; but Vichy's documentaries were cleansed of any mention of the war, as if the Fall of France had never happened. The consistent message was of continuity with French life before war broke out, and a total ignoring of the brief period when France had been fighting. The shift from an educational to a more propagandist medium occurred therefore in stages which ran alongside current events: from initial attempts to mobilize public opinion first behind the Munich Agreements, then behind the war effort, and finally behind the policies and values of Marshal Pétain's new regime.

This is crucial to understanding how films like *Nourrir la France* were made, how they were received and, above all, why they showed a very selective image of everyday life. Unlike Nazi Germany, France did not have a well-oiled propaganda machine.[16] The Third Republic's attempts to develop a propaganda ministry were arduous and, in comparison to Great Britain's own comparatively young Ministry of Information, which could draw on the General Post Office film unit, France lagged behind at the outbreak of war.[17] Thus the politicization of French cinema was not instantaneous, and the government was hindered by the existence of several competing newsreels over which to assert its influence. After July 1940, the best filmmakers, who arguably would have made the most professional documentaries, were not available to the Vichy authorities, who thus had to rely on the personnel they had to hand in the 'Free' Zone south of the demarcation line. In some cases these were experienced men and women, such as Philippe Este, the director of the pre-war Pathé newsreel and subsequent director of France-Actualités Pathé-Gaumont (FAPG), the first Vichy newsreel.[18] In others, however, documentaries were produced by relative newcomers, like Jean Masson, with little filmmaking experience.

In fact, there was a clear distinction between the more professional wings of the SGI, such as its dedicated radio and poster producers, and the altogether more cottage-industry approach of documentary makers. Like Jean Giraudoux under Daladier, Tixier-Vignancour's training was not in filmmaking and the pressure fell above all on the French newsreel makers of FAPG to compete with German newsreel, and not on documentary makers.[19] Guy de Carmoy, the interzone liaison officer for cinema, was sympathetic to documentary producers, and this combined with Tixier-Vignancour's relative inexperience to accord a far greater autonomy to documentary makers than to other propagandists. The records of the Vichy authorities concerning documentary film demonstrate that they were frequently more concerned with finances and with avoiding overlap between documentaries than with content.[20] Although the SGI did censor documentaries, in many ways the censorship came with the approval of funding or the permission to film in the first place. As such, requests to produce documentaries flooded into the offices of the Direction du Cinéma, often with wide-ranging and largely informative topics.[21] While clearly documentary film was now subjected to greater scrutiny than in previous years, and funding and approval normally granted only for films which reflected the aims and values of the Vichy regime, there was also a sense that documentary makers wished to continue as they had before and were often granted the freedom to do so: making educational and informative films. There was, therefore, a tension between the propagandist structures of documentary making under Vichy and the desire to make informative film on the part of filmmakers. *Nourrir la France* illustrates the compromise: documentaries did show aspects of real life, but did so in a circumscribed way which avoided many aspects of reality. Arguably, they thus reflected Joseph Goebbels's conviction that the best propaganda conveyed *some* factual truth, but not all.[22]

Experiences of food in everyday life

By the time *Nourrir la France* was released across the 'Free' Zone and North Africa in the summer of 1942, much had changed since the establishment of the Vichy regime in 1940. Pétain had promised to bring stability, but two years later food supplies were short, rationing was tighter and it was clear that the war was not going to end any time soon. Indeed, cinema audiences had a number of considerable concerns by 1942; but of all their preoccupations, the greatest was food.[23] Prefectoral reports for 1942 betray the hunger experienced by so much of the French population. In June 1942, the 'Free' Zone summary noted that:

> Rationing remains at the top of everyday concerns [...]. The criticisms made with regard to those responsible for rationing remain at the same level. Rationing continues to play a preponderant role in the mind of the public, and is indeed the source of legitimate worries. The coming winter is awaited with apprehension and many are worried about problems if a particularly strong effort is not made to improve the supply of food for urban areas compared with last year.[24]

Such sentiments were not new and far from unique to June 1942, but they demonstrate real anxieties among the population. As this book has made clear, there is no standard French experience of war, but hunger was a major concern, and particularly for those in urban areas. Jean Guéhenno, resident in Paris during the war, wrote in his diary on 14 February 1942 that 'if I haven't written anything for a while it's because I'm hungry'.[25] Food is a common theme in other wartime diaries, such as that of student Madeleine Blaess: in December 1942 she lamented the absence of eggs and milk with which to make crêpes.[26] Yet as Kay Chadwick has pointed out, Paris was at least able to draw on its relatively self-sufficient agricultural hinterlands, even if supplies were frequently disrupted and transport difficult.[27] In the largely rural 'Free' Zone, big cities like Toulouse and Marseille, where *Nourrir la France* is believed to have been distributed initially, suffered disproportionately. In Toulouse, Marseille, Clermont-Ferrand and Montpellier, children weighed on average seven kilograms less in 1942 than they had in 1938.[28] Rationing allowances had decreased considerably in the same year: in the A (Adult) category, rations were reduced to just 275 grams of bread and 21.9 grams of meat per day, amongst equally meagre allowances of dairy products.[29]

But the contrast between city and country was not always clear-cut, and charitable intervention helped. For example, in Marseille, as Shannon Fogg has shown in this volume, some needy children were fortunate to be helped by the American Friends Service Committee. In other parts of the 'Free' Zone, including *départements* with polycultural farming, the population as a whole ate better than those living in more monocultural *départements*. This was the case, for example, with the Dordogne, whose inhabitants managed, by and large, to eat reasonably well without too much difficulty,[30] or the Creuse which Lindsey Dodd has shown managed to feed itself and a substantial number of refugees. However, in the wine-producing Hérault, a surplus of vineyards meant the availability of good, though expensive, *Appellation d'Origine Contrôlée* (AOC) wine, the only type approved by the Vichy authorities, but not a plentiful supply of food whether in Montpellier or the surrounding countryside.[31] And while Jean Guéhenno and Madeleine Blaess spoke of hunger, others, like Jean Galtier-Bossière noted in 1941 that whole chickens could be bought for 200 francs if one knew where to look.[32] The black market meant that food could generally be found, though at a sizeable cost. The price of milk on the black market in Marseille had increased by 110 per cent between the declaration of war in 1939 and the end of 1940.[33] Jean Dutourd's literary classic *Au Bon Beurre* captures the scheming profit-driven plans of the Poissonnard family who thrive during the Occupation: in one notable scene the Poissanards capitalize on a gluttonous Pétainist who cannot resist buying illicit butter – 'Were they not, after all, shopkeepers, whose occupation was selling things, even on the black market'.[34] Thus while inequalities existed across both zones, food remained a serious concern.

Nourrir la France and the selective definition of the everyday

None of these geographical disparities, nor the near-starvation experienced in some major cities across France, nor indeed the existence of the black market, is mentioned in *Nourrir la France*. Yet these realities were not only acknowledged, they were tackled head-on in other forms of propaganda. Radio Vichy frequently noted the difficulties faced by people across the country when it came to food and by 1942 the radio station was broadcasting speeches and programmes denouncing the black market, using the topic to attack the Allies and the Free French. Philippe Henriot's frequent broadcasts in 1942 and thereafter,[35] sought, in Chadwick's terms, 'to alienate the inhabitants of metropolitan France from the Free French in London'.[36] Both Pétain and Laval gave radio broadcasts condemning the black market and urging farmers to ensure that any surplus was handed over to the rationing authorities.[37] The French Service of the BBC also sought to recognize the hardships of the French people and to encourage solidarity between farmers and townspeople in order to better the situation, while consistently pointing to collaboration as the source of this inequality.[38] Meanwhile, recipe suggestions for cooking without previously essential ingredients were printed in magazines newspapers such as *Rustica, La Revue horticole* and *La Depêche du Centre*, as well as household management guides like Hachette's *Almanach*, which opened this book.[39] The poster branch of the SGI denounced the black market and the damage it was causing to food supplies; one 1943 poster famously depicted two caricature criminals exchanging a baguette behind one another's backs while staring ahead at a noose; the caption read 'black market, crime against the community'.[40]

The poster and radio branches of the SGI were willing to engage with the general concerns around food supply and rationing, seeking to use this theme as a way of rallying the population not only around Pétain but against the Allies. The importance of these real, everyday considerations about feeding the family and the inconsistencies between town and country and from one *département* to another were not lost on the Vichy authorities, and it was very clear from the broadcasts of the regime's leadership that they recognized, or at least claimed to recognize, that many people were suffering extreme hardship.

The SGI's cinema branch, and its documentary makers, however, took a different line. Although very little is known about the distribution of *Nourrir la France* – it is noted in the Archives Nationales that a fire in the post-war period destroyed certain evidence[41] – it is very likely that the documentary followed a similar distribution pattern to its contemporaries in 1942, being sent first to the larger cities in the 'Free' Zone and then to more rural locations, before finally ending up in urban centres in North Africa, particularly Algeria.[42] The first audiences for Masson's film, then, would have been urban-dwellers in cities like Marseille (generally the first on the list for distribution), Toulouse, Clermont-Ferrand and Lyon: in short, those cities where children were notably underweight. Food shortages were part of the fabric of everyday life in these places, but Masson's film does little to acknowledge this.

The film opens with a lingering shot over an empty farmhouse, as if to note that the French countryside has been depopulated. Although there is no explicit acknowledgement in the film of the absence of 1.8 million prisoners of war, of whom 36 per cent were farmers or farm labourers, there is at least a sense that the countryside is not quite as populated as it ought to be.[43] As the camera cuts to the interior of the farmhouse and zooms in on the window frame, the narrator announces that 'through the open window let us consider the surrounding areas. The farm is abandoned'. This opening sequence, however, jars with what comes after: it appears to give the message that there is no-one to do the farming anymore. To some extent this is a reflection of traditional documentary film in that it seeks to convey 'reality' and to take into account farmers' concerns about their workforce, as noted in Prefects' reports across the summer of 1942.[44] Of course, this could be viewed as an attempt to encourage urban populations to return to the land, in exchange for financial incentives – a central policy of the National Revolution in its early days, though by 1942 largely defunct.[45] But this opening sequence seems at odds with the real message of the film, which is that there is in fact a vibrant rural workforce who can happily provide food for France. The contrast between the ruined, empty farmhouse and the scenes of subsequent agricultural labour and plentiful supply is an odd one and seems rather contrived. Nevertheless, in the following scene, the camera cuts to a field where middle-aged male farmers undertake various agricultural tasks like ploughing and grape-picking, developing the sense that this food is in plentiful supply and that these mundane, if essential, agricultural tasks continue as normal. In the next sequence, this continuity of rural life is developed with shots of a variety of produce, again emphasizing the capacity of French farmers to produce a range of goods under Pétain's watchful eye. In the subsequent scene, a farmer is pictured scything the field by hand, demonstrating the regime's continued protection of rural traditions, and the importance of the land. The narrator affirms that 'the land is always there, always in its place'. There is, again, no suggestion that anything is out of the ordinary, with farmers continuing to work the land and to produce food for the nation. In the final scene, Masson emphasizes the continuity of the gentle rhythms and beauty of rural life, as a shot of a field appears on screen, with thriving crops blowing in the wind. To accompany this final, reassuring image of French traditions protected by Vichy, Masson establishes a direct link between the Marshal and this vision of an eternal France, tangible in the continuities of rural life: the narrator concludes the film with a reference to Pétain's 25 June 1940 speech, assuring the audience that 'we learnt a long time ago that the land does not lie'.[46]

As a whole, then, the film promotes an image of life in the countryside which continues more or less as 'normal'. There are no references to wartime, no mentions of rationing and no suggestion of Occupation. While the film contains something of the educational in its opening allusions to rural depopulation, harking back to the genre before it became politicized, and shows a selective reality – that of the labourers producing foods through traditional methods – its message is mixed. The later scenes of abundant agricultural produce echo those of other Vichy documentaries, such as the 1941 film *Jeunes de France*, in which young men from the Chantiers de la Jeunesse are shown being rewarded for their labour by indulging in a plentiful feast. Yet the film reflects little of the real hardships across the nation as a whole.

Conclusion: the fiction of documentary in wartime France

Nourrir la France was by no means the only film to follow this pattern; many others presented a highly selective version of reality: contemporary films such as *Travail* avoided any mention of war, preferring instead to focus on financial and material reward for traditionalized images of hard work. While these films touched on the values of the Vichy regime of work and the family, they only ever made vague reference to actual policies, such as the subsidies for 'returning to the land', and ignored any mention of the framework around those policies, such as collaboration. In many ways, this is the key to understanding this trend of selective reality in documentary making: such films take into account *some* of the experiences of *some* people; *Nourrir la France* depicts the reality of *some* rural people.

At the same time, Masson and his colleagues, along with their immediate supervisors at the Direction du Cinéma of the SGI, were arguably reflecting the audience's understanding of documentary and indeed of the cinema. Much of the discussion in the SGI's remaining papers revolves around the need to make, in the words of Henri Clerc, the director of the joint Franco-German newsreel France-Actualités, a 'real' film.[47] Clerc was joined in this thinking by Tixier-Vignancour, who wrote of the need for 'cinema propaganda which need not be too aggressive',[48] Guy de Carmoy, who recorded that 'propaganda [ought to be] carefully dosed, sagely-presented',[49] and Louis-Émile Galey, Tixier's successor, who thought of 'cinema [as the] reflection of wider French mindset'.[50] What little we know about Masson's motivations, based on the scant remaining archival evidence, would suggest that he, too, was inclined to make documentaries which touched on topics somewhat removed from most people's experiences. Given subsequent concerns over financial irregularity in the production of *Nourrir la France*, Masson also, like some of his contemporaries, appeared to be happy to make whatever film he could get commissioned, provided he was well paid. Masson is by no means alone in this regard: many of his contemporaries were quick to pitch documentary films which followed the same trend as *Nourrir la France*, focussing in some cases on aspects of Vichy ideology, but rarely with an attempt to promote concrete policies. In some cases filmmakers wanted simply to make entirely apolitical films.

Millions of people flocked to the cinema during the Occupation not only because it was a relatively inexpensive place to spend time (and warm in the winter) but because of the lure of escapism.[51] Having only recently and gradually become politicized, documentary film was not tainted by the same overtly political nature of newsreel. As a result, audiences appear to have viewed these films as part of the wider package of the feature film: a chance to learn something new while also escaping from the hardships of the everyday. This would justify why the very hardships audiences were seeking to avoid were not represented directly on screen. Kay Chadwick notes that 'many people saw only too well the inconsistency between the dismal reality of their daily lives and propaganda films such as *Nourrir la France*'.[52]

Yet this would suggest that audiences reacted negatively to this film and indeed to other documentaries. The very fact that so little has been recorded about audience reception of this material, in sharp contrast to the very negative responses that greeted the German-produced newsreel Actualités-Mondiales, and subsequently France-Actualités, suggests that audience reactions to documentary were not noteworthy, or at least not sufficiently negative to warrant recording. It is clear that radio and poster propaganda, in acknowledging food shortages and seeking to attack those responsible for increasing inequality (though notably not the Germans), made a real attempt to follow Goebbels's maxim around basing the best propaganda in truth. For the makers of poster and radio propaganda, especially Philippe Henriot, it was important to tackle hardships and realities directly in order to increase the standing of the Vichy regime and raise public opinion against its enemies. It could be that such material was effective, as it appeared to take people's everyday concerns seriously, and demonstrate that the regime was on the side of ordinary people.

By ignoring food shortages, and even flaunting abundance, *Nourrir la France*, could seem to do just the opposite. But its appeal was arguably more rooted in the context of the cinema, and of escapism; it belonged to a world already removed from the everyday. The relative autonomy granted to documentary filmmakers meant that they could ape the style and tone of the feature films, and in many ways to present highly fictionalized films which documented aspects of everyday life that reflected well on the Vichy regime. This was a fine line to walk, and indeed Chadwick's argument that *Nourrir la France* had the potential to alienate audiences is valid. Yet while the representation of France put forward in *Nourrir la France* ignored certain realities, it engaged with others – in this case, the hard labour and successful work of farmers – and thus carried the recognition of those parts of the population. By ignoring all the hardships that the Second World War brought to France, documentaries could develop a notion of continuity that, far from being divisive, could reassure audiences of normality, as Steve Wharton has argued in the previous chapter. Rather than holding up a mirror to the genuine lived experiences of French people across the entire nation, Vichy documentary film pushed the boundaries of the genre; although these films depicted a kind of everyday Frenchness rooted in reality, albeit selectively, these films were, in essence, works of fiction.

Notes

1 The Relève was Pierre Laval's attempt to head off the requisitioning of French labour for the German war effort; it called upon skilled workers to volunteer for work in Germany, and in return for every three who went, one French prisoner of war would be released. See, for example, H. Rousso, 'L'écomomie: pénurie et modernisation,' in J.-P. Azéma and F. Bédarida (eds), *La France des années noires 1* (Paris: Seuil, 2000), p. 470; and R. O. Paxton, *Vichy France: Old Guard and New Order* (New York:

Columbia University Press, 2001), pp. 281–2. On the impact of the Relève inside families, see L. Dodd, '"Mon petit papa chéri": children, fathers and family separation in Vichy France', *Essays in French Literature and Culture*, 54 (2017), 97–116.

2 *Nourrir la France* (dir. J. Masson, 1942), available for viewing in the Centre National de la Cinématographie (CNC) or at the CNC collections in the Bibliothèque Nationale de France (BNF).

3 This figure is used here to apply specifically to Vichy-backed films and not those produced or commissioned by the German propaganda authorities and their studios at Continental Films.

4 This is the case, most notably for some high-profile documentary films such as *Jeunes de France* (dir. P. Este, 1941), *Méditerrannée/Niger* (dir. unknown, 1941), *Travail* (dir. J. Morel, 1942), *Chefs de demain* (dir. R. Clément, 1943), amongst others. All films can be viewed at the CNC. Further examples are explored in D. Lees, 'Vichy on film: the portrayal in documentary propaganda of life under Occupation, 1940–1944' (unpublished PhD thesis, University of Warwick, 2014).

5 Pertinent recent examples, beyond the chapters in this book, include C. Moorehead, *Village of Secrets: Defying the Nazis in Vichy France* (New York: HarperCollins, 2014); D. Lee, *Pétain's Jewish Children: French Jewish Youth and the Vichy Regime, 1940–1944* (Oxford: Oxford University Press, 2014); L. Broch, *Ordinary Workers, Vichy and the Holocaust: French Railwaymen and the Second World War* (Cambridge: Cambridge University Press, 2016); L. Dodd, *French Children under the Allied Bombs, 1940–45: An Oral History* (Manchester: Manchester University Press, 2016).

6 *Nourrir la France* is the subject of just one line of analysis in the existing work on Vichy documentary film, whereas existing studies of Vichy propaganda film more broadly have not compared other forms of propaganda. For the very brief mention of *Nourrir la France* in academic work on documentary see J.-P. Bertin-Maghit, *Les Documenteurs des années noires* (Paris: Nouveau Monde Éditions, 2004) p. 196. On documentary and newsreel film under Vichy more broadly, see J.-P. Bertin-Maghit, 'Encadrer et contrôler le documentaire de propagande sous l'Occupation', *Vingtième siècle*, 63 (1999), 23–49; J. Gili, 'Les journaux d'actualités cinématographiques de 39 à 44', *Cahiers de la Cinémathèque*, 8 (1973); S. Wharton, *Screening Reality: French Documentary Film during the German Occupation* (Bern: Peter Lang, 2006); B. Bowles, 'Accommodating Vichy: the politics of Marcel Pagnol's *La Fille du puisatier*', *Historical Reflections*, 35.2 (2009), 84–107; B. Bowles, '*La Tragédie de Mers-el-Kébir* and the politics of filmed news in France, 1940–1944', *Journal of Modern History*, 76.2 (2004), 347–88; B. Bowles, 'The attempted nazification of French cinema, 1934–1944', in R. Vande Winkel and D. Welch (eds), *Cinema and the Swastika: The International Expansion of Third Reich Cinema* (London: Palgrave Macmillan, 2011), 130–45; B. Bowles, 'Newsreels, ideology and public opinion under Vichy: the case of *La France en Marche*', in *French Historical Studies*, 27.2 (2004), 419–63.

7 Wharton, *Screening Reality*, p. 206.

8 Bowles, 'Newsreels, ideology and public opinion', p. 422.

9 Wharton, *Screening Reality*, p. 30.

10 J. Grierson, 'Documentary: the bright example', in J. Grierson, *Grierson on Documentary* (London: Faber and Faber, 1973) p. 191.

11 Wharton, *Screening Reality*, p. 24.

12 Wharton, *Screening Reality*, p. 30; Bowles, '"*La Tragédie de Mers-el-Kébir*"', p. 351.

13 Bowles, 'Newsreels, ideology and public opinion', p. 431.

14 Bowles, '"*La Tragédie de Mers-el-Kébir*"', p. 351; D. Rossignol, *Histoire de la propagande en France de 1940 à 1944* (Paris: Presses universitaires de France, 1991), pp. 12–25; P. Amaury, *Les Deux Premières Expériences d'un 'Ministère de l'Information' en France* (Paris: Librairie Générale de Droit et de Jurisprudence, 1969).

15 G. Jowett and V. O'Donnell, *Propaganda and Persuasion* (London: Sage Publications Ltd, 2015; 6th edn), p. 7.

16 On the subject of cinema propaganda in Nazi Germany see for example I. Garden, *The Third Reich's Celluloid War: Propaganda in Nazi Feature Films, Documentaries and Television* (Stroud: The History Press, 2012); and R. Vande Winkel and D. Welch (eds), *Cinema and the Swastika*.

17 S. Anthony and J. G. Mansell (eds), *The Projection of Britain: A History of the GPO Film Unit* (London: Palgrave Macmillan, 2011).

18 Much of the details around FAPG can be found in the Archives Nationales de France (AN), F/42 series. See for example AN, F/42 119: Memorandum on 'Journal France-Actualités-Pathé,' 18 Oct.1940; AN, F/42 118: 'Note concernant "*FAPG*"', 16 May 1941.

19 This was reflected in the involvement of Pierre Laval in demanding a quick turnaround in production of the weekly newsreel. See AN, F/42 119: Memorandum on 'Journal France-Actualités-Pathé,' 18 October 1940. Vichy authorities likewise funded FAPG to the sum of 15 million francs between October 1940 and December 1941 and expected results. See AN, F/42 119: 'Ventilation du bilan à fin juin 1941–en 1940 et 1941. Comptes d'exploitation', 30 June 1941 and AN, F/42 119: '*France-Actualités Pathé-Gaumont*, Marseille: Compte d'exploitation au 31 décembre 1941', 31 December 1941.

20 See the copious correspondence surrounding the finances of *Nourrir la France* and the absence of any documentation around the commissioning or production of the film. See AN F/41 92: 'Rapport de M. Thuillier, Expert-Comptable à Monsieur l'Inspecteur des Finances, Directeur de l'Administration Générale,' 8 May 1943.

21 See, for example, the discussion around commissioning a film on the *Eaux du Rhône*, specifically AN, F/41 365: contract between the SGI and the *Artisans d'art et du cinéma*, 31 October 1941.

22 N. Cull, D. Holbrook and D. Welch, *Propaganda and Mass Persuasion: A Historical Encyclopedia, 1500 to the Present* (Santa Barbara: ABC Clio, 2003), pp. 39–40.

23 See the *synthèse* of the Prefect reports for the 'Free' Zone, June 1942: Institut d'Histoire et du Temps Présent (IHTP), Centre national de la recherche scientifique (CNRS), Paris: 'Synthèse des rapports de Préfets: zone libre', June 1942.
24 'Synthèse des rapports de Préfets: zone libre', June 1942.
25 J. Guéhenno, *Journal des années noires* (Paris: Gallimard, 2002), p. 239.
26 M. Blaess, University of Sheffield Library Special Collections, MS296, Unpublished war diaries, 11 December 1942.
27 K. Chadwick, 'An appetite for argument: radio propaganda and food in occupied France', *French History*, 31.1 (2017), 85–106, p. 89.
28 E. Alary, B. Vergez-Chaignon, G. Gauvain, *Les Français au quotidien, 1939–1949* (Paris: Perrin, 2006), p. 161.
29 Alary, Vergez-Chaignon, Gauvain, *Les Français au quotidien*, p. 207.
30 Alary, Vergez-Chaignon, Gauvain, *Les Français au quotidien*, p. 186.
31 Concerns over the cost of AOC wine were raised in the *synthèse* of the Prefect reports for June 1942 (IHTP/CNRS: 'Synthèse des rapports de Préfets: zone libre', June 1942); on the banning of *vin de table* in favour of AOC wines see E. Alary, B. Vergez-Chaignon, G. Gauvain, *Les Français au quotidien*, p. 159; on the Hérault see Chadwick, 'An appetite for argument', p. 89.
32 J. Galtier-Boissière, *Mon journal pendant l'Occupation* (Paris: Libretto, 2016), p. 79.
33 Alary, Vergez-Chaignon, Gauvain, *Les Français au quotidien*, p. 222.
34 J. Dutourd, *Au Bon Beurre* (Paris: Gallimard, 1952), p. 239.
35 Henriot became Minister of Propaganda in January 1944
36 Chadwick, 'An appetite for argument', p. 99.
37 P. Pétain, 'Discours du 29 mars 1942', in *Discours aux Français* (Paris: Albin Michel, 1949), pp. 243–4; Bibliothèque Nationale de France, 8-LB58-62: P. Laval, 'Message aux Français prononcé le 20 avril 1942' (Paris, 1942). On this point see Chadwick, 'An appetite for argument,' p. 97.
38 Chadwick, 'An appetite for argument', p. 98.
39 Alary, Vergez-Chaignon, Gauvain, *Les Français au quotidien*, p. 192.
40 Archives départementales de la Savoie (ADS), 06-01MNA: A. Fournier, 'Marché noir: crime contre la communauté', 1943.
41 AN, F/42 1-37: J. Mady, 'Introduction aux fonds "Information"'.
42 This was the case, for example, with films such as *Travail* and *Fidélité* (dir. Y. Naintré, 1941). See AN, F/41 92: Note from E. Lagneau at Pathé to L.-E. Galey, then head of the Direction du Cinéma, 18 June 1943.
43 See R. Vinen, *The Unfree French: Life under the Occupation* (London: Penguin, 2007), p. 209.
44 IHTP/CNRS: 'Synthèse des rapports de Préfets: zone libre' for July and August 1942
45 On the failure of Vichy's 'back to the land' policies, see Paxton, *Vichy France*, p. 208.

46 P. Pétain, 'Appel du 25 juin 1940', in Pétain, *Discours aux Français*, p. 66.

47 AN, F/42 119: Correspondence between Clerc and Galey, 6 March 1943.

48 AN, F/41 368: 'Note sur les actualités cinématographiques', 3 August 1940.

49 AN, F/42 133: Memorandum on cinema propaganda (undated, but before February 1941).

50 *Ciné-Mondial*, 5, 14 November 1941

51 See, for example, O. Barrot and R. Chirat, *La Vie culturelle dans la France occupée* (Paris: Gallimard, 2009), p. 88.

52 Chadwick, 'An appetite for argument', p. 101.

Select Bibliography

Adler, K. H., 'Reading national identity. Gender and "prostitution" during the Occupation', *Modern and Contemporary France*, 7.1 (1999), 47–57.

Aglan, A. and R. Frank (eds), *La Guerre-monde* (Paris: Gallimard, 2015).

Alary, E., B. Vergez-Chaignon and G. Gauvain, *Les Français au quotidien, 1939–1949* (Paris: Perrin, 2006).

Aubert, N., '"We have nothing better than testimony": History and memory in French war narratives', *Journal of European Studies*, 45.5 (2015), 287–300.

Azéma, J.-P., 'Les Libérations de la France: prologue', *French Cultural Studies*, 15.5 (1994), 223–6.

Azéma, J.-P. and F. Bédarida (eds), *Vichy et les Français* (Paris: Fayard, 1992).

Baldoli, C. and A. Knapp, *Forgotten Blitzes: France and Italy under Allied Air Attack* (London, Continuum, 2012).

Barzman, J. and C. Malon (eds), *Les Enjeux des bombardements du Havre: résultats et nouvelles pistes* (Le Havre, Presses universitaires de Rouen et du Havre, 2016).

Barzman, J., C. Bouillot and A. Knapp (eds), *Bombardements 1944. Le Havre, Normandie, France, Europe* (Rouen: Presses universitaires de Rouen et du Havre, 2016).

Bertin-Maghit, J.-P., *Les Documenteurs des années noires* (Paris: Nouveau Monde Éditions, 2004).

Besson, J.-L., *Paris Rutabagas* (Paris, Gallimard Jeunesse, 2005).

Boegner, P., *Carnets du pasteur Boegner (1940–1945)*, présentés et annotés par Philippe Boegner (Paris: Fayard, 1992).

Boldorf, M. and J. Scherner, 'France's Occupation costs and the war in the East: the contribution to the German war economy, 1940–44', *Journal of Contemporary History*, 4.2 (2012), 291–316.

Boninchi, M., *Vichy et l'ordre moral* (Paris: Presses universitaires de France, 2005).

Bowles, B., 'German newsreel propaganda in France, 1940–1944', *The Historical Journal of Film, Radio, and Television*, 24.1 (2004), 45–67.

Bowles, B., 'Newsreels, ideology and public opinion under Vichy: the case of *La France en Marche*', *French Historical Studies*, 27:2 (2004), 419–63.

Bowles, B., 'Accommodating Vichy: the politics of Marcel Pagnol's *La Fille du puisatier*,' *Historical Reflections*, 35:2 (2009), 84–107.

Broch, L., *Ordinary Workers, Vichy and the Holocaust: French Railwaymen and the Second World War* (Cambridge: Cambridge University Press, 2016).

Brossat, A., *Libération, fête folle, 6 juin 1944 – 8 mai 45: mythes et rites ou le grand théâtre des passions populaires* (Paris: Éditions autrement, 1994).

Bueltzingsloewen, I., L. Douzou, J.-D. Durand, H. Joly and J. Solchany (eds), *Lyon dans la Seconde Guerre mondiale. Villes et métropoles à l'épreuve du conflit* (Rennes: Presses universitaires de Rennes, 2016).

Capdevila, L., F. Rouquet, F. Virgili and D. Voldman, *Hommes et femmes dans la France en guerre, 1914–1945* (Paris: Payot, 2003).

Capuano, C., *Vichy et la famille: réalités et faux-semblants d'une politique publique* (Rennes: Presses universitaires de Rennes, 2009).

Catherine, J.-C. (ed.) *La Captivité des prisonniers de guerre: histoire, art et mémoire 1939–1945: Pour une approche européenne* (Rennes: Presses universitaires de Rennes, 2008).

Chadwick, K., 'An appetite for argument: radio propaganda and food in occupied France,' *French History*, 31.1 (2017), 85–106.

Condette, J. F. (ed.), *Les Écoles dans la guerre: acteurs et institutions éducatives dans les tourmentes guerrières (*XVIIe-XXe* siècles)* (Lille: Presses universitaires du Septentrion, 2014).

Connolly, J., 'Encountering Germans: the experience of Occupation in the Nord, 1914–1918' (unpublished PhD dissertation, King's College London, 2012).

Copeau, P., *La Libération de la France, actes du colloque international tenu à Paris du 28 au 31 octobre 1974* (Paris: CNRS, 1976).

Corcy, S., *La Vie culturelle sous l'Occupation* (Paris: Perrin, 2005).

Crew, D. F., 'Alltagsgeschichte: a new social history "from below"?' *Central European History*, 22.3/4: German histories: challenges in theory, practice, technique (1989), 394–407.

Cyrulnik, B., *Je me souviens* (Paris: Odile Jacob, 2010).

Cyrulnik, B., *Sauve-toi, la vie t'appelle* (Paris: Odile Jacob, 2014).

Devigne, M., 'Classe de guerre: une histoire de l'École entre Vichy et République' (unpublished PhD dissertation, Université Paris Sorbonne, 2015).

Diamond, H., *Women and the Second World War in France, 1939–48. Choices and Constraints* (London: Longman, 1999).

Diamond, H., *Fleeing Hitler: France 1940* (Oxford and New York: Oxford University Press, 2007).

Diamond, H. and S. Kitson (eds), *Vichy, Resistance, Liberation. New Perspectives on Wartime France* (Oxford and New York: Berg, 2005).

Dodd, L., *French Children under the Allied Bombs, 1940–45: An Oral History* (Manchester, Manchester University Press, 2016).

Dodd, L., 'Children's citizenly participation in the National Revolution: the instrumentalization of children in Vichy France', *European Review of History: Revue d'Histoire Européenne*, 24.5 (2017), 759–80.

Dodd, L., '"Mon petit papa chéri": children, fathers and family separation in Vichy France', *Essays in French Literature and Culture*, 54 (2017), 97–116.

Dodd, L. and A. Knapp, '"How many Frenchmen did you kill?" Allied bombing policy towards France (1940–1945)', *French History*, 22.4 (2008), 469–92.

Douart, G., *Les civils sous l'Occupation. Nantes dans la guerre* (Maulévrier: éditions Hérault, 1993).

Douzou, L., *La Résistance française- une histoire périlleuse* (Paris: Seuil, 2005).

Downs, L. L., *Childhood in the Promised Land: Working Class Movements and the* Colonies de Vacances *in France, 1880–1960* (Durham, NC and London: Duke University Press, 2002).

Downs, L. L., 'Au revoir les enfants. Wartime evacuation and the politics of childhood in France and Britain', *History Workshop Journal*, 82.1 (2016), 121–50.

Durand, Y., *La Vie quotidienne des prisonniers de guerre dans les Stalags, les Oflags, et les Kommandos 1939–1945* (Paris: Hachette, 1987).

Echenberg, M., *Colonial Conscripts: the Tirailleur Sénégalais in French West Africa, 1857–1960* (London: James Currey, 1991).

Faure, L. H., *Un 'plan Marshall juif:' La présence juive américaine en France après la Shoah, 1944–1954* (Paris: Armand Colin, 2013).

Feiertag, O. (ed.), *Histoire et Mémoire de la Résistance en Seine-Inférieure* (Rouen: Presses universitaires de Rouen et du Havre, 2017).

Fishman, S., *We Will Wait: Wives of French Prisoners of War, 1940–1945* (New Haven and London: Yale University Press, 1991).

Fishman, S., *The Battle for Children: World War II, Youth Crime, and Juvenile Justice in Twentieth-Century France* (Cambridge, MA and London: Harvard University Press, 2002).

Fogg, S. L., *The Politics of Daily Life in Vichy France: Foreigners, Undesirables and Strangers* (Cambridge and New York: Cambridge University Press, 2008).

Fogg, S. L., *Stealing Home. Looting, Restitution, and Reconstructing Jewish Lives in France, 1942–1947* (Oxford: Oxford University Press, 2016).

Footitt, H. and A. Knapp (eds), *Liberal Democracies at War. Conflict and Representation* (London: Bloomsbury, 2013).

François, J.-J., *La Guerre de 1939–1940 en Eure-et-Loir: le courrier des lecteurs* (Luisant: La Parcheminière, 1996).

Gallot, F., *En Découdre* (Paris: La Découverte, 2015).

Gardiner, M., *Critiques of Everyday Life: An Introduction* (London: Routledge, 2002).

Gervereau, L., and D. Peschanski, *La Propagande sous Vichy* (Nanterre: BDIC, 1990).

Gildea, R., *Marianne in Chains: Daily Life in the Heart of France during the German Occupation* (New York: Picador, 2002).

Gildea, R., O. Wieviorka and A. Waring (eds), *Surviving Hitler and Mussolini: Daily Life in Occupied Europe* (London: Bloomsbury, 2006).

Ginio, R., *French Colonialism Unmasked: the Vichy years in French West Africa* (Lincoln, NE: University of Nebraska Press, 2006).

Goldsztejn, I., 'Le rôle de l'American Joint dans la reconstruction de la communauté', *Archives Juives*, 28.1 (1995), 23–37.

Gregory, B., 'Is small beautiful? Microhistory and the history of everyday life', *History and Theory*, 38.1 (1999), 100–10.

Grenard, F., *La France du marché noir 1940–1949* (Paris: Payot, 2008).

Grenard, F., *Une Légende du Maquis: Georges Guingouin, du mythe à l'histoire* (Paris: Vendémiaire, 2014).

Guillon, J.-M., P. Laborie and J. Sainclivier (eds), *Images des comportements sous l'Occupation: mémoires, transmission, idées reçues 1940–1945* (Rennes: Presses universitaires de Rennes, 2015).

Guingouin, G., *Quatre ans de lutte sur le sol Limousin* (Paris: Hachette, 1974).

Hallie, P. P., *Lest Innocent Blood Be Shed: The Story of Le Chambon and How Goodness Happened There* (New York: Harper & Row, 1979).

Harootunian, H., 'Shadowing history: national narratives and the persistence of the everyday', *Cultural Studies*, 18.2/3 (2004), 181–200.

Henry, P., *We Only Know Men: The Rescue of Jews in France during the Holocaust* (Washington, DC: The Catholic University of America Press, 2007).

Herzog, D. (ed.), *Brutality and Desire. War and Sexuality in Europe's Twentieth Century* (Basingstoke, New York: Palgrave Macmillan, 2009).

Jamet, F., *One Two Two* (Paris: Olivier Orban, 1975).

Kedward, H. R., *Resistance in Vichy France* (Oxford: Oxford University Press, 1978).

Kedward, H. R., *In Search of the Maquis* (Oxford: Clarendon Press, 1993).

Kedward, H. R. and N. Wood (eds), *The Liberation of France: Image and Event* (Oxford and Washington DC: Berg, 1995).

Keith, S., 'Collective memory and the end of Occupation: remembering (and forgetting) the Liberation of Paris in images', *Visual Communication Quarterly*, 17.3 (2010), 134–46.

Kershner, H. E., *Quaker Service in Modern War: Spain and France, 1939–1940* (New York: Prentice-Hall, 1950).

Kitchen, R., *A Legacy of Shame: French Narratives of War and Occupation* (Oxford: Peter Lang, 2013).

Knapp, A., *Les Français sous les bombes allies* (Paris: Tallandier, 2014).

Laborie, P., *L'opinion française sous Vichy* (Paris: Seuil, 1990; 2001).

Laborie, P. and F. Marcot (eds), *Les comportements collectifs en France et dans l'Europe allemande, 1940–1945* (Rennes: Presses universitaires de Rennes, 2015).

Lawler, N., *Soldiers of Misfortune: Ivorien Tirailleurs of World War II* (Ohio: Ohio University Press, 1992).

Leclerc, F. and M. Weindling, 'La répression des femmes coupables d'avoir collaboré pendant l'Occupation', *Clio. Femmes, Genre, Histoire*, 1 (1995).

Le Crom, J.-P., *Syndicats nous voilà! Vichy et le corporatisme* (Paris, Éditions de l'atelier), 1995.

Le Crom, J.-P., *Au secours, Maréchal! L'instrumentalisation de l'humanitaire (1940–1944)* (Paris: Presses universitaires de France, 2013).

Lee, D., *Pétain's Jewish Children: French Jewish Youth and the Vichy Regime* (Oxford: Oxford University Press, 2014).

Lefébure, A., *Les Conversations secrètes des Français sous l'Occupation* (Paris: Plon, 1993).

Lefebvre, H., *Critique of Everyday Life* (London: Verso, 1991; transl. J. Moore).
Léglise, P., *L'Histoire de la politique du cinéma français* (Brive: Filméditions, 1977).
Leleu, J.-L., F. Passera and J. Quellien (eds), *La France pendant la seconde guerre mondiale, atlas historique* (Paris: Fayard and Ministère de la Défense, 2010).
Lieb, P. and R. O. Paxton, 'Maintenir l'ordre en France occupée. Combien de divisions?', *Vingtième Siècle. Revue d'histoire*, 112 (2011), 115–26.
Lowrie, D. A., *The Hunted Children* (New York: W.W. Norton & Company, 1963).
Lüdtke, A. (ed.), *The History of Everyday Life* (Princeton: Princeton University Press, 1995; transl. W. Templer).
Luneau, A., J. Guérot and S. Martens, *Comme un allemand en France. Lettres inédites sous l'occupation 1940–1944* (Paris: Vendémaire 2016).
Mabon, A., *Prisonniers de guerre 'Indigènes': visages oubliés de la France occupée* (Paris: La Découverte, 2010).
Mahé, C., 'Des éclats de rire entre les bombes, les expériences enfantines de la guerre à travers le jeu et les jouets dans la France occupée (1939–1945)' (unpublished Masters dissertation, Sciences Po, Paris, 2014).
Marcot, F. et al. (eds), *Dictionnaire historique de la Résistance* (Paris: Robert Laffont, 2006).
Meinen, I., 'La réglementation de la prostitution et des relations sexuelles par les occupants', *Travail, Genre et Sociétés*, 10.2 (2003), 69–82.
Meinen, I., *Wehrmacht et prostitution sous l'Occupation* (1940–1945) (Paris: Payot, 2006).
Mexandeau, L., *Nous, nous ne verrons pas la fin. Un enfant dans la guerre (1939–1945)* (Paris, Éditions Le Cherche midi, 2003).
Miller, G., *Les Pousse-au-jouir du maréchal Pétain* (Paris: Seuil, 1975).
Moorehead, C., *Village of Secrets: Defying the Nazis in Vichy France* (New York: HarperCollins, 2014).
Muel-Dreyfus, F., *Vichy et l'éternel féminin* (Paris: Le Seuil, 1996).
Nettelbeck, C., 'A forgotten zone of memory? French primary school children and the history of the Occupation', *French History and Civilization*, 14 (2011), 157–66.
Norton, M., 'Resistance in Upper Normandy, 1940–44' (unpublished PhD thesis, Edge Hill University, 2017).
Olivier, C., 'Un proxénète écrit à Suzy en 1941', *Clio. Femmes, Genre, Histoire*, 17 (2003), 115–36.
Olivier, C., 'Bucoliques et emmurées. Les prostituées et le régime de Vichy', *Travail, Genre et Sociétés* (2003), 55–68.
Ory, P., *Les Collaborateurs* (Paris: Seuil, 1976).
Paxton, R. O., *Vichy France: Old Guard and New Order* (New York: Columbia University Press, 2nd edn, 2001).
Pédron, P., *La Prison sous Vichy* (Paris: L'atelier, 1993).
Pérotin, Y., *La Vie inimitable* (Grenoble: Presses universitaires de Grenoble, 2014).
Peschanski, P., *Vichy 1940–1944. Contrôle et exclusion* (Brussels: Complexe, 1997).

Picaper, J.-P. and L. Norz, *Enfants maudits. Ils sont 200,000, on les appelait les enfants de Boches* (Geneva: Éditions des Syrtes, 2004).

Place, E. M., 'Wehrmacht soldiers in Paris 1940–1944' (unpublished PhD dissertation, University of Birmingham, 2007).

Pollard, M., *Reign of Virtue, Mobilizing Gender in Vichy France* (Chicago and London: University of Chicago Press, 1998).

Proud, J., *Children and Propaganda: Il Etait une Fois . . . Fiction and Fairy Tale in Vichy France* (Bristol: Intellect, 1999).

Ragache, G., *Les Enfants de la guerre; vivre, survivre, lire et jouer en France (1939–1949)* (Paris: Perrin, 1997).

Risser, N. D., *France under Fire: German Invasion, Civilian Flight, and Family Survival during World War II* (Cambridge and New York: Cambridge University Press, 2012).

Roberts, M.-L., 'La photo du GI viril: genre et photojournalisme en France à la Libération', *Le Mouvement social,* 219 (2007), 35–56.

Roberts, M. L., *What Soldiers Do: Sex and the American GI in World War II France* (Chicago and London: University of Chicago Press, 2013).

Röger, M. and E. Debruyne, 'From control to terror: German prostitution policies in eastern and western European territories during both World Wars', *Gender & History,* 28.3 (2016), 687–708.

Rossignol, D., *Histoire de la Propagande en France de 1940 à 1944* (Paris: Presses universitaires de France, 1991).

Rousso, H., *The Vichy Syndrome: History and Memory in France since 1944* (Cambridge MA and London: Harvard University Press, 1991; transl. A. Goldhammer).

Ryan, D. F., *The Holocaust and the Jews of Marseille: The Enforcement of Anti-Semitic Policies in Vichy France* (Urbana and Chicago: University of Illinois Press, 1996).

Sanders, P., *Histoire du marché noir 1940–1946* (Paris: Perrin, 2001).

Sauvy, A., *La Vie économique des Français de 1939 à 1945* (Paris: Flammarion, 1978).

Scheck, R., *Hitler's African Victims: The German Army Massacres of Black French Soldiers in 1940* (Cambridge: Cambridge University Press, 2006).

Scheck, R., 'French colonial soldiers in German prisoner of war camps 1940–1945', *French History,* 24.3 (2010), 420–46.

Schilling, D., 'Everyday life and the challenge to history in postwar France: Braudel, Lefebvre and Certeau', *Diacritics,* 33.1 (2003), 23–40.

Scott, J. C., *Weapons of the Weak* (New York: Oxford University Press, 1985).

Stargardt, N., *Witnesses of War: Children's Lives Under the Nazis* (New York: Vintage Books, 2005).

Steege, P., A. S. Bergerson, M. Healy and P. E. Swett, 'The history of everyday life: a second chapter', *The Journal of Modern History,* 80.2 (2008), 358–78.

Thomas, M., 'The Vichy Government and French Colonial POWs, 1940–1944', *French Historical Studies,* 25.4 (2002), 657–92.

Thuin, F., *Pétain et la dictature de l'image, Enfance et jeunesse, cinq ans de propagande* (Clermont-de-l'Oise: Éditions Daniel Bordet, 2011).

Torrie, J. S., *'For Their Own Good': Civilian Evacuations in Germany and France, 1939–1945* (New York and Oxford: Berghahn, 2010).

Touroude, G., *Les Braconniers de l'espérance* (Royan: Éditions de la Langrotte, 1995).

Veillon, D., *Vivre et survivre en France 1939–1947* (Paris: Payot, 1995).

Vinen, R., *The Unfree French. Life under the Occupation* (London: Penguin, 2007).

Virgili, F., *Shorn Women, Gender and Punishment in Liberation France* (Oxford: Berg, 2002).

Wharton, S., *Screening Reality: French Documentary Film during the German Occupation* (Bern: Peter Lang, 2006).

Wieviorka, O., *La Mémoire désunie. Le souvenir politique des années sombres, de la Libération à nos jours* (Paris: Seuil, 2013).

Index

Lightning Source UK Ltd.
Milton Keynes UK
UKHW020735241219
355953UK00004B/168/P

9 781350 143791